SOUNDS – MEANING – COMMUNICATION

LANDMARKS IN PHONETICS, PHONOLOGY AND COGNITIVE LINGUISTICS

Edited by Jolanta Szpyra-Kozłowska

VOLUME 7

Notes on the quality assurance and peer review of this publication

Prior to publication, the quality of the work published in this series is reviewed by an external referee appointed by the editorship.

Polish consonant clusters in the British mouth

Marek Radomski

Polish consonant clusters in the British mouth

A study in online loanword adaptation

PETER LANG

Bibliographic Information published by the Deutsche Nationalbibliothek
The Deutsche Nationalbibliothek lists this publication in the
Deutsche Nationalbibliografie; detailed bibliographic data is available
in the internet at http://dnb.d-nb.de.

Library of Congress Cataloging-in-Publication Data
Names: Radomski, Marek, author.
Title: Polish consonant clusters in the British mouth : a study in online
  loanword adaptation / Marek Radomski.
Description: Berlin ; New York : Peter Lang, [2019] | Series: Sounds -
  meaning - communication: Landmarks in phonetics, phonology and cognitive
  linguistics ; Vol. 7 | Includes bibliographical references.
Identifiers: LCCN 2018057403 | ISBN 9783631770443
Subjects: LCSH: English language--Foreign words and phrases--Polish. |
  English language--Foreign elements--Polish. | Optimality theory
  (Linguistics)
Classification: LCC PE1582.P65 R34 2019 | DDC 422/.491851--dc23 LC
record available at https://lccn.loc.gov/2018057403

This publication was financially supported by
Maria Curie-Skłodowska University in Lublin, Poland.

Reviewed by Prof. Haike Jacobs.

Cover illustration printed with kind permission of Jerzy Durczak.

Printed by CPI books GmbH, Leck.

ISSN 2365-8150
ISBN 978-3-631-77044-3 (Print)
E-ISBN 978-3-631-77225-6 (E-PDF)
E-ISBN 978-3-631-77226-3 (EPUB)
E-ISBN 978-3-631-77227-0 (MOBI)
DOI 10.3726/b14998

© Peter Lang GmbH
Internationaler Verlag der Wissenschaften
Berlin 2019
All rights reserved.

Peter Lang – Berlin · Bern · Bruxelles · New York ·
Oxford · Warszawa · Wien

Acknowledgements

I would like to express my profound gratitude to my research supervisor, Professor Jolanta Szpyra-Kozłowska, for her expert and patient guidance, positive encouragement and valuable criticism of this work.

I would also like to extend my thanks to Prof. Haike Jacobs and Prof. Geoffrey Schwartz, who reviewed the manuscript, for their insightful comments and criticism which have helped to improve its quality.

My sincere thanks also go to my colleagues from the Phonetics and Phonology Unit at the Institute of English Studies, Maria Curie-Skłodowska University in Lublin: Dr Agnieszka Bryła-Cruz, Dr hab. Wiktor Gonet, Ms Kateryna Laidler and Dr Radosław Święciński, for stimulating discussions and continued support.

I am particularly grateful to the following persons for their invaluable assistance with the collection of my data: Prof. Pauline Foster, Dr Joanna Przedlacka, Prof. Jane Setter and Mr Jan Trębacz.

Last but not least, I wish to thank my wife, Marzena, for her unwavering support and endless patience, and my daughters, Hanna and Karolina.

Contents

X

Introduction

Recent years have brought a considerable interest in the issue of phonological loanword adaptation. Various theoretical approaches to this phenomenon have been put forward with a view to accounting for the mechanisms which govern modifications in the sound structure of loans resulting from the differences between the sound systems of the source and the target languages. Given the variety of phenomena attested in loan nativisation, it comes as no surprise that different factors, e.g. phonology, perception and orthography, assume key importance in specific proposals. Three main approaches to loan assimilation have developed in the relevant literature. The phonological approximation view claims that loanword adaptation is performed mainly in the phonological component of grammar (e.g. Itô and Mester 1995, Paradis and LaCharité 1997). According to the phonetic approximation view, the majority of sound modifications occurring in borrowings take place at the perception stage (e.g. Peperkamp *et al.* 2008, Boersma and Hamann 2009). Finally, under the phonetic-phonological adaptation view, both perception and phonology are involved in computing loanword adaptation to different degrees (e.g. Silverman 1992, Kang 2003). All these theoretical proposals constitute the subject of an ongoing debate. This discussion is further complicated by numerous linguistic as well as extra-linguistic factors that may bear upon loan assimilation, such as the nature of the input representation, the role of bilingualism or the impact of spelling.

The present monograph is intended as a contribution to this debate. Its main focus is on online adaptation of Polish initial and final clusters consisting of two consonants (CC) and three consonants (CCC) by native speakers of Standard Southern British English. This is the first analysis of the nativisation of Polish consonant clusters found in the literature, which provides a new and rich body of data from English, the most studied language whose phonological structure has been examined in numerous works. The study reveals several completely new aspects of the phonological competence of native English speakers. Its major goal is to propose an adequate, in-depth formal analysis of the experimental results within the framework of Optimality Theory (OT) (Prince and Smolensky 1993/2004, McCarthy and Prince 1995). The monograph offers strong empirical evidence for the validity of OT as a model of phonology capable of providing a coherent theoretical interpretation of the data obtained in the experiments. We identify the most frequent repair strategies used to adapt foreign phonotactic structures as well as uncover the mechanisms governing the nativisation process. In particular, our goal is to determine whether loan assimilation takes place in phonological production or in perception. Another aim is to verify the validity of various loan adaptation models. To this end, we confront the results of our experiments with the predictions made by the major approaches to loan assimilation.

The study focuses on online adaptations, i.e. loanwords adapted in real time in a repetition task, rather than on established borrowings since the former offer a unique insight into the source language phonology. On the other hand, the phonological shape of the latter is usually a combined effect of various sound changes, including those that took place at the moment of adaptation as well as at later stages. In some cases it may be difficult to determine exactly how a given item entered the target language and whether or not some other factors, such as orthography, played a role in its modification. Such problems do not exist in research on online adaptations, which offers unambiguous evidence for synchronic phonological phenomena.

Chapter 1 contains a brief introduction to the basic concepts and the most important issues relevant to the study of loanwords and phonological loan nativisation. It starts with a definition and a general classification of borrowings. Then, the major controversial issues in phonological loan adaptation are discussed, including the main factors shaping this phenomenon, such as the nature of the input representation, the channel of borrowing, the influence of spelling and the degree of community bilingualism, as well as some problematic patterns which may emerge in this process, e.g. the too-many-solutions problem, divergent repair, unnecessary repair, differential importation and retreat to the unmarked. Finally, since the present monograph deals with the phonological adaptation of loanwords into English, we find it useful to outline a general historical background of foreign lexical influence on this language.

Chapter 2 is devoted to a survey of various contemporary theoretical models of phonological loanword adaptation. We start with a presentation of selected analyses belonging to the phonological approximation view where loanword nativisation is claimed to be a function of the phonological production grammar, e.g. the Theory of Constraints and Repair Strategies Loanword Model (e.g. Paradis and LaCharité 1997) and Itô and Mester's (1995, 1999, 2001) Optimality Theory account of lexical stratification in Japanese. Next, we focus on the phonetic approaches to the process in question which maintain that loan assimilation originates in perception and that the role of phonology is limited, i.e. a psycholinguistic three-level model of speech processing (Peperkamp and Dupoux 2002, 2003, Peperkamp 2005, Peperkamp et al. 2008) and a bidirectional three-level

2

model for L1 processing and loanword adaptation proposed by Boersma and Hamann (2009). Finally, a variety of mixed models involving both the perception grammar and the production grammar are examined, such as Silverman's (1992) two-tier model of loanword adaptation and the perceptual similarity approach (e.g. Kang 2003).

The primary aim of Chapter 3 is to put the experiments on online adaptation of Polish CC and CCC consonant clusters by native speakers of English in a broader theoretical perspective by investigating relevant aspects of the phonotactics and syllable structure of English as well as previous research on online adaptation. First, an overview of the phonotactic restrictions on the initial and final consonant sequences in English and Polish is provided. Next, we examine the notion of sonority and sonority-based cross-linguistic principles, such as the Sonority Sequencing Principle (e.g. Selkirk 1984), the Minimum Sonority Distance (e.g. Steriade 1982), the Syllable Contact Law (e.g. Murray and Vennemann 1983) and the Sonority Dispersion Principle (e.g. Clements 1990). We also briefly discuss selected frameworks in which the traditional notion of sonority is criticised or even rejected. The second goal of the Chapter is to provide an introduction to the model of Optimality Theory within which an analysis of the experimental data will be carried out in Chapters 4 and 5.

Chapter 4 reports on an online loanword adaptation experiment in which 30 native speakers of British English reproduced authentic Polish words containing word-initial and word-final CC consonant clusters which do not occur in English. First, the data belonging to each category of responses, i.e. target-like reproduction, vowel epenthesis, segment change and consonant deletion, are presented and examined. Next, the experimental results are confronted with the predictions made by the major approaches to loan assimilation discussed in Chapter 2. It is argued that the relevant data can receive a straightforward explanation in an Optimality Theory analysis similar to Itô and Mester's (1995, 1999, 2001) account of lexical stratification in Japanese. The results of the study thus lend support to a claim that there is no need for a separate loan phonology component if native phonology is understood as a partial ranking with floating faithfulness constraints.

Chapter 5 deals with the patterns of adaptation of Polish CCC clusters by native speakers of Standard Southern British English. Its major aim is to confront and compare the findings concerning CC sequences with another set of experimental data. The presentation of the results is followed by a formal OT account of the observed phenomena based on the same constraint rankings which were used for the analysis of CC clusters in Chapter 4. It is argued that both

3

experiments confirm that loanword phonology is mainly native phonology in action supplemented with the mechanism of FAITH promotion or demotion. The role of perception in loanword integration is claimed to be relatively limited. Finally, we investigate the similarities and differences between the nativisation patterns of consonant clusters found in online adaptations and in established loanwords in English.

We sum up the results and the findings in Conclusion, which is followed by Appendices 1–6 with the full list of the experimental stimuli and results as well as details concerning the participants. The cited works are enumerated in the References.

1 Introduction to linguistic borrowing and phonological loanword adaptation

1 Introduction

This Chapter introduces the basic concepts and the most important issues relevant to the study of loanwords and phonological loan adaptation. It starts with a definition and a general classification of borrowings. Next, the major controversial issues in phonological nativisation are briefly examined, including the main factors shaping adaptation as well as some problematic patterns which may emerge in the process under discussion. Finally, since the present monograph deals with the phonological adaptation of loanwords into English, we find it useful and justified to outline a general historical background of foreign lexical influence on this language.

In Section 2 we introduce the issue of borrowings and their phonological nativisation, pointing to a variety of modifications they may undergo while being adapted into the target language. Then, a distinction between online adaptations and integrated loanwords is briefly explained. Finally, we discuss the definition as well as the classification of borrowings proposed in Haugen's (1950) seminal work.

Section 3 deals with the main controversial issues in phonological loan adaptation. First, we address the major factors which, to varying degrees, influence the process in question. These include the nature of the input to loanword nativisation, with different predictions made by the phonological vs. the phonetic input views, the role of the channel of borrowing (spoken vs. written) and the related issue of the impact of orthography as well as the question of the borrowers' level of bilingualism and its bearing on loanword integration. Next, we present and discuss several problematic patterns, identified by Kang (2011), emerging in phonological loanword adaptation, such as the too-many-solutions problem, divergent repair, unnecessary repair, differential importation and retreat to the unmarked. It is pointed out that the existence of all these phenomena further complicates the study of loanword assimilation and poses a considerable challenge to any theory of loan adaptation.

Section 4 is devoted to a succinct presentation of the history of borrowings into English. We identify the major sources of foreign influence in four periods frequently isolated in the development of this language, i.e. Old English, Middle English, Early Modern English and Present-Day English. Furthermore, the

5

impact of borrowing on the vocabulary as well as on the phonology of English is briefly examined. Finally, we discuss the Polish contribution to the English lexicon.

Section 5 concludes the discussion with a brief summary of the main points made in this Chapter.

2 Definition and classification of borrowings

Loanwords are lexical items borrowed from one language into another linguistic system. The language from which a particular word is taken is usually referred to as L2, the source or the donor language, whereas the one into which a loanword is incorporated is termed L1, the target or the recipient language. In the course of borrowing, source items may undergo various modifications so as to conform to L1 grammar, a process called loanword adaptation (also integration, assimilation, accommodation or nativisation). These changes may affect different properties of a borrowed word, including its morphology, semantics, orthography as well as phonology.

Morphological adaptation takes place, for example, when a loanword is made to conform to the inflectional system of the target language by adopting its inflectional endings for different grammatical categories such as tense, case, number or gender. For instance, when English verbs are borrowed into Polish, they are usually d with the verbal suffix *-ować* [ɔvaʨ], as in *surfować* [sɛrˈfɔvaʨ] 'to surf' and *parkować* [parˈkɔvaʨ] 'to park' (Witalisz 2013: 335–336). Furthermore, English nouns receive grammatical gender in Polish (masculine, feminine or neuter), e.g. *panel* [ˈpãnɛl] (masculine) and *maskara* [maˈskara] 'mascara' (feminine) (see e.g. Fisiak 1975 and Mańczak-Wohlfeld 2007, 2008 for more detailed discussions on the morphological adaptation of anglicisms in Polish).

Semantic adaptation concerns any modifications in the meaning of a borrowed item which occur in the process of loan assimilation, such as semantic narrowing or broadening. For example, English *cake* was borrowed into Polish as *keks* [kɛks] with a narrowed meaning of 'fruit cake' (Fisiak 1970: 41). A comprehensive account of the semantics of English loanwords in Polish can be found in Mańczak-Wohlfeld (1995).

Orthographic adaptation affects the spelling of loanwords, which is usually necessary when the donor and the recipient languages use different alphabets.[1] However, even if the writing systems are similar, some orthographic modifications

---

1 As pointed out by Haspelmath (2009), the necessity of orthographic adaptation crucially depends on the borrowers' familiarity with the writing system of the source

may take place. For instance, the English words *jeans* and *dealer* are very frequently spelt in Polish as *dżinsy* ['d͡ʐinsɨ] and *diler* ['dʲilɛr] respectively (Witalisz
2013: 334), in accordance with the way they are pronounced in Polish. It should
be pointed out that orthographic adaptation is usually assumed to be a marker of
a high degree of nativisation of loanwords.

The present monograph deals with the phonological aspect of loanword adaptation, i.e. any changes in the sound structure of borrowings which result from
the differences between the phonetic and phonological systems of the source
and the target languages. As observed by Haunz (2007), these modifications may
affect different aspects of phonological organisation, namely the phonemic, phonotactic and prosodic levels.[2]

Phonemic adaptation takes place when a source word contains a phoneme
which is not part of the target language inventory. In such cases, illicit segments
are usually substituted with their closest native equivalents. For example, Paradis
and LaCharité (1997) demonstrate that when French words containing /z/ are
borrowed into Fula, whose inventory lacks /z/, the segment in question is invariably adapted as /s/. Once the phonemes of the donor language have been replaced
with those of the recipient language, they can be phonetically realised as appro-
priate L1 allophones. It is important to note that in some cases foreign segments
are not substituted with native ones but enter the target language unadapted, a
phenomenon referred to as importation, e.g. English /r/ is frequently borrowed
as such in Quebec French and Montreal French (Paradis and LaCharité 1997).

Apart from the segmental level, the phonotactics of borrowed words is frequently adapted in loanword integration. As is well-known, languages differ
significantly in terms of their phonotactic restrictions, i.e. permitted contexts
in which particular sounds may occur as well as acceptable sequences of segments. If a loanword contains a phonotactic structure which is ill-formed from
the point of view of the borrowing language, it is usually modified so as to fit the
phonology of the target language. Thus, when words with consonant clusters
are borrowed into a language with only CV syllables, the problematic structure
may be repaired by means of either vowel epenthesis or consonant deletion.
The former strategy is applied, for instance, to English words borrowed into

---

language. For example, some English loans are not always orthographically adapted
in Russian or Japanese because borrowers are familiar with the Latin alphabet.

2   It is important to keep in mind the distinction between loanword adaptation, i.e. modifying a foreign word so that it fits the borrowing language phonology, and loanword
lexicalisation, a process whereby loanwords enter the lexicon of the target language
(Winter-Froemel 2008: 156).

Sesotho, e.g. *football* is adapted as [futubɔlɔ] and *box* emerges as [bɔkɔsɛ] (Rose and Demuth 2006: 1118). The latter repair may be found in the adaptation of English loanwords in White Hmong, e.g. *house* and *juice* are borrowed as [háù] and [ndʑû] respectively (Golston and Yang 2001).[3]

Finally, the prosodic structure of loanwords may undergo changes in the process of adaptation, especially when borrowing into tone languages or differences in stress placement are involved. Thus, when English words are borrowed into Cantonese, which is a tone language, they are assigned one of the six tones, depending on the stress pattern of the source item, e.g. English syllables bearing primary stress receive a high tone (Silverman 1992). On the other hand, in some cases no prosodic adaptation takes place, e.g. in certain French loanwords in Polish the segments are nativised, but the original final stress is preserved, as in *menu* [mɛ̃ˈɲi] (*[ˈmɛ̃ɲi]).

In an analysis of any modifications occurring during loan adaptation it is necessary to keep in mind the distinction between two types of loanwords, namely established or integrated borrowings and online adaptations (Peperkamp 2005, Haunz 2007). The former include foreign items which entered the lexicon of the target language. Such loans should be understood as products of "a completed language change, a diachronic process that once started as an individual innovation but has been propagated throughout the speech community" (Haspelmath 2009: 38). As argued by Peperkamp (2005), a phonological investigation of integrated loanwords is necessarily diachronic as it explains the modifications applied by the speakers who originally introduced these items. Moreover, the phonological shape of such borrowings may be a combined effect of various sound changes, including those that took place at the moment of adaptation as well as at later stages. In some cases it is also difficult to determine exactly the way in which a given item entered the target language and whether or not some other factors, such as orthography, played a role (Haunz 2007).

On the other hand, online adaptations are loanwords adapted in real time, here and now. An examination of the sound changes taking place during online adaptation offers a unique insight into the target language phonology in that it may reveal generalisations which frequently cannot be made on the basis of the native data alone. In other words, it allows us to observe "hidden constraint rankings" (Haunz 2007: 5) or "otherwise latent constraints in action" (Paradis and LaCharité 1997: 382). In contrast to an analysis of integrated loanwords, research on online adaptations provides unambiguous evidence for synchronic

---

3   Further examples of both repairs are listed in Kang (2011).

phonological phenomena. In addition, as indicated by Kang (2011: 2275), loanword adaptation research in general sheds light on such phonological issues as "the role of output constraints vs. processes, the phonetics–phonology interface (more specifically, the role of perceptual factors in shaping phonological patterns), the role of native phonological contrasts in phonological processes, the productivity of stochastic generalisations and the role of innate vs. acquired knowledge." Furthermore, since a number of sociolinguistic factors, such as the level of bilingualism, are involved in loanword integration, the study of loans may facilitate an inquiry into the interface between sociolinguistics and phonology.

In the light of these facts, it comes as no surprise that borrowings have attracted considerable attention in the linguistic literature. As a matter of fact, an interest in borrowing or language contact-induced changes in lexicons of various languages dates back to the nineteenth century study of Paul (1891). Research into borrowing continued in the first half of the twentieth century with works of Jespersen (1912), Sapir (1921) and Bloomfield (1933), among others. However, as pointed out by Hoffer (2002), it is Haugen's (1950) article that serves as the major reference point for the current studies on the subject.

Haugen defines borrowing as "the attempted reproduction in one language of patterns previously found in another" (p. 212). He distinguishes between two basic types of linguistic borrowing, namely substitution and importation. The former pertains to the phenomenon whereby foreign structures are replaced by native ones, whereas the latter refers to the situation in which certain patterns of the source language are introduced into the target language. Substitution may be further subdivided into morphemic and phonemic, i.e. replacement of morphemes and phonemes respectively. As noted by Haugen, when a borrowing contains no structures which are innovations in the target language, it is virtually impossible to differentiate between substitution and importation.

Haugen's taxonomy of borrowings, summarised in Tab. 1, is based on the degree of morphemic substitution found in various types of loans. Drawing on this, he establishes three main categories of borrowed items, namely loanwords, loanblends and loanshifts.[4]

---

4 This classification has been modified by Winford (2003), who maintains that borrowings fall into two main types, that is loanwords and loanshifts. The former are items in which at least part of the original morphemic shape is retained (this category includes 'pure' loanwords and loanblends). The latter consist of native morphemes exclusively but their meanings are at least partly derived from the foreign source (they are subdivided into loan translations and semantic loans). Creations are not included in Tab. 1 since, although undeniably lexical contact phenomena, they are not strictly

Tab. 1: Taxonomy of borrowings (Haugen 1950)

TYPE	DESCRIPTION	EXAMPLE
loanword	no morphemic substitution + some degree of phonemic substitution	English *rendezvous* ['rɒndɪvuː] from French *rendezvous* [ʁãdevu]
loanblend (hybrid) a) blended stem b) blended derivative c) blended compound	partial morphemic substitution (a foreign morpheme + a native one) a) a combination of a native and a foreign stem into a single item b) foreign stem + native affix c) native stem + foreign stem	a) American Norwegian *kårna* from English *corner* and Norwegian *hyrrna* b) Pennsylvania German *bassig* from English *boss* + German *-ig* c) Pennsylvania German *bockabuch* from English *pocket* + German *buch*
loanshift a) loan translation (calque) b) semantic loan	complete morphemic substitution without importation a) translating a foreign pattern into a combination of native morphemes b) shift in the meaning of a native word under the foreign influence	a) Spanish *rascacielos* modelled on English *skyscraper* b) American Portuguese *humoroso* (1. Portuguese 'capricious' + 2. English 'humorous')

The first group, i.e. loanwords, are characterised by the lack of morphemic sub-stitution, which means that a given loan's morphemes are imported during the process. This is not to say, however, that the borrowing remains unchanged as the lack of morphemic substitution means solely that no part of the source item is replaced with a native morpheme. The loan itself frequently undergoes modi-fications with respect to its phonemic shape in that borrowers replace foreign sounds with closest native equivalents.[5] Another frequent adjustment concerns the spelling of such items which is made to conform to the target language or-thography.[6] A representative example of a loanword given by Haugen (1950) is American English *shivaree* from French *charivari* 'an uninvited serenade of newlyweds.' Some English loanwords in Polish include *brydż* [brɨʧ] 'bridge,' *dżentelmen* [ʤɛn'tɛlmẽn] 'gentleman,' *piknik* ['pʲikʲɲik] 'picnic' and *werdykt* ['vɛrdɨkt] 'verdict' (Fisiak 1970).

---

borrowings. Examples in Tab. 1 have been taken from Haugen (1950) and Winford (2003).

5 Haugen (1950) does not specify on what 'closeness' should be based.

6 Winford (2003) also mentions the possibility of semantic change in loanwords, e.g. English *corner* was borrowed into Dutch and Polish only with reference to 'a corner kick in football.'

Loanblends or hybrids show partial morphemic substitution, i.e. only a part of the original morphemic shape is imported and a native morpheme is substituted for the rest. Loanblends are further classified into blended stems, derivatives and compounds. Blended stems arise as a result of combining both a native and a foreign stem into a single item, for instance American Norwegian *kårna* is a mixture of English *corner* and Norwegian *hyrrna* 'corner'.[7] Blended derivatives substitute native affixes for foreign ones, as in Pennsylvania German *bassig* 'bossy' or *fonnig* 'funny', in which the native suffix *-ig* replaces English *-y*. Blended compounds consist of both a native and a foreign stem, for example in Pennsylvania German *bockabuch* 'pocketbook' English *book* was replaced with German *buch*. Examples of English loanblends in Polish include *cyberprzestrzeń* [t͡ɕibɛrˈpʂɛstʂɛ̃ɲ] 'cyberspace', *megaprzebój* [mɛgaˈpʂɛbuj] 'mega hit' and *pracoholik* [praˈt͡ɕɔˈxɔlʲik] 'workaholic' (Witalisz 2013: 332).

Loanshifts display complete morphemic substitution, which means that no morphemes are imported from the source language and only native ones are used instead. Loanshifts fall into two types, namely loan translations (calques) and semantic loans. As regards the former, a source item is not imported but translated into an equivalent target item, for example Spanish *rascacielos*, German *Wolkenkratzer* and Polish *drapacz chmur* [ˈdrapat͡ʂ xmur] are all modelled on English *skyscraper*. Further examples of English calques in Polish are *jajogłowy* [jajɔˈgwɔvɨ] 'an egghead', *nowomowa* [nɔvɔˈmɔva] 'newspeak', *gabinet cieni* [gaˈbʲinɛt ˈt͡ɕɛɲi] 'shadow cabinet' and *gorący ziemniak* [gɔˈrɔnt͡ɕi ˈʑɛmʲɲak] 'hot potato' (Witalisz 2013: 331). In the case of semantic loans, the only result of borrowing is a change in the semantics of a native word, for instance the meaning of English *humorous* has been added to American Portuguese *humoroso* 'capricious'. Similarly, the meanings of Polish words *mysz* [mɨʂ] 'a mouse' and *sieć* [ɕɛt͡ɕ] 'a web' have been extended under the influence of English so that they refer also to 'a computer device' and 'the Internet' respectively. Haugen (1950) further subdivides semantic loans into loan homonyms, where the new meaning is completely different than the original one, and loan synonyms, where there is some degree of similarity between the two meanings.

As illustrated in Tab. 1, the term 'borrowing' may refer to a wide range of phenomena. In the present monograph, our primary interest is in the phonological nativisation of loanwords in English. In particular, we would like to examine the

---

7   Winford (2003) excludes blended stems from his classification, maintaining that such cases are infrequent and may be interpreted as instances of morphemic importation with phonemic substitution.

patterns of adaptation of Polish consonant clusters by native speakers of Standard British English in online loan adaptation experiments. We hope that the obtained results will shed light on some important synchronic aspects of English phonology as well as contribute to the loan phonology debate.

3 Controversial issues in phonological loanword adaptation

Phonological loanword adaptation is a complex phenomenon, shaped by numerous linguistic as well as extra-linguistic factors (Szpyra-Kozłowska 2015, 2016a, 2016b). The main debate in the literature seems to be focused on whether the nature of the process in question is primarily phonetic or phonological, i.e. whether it takes place in perception or in production. In addition, other issues relevant to loan integration, such as the role of orthography or the degree of community bilingualism, are frequently discussed. In this Section, we provide a brief overview of the most significant factors influencing phonological loanword nativisation, namely the nature of the input representation (3.1), the channel of borrowing and the impact of spelling (3.2) as well as the role of the degree of community bilingualism (3.3). Given the variety of factors involved in phonological loan adaptation, it comes as no surprise that its results display a high degree of variation, sometimes revealing certain puzzling patterns which are difficult to account for in terms of native phonological processes or constraints. In Section 3.4 we briefly introduce and discuss five such patterns identified by Kang (2011).

3.1 The nature of the input representation

One of the most hotly debated current issues related to phonological loanword adaptation is the nature of the input to this process. In the literature on the subject, there are two main views concerning the nature of the input representation. They are based on different assumptions about the agents of adaptation and therefore make different predictions about nativisation patterns.

On the one hand, some researchers advocate the phonological input view (Paradis 1996, Paradis and LaCharité 1997, 2008, LaCharité and Paradis 2005), i.e. the idea that loanword integration takes as its input an abstract phonological representation of a source item, which is subsequently modified so as to conform to the target language phonology. This approach usually rests on the assumption that borrowing is performed by competent bilinguals who have access to both L1 and L2 phonology. However, some researchers implicitly assume that the input to loan adaptation is phonological irrespective of the adapters' proficiency in L2. For instance, Jacobs and Gussenhoven (2000: 198) claim that "language users analyse speech signals in terms of a universal phonological vocabulary, which is of course much larger than the subset that is incorporated in their native language." Under this view, borrowers faithfully perceive non-native structures and construct the input to loan nativisation by means of the universal segment parser which assigns a phonological representation to foreign items. According to the phonological input view, the contrastive features of source language phonemes assume key importance in the process and their allophonic variants are irrelevant. It therefore follows that a given L2 phoneme should be uniformly adapted in the target language irrespective of its phonetic realisation in various contexts (phonemic uniformity). Such an approach to the input of adaptation constitutes the basis of the phonological approximation view to loan nativisation (see Chapter 2, Section 2.2 for a detailed discussion).

For instance, English voiceless plosives are invariably adapted as aspirated voiceless plosives in Korean regardless of whether they are aspirated or unaspirated in the source item, as in [tʰ]*oy* s[t]*ory* → /tʰoi sitʰori/. As argued by Oh (2004), this pattern can be accounted for under the assumption that the input to loanword nativisation is phonological rather than phonetic. In the case under discussion, both *toy* and *story* contain the underlying /t/, which is mapped onto /tʰ/ in Korean irrespective of the phonetic realisation of that phoneme in English.[8]

The opposite approach, i.e. the phonetic input view (e.g. Silverman 1992, Yip 1993, Peperkamp and Dupoux 2002, 2003, Peperkamp 2005, Peperkamp *et al.* 2008), claims that the input to loanword assimilation is a detailed acoustic representation of a source word as pronounced by L2 speakers, which is then filtered through the perceptual system of borrowers. According to this view, the majority of modifications that loanwords undergo result from misperception of L2 items by L1 speakers, both mono- and bilinguals. Given this assumption, the adaptation of a given source phoneme varies depending on the phonetic realisation of that segment in a particular context in the donor language. In other words, loan assimilation patterns are sensitive to allophonic variants of phonemes in L2. The concept of the phonetic input is the fundamental assumption underlying the phonetic approximation view to loan nativisation (see Chapter 2, Section 2.3 for a detailed discussion).

For example, the adaptation of English voiceless stops in Thai seems to be based on the phonetic rather than the phonological input, as argued by Kenstowicz and Suchato (2006). The segments in question are adapted as voiceless

---

8   See Kang (2011) for more examples of adaptations based on the phonological and the phonetic input.

aspirated stops initially in monosyllabic words but as unaspirated voiceless stops in /sC/ clusters, which reflects the allophonic realisation of voiceless plosives in English (1) (Kenstowicz and Suchato 2006: 928–929).

(1) Adaptation of English voiceless stops in Thai

English	Thai		English	Thai
[pʰ]*in*	[phīn]		s[p]*are*	[səpēe]
[tʰ]*est*	[thées]		s[t]*yle*	[sətãaj]

Crawford (2009) suggests that, apart from the phonological and the phonetic input, loanword adaptation can be based on an orthographic representation of a source item, which is interpreted by borrowers as a sequence of phonemes in the target language. He maintains that in many cases it is impossible to determine whether a given nativisation pattern is phonologically- or orthographically-based. For instance, the uniform adaptation of English voiceless stops as aspirated voiceless stops in Korean can be viewed as the result of applying a phonological rule converting /t/ into [tʰ] in English loanwords. On the other hand, the regularity in question can be attributed to the influence of spelling in that Korean borrowers may rely on a grapheme-to-phoneme correspondence rule according to which <t> is pronounced as [tʰ]. Another similar case is provided by the Japanese adaptation of American English *writer* and *rider*, both pronounced /ɹɑɪɾɹ/ in the source language, as /ɹaita:/ and /ɹaida:/ respectively (Crawford 2009). This fact can be interpreted as a case of the phonological approximation, with the adapters relying on the abstract phonemic representations of the words in question, or as an orthographically-based adaptation. As demonstrated by Szpyra-Kozłowska (2016c), a similar difficulty arises in the nativisation of the English vowel /ɪ/ in Polish. This segment is usually realised as /i/, which might be interpreted as a phonologically minimal repair (/ɪ/ → /i/ mapping involves only the deletion of [-tense]) or as a spelling-based adaptation since Polish borrowers may rely on the grapheme-to-phoneme correspondence rule where English <i> → Polish /i/. It may well be the case that both phonology as well as orthography play a role and mutually reinforce each other. Crawford (2009: 94) suggests that cases of loanword nativisation conditioned solely by phonological factors are unlikely in that "a purely phonological borrowing situation would have to involve borrowers who are bilingual in both L1 and L2, allowing them access to L2 phonological representations, but who are not also literate in L2, ruling out any influence of L2 orthography." He concludes that such situations are extremely rare and, as a result, purely phonological adaptations should be regarded as uncommon.

To sum up, it has been argued that loanword assimilation is not a uniform process since evidence can be found in support of the phonetic as well as the phonological and the orthographic input view. Given the variety of nativisation patterns as well as the multiple factors conditioning the process under examination, it seems reasonable to acknowledge that a foreign item can be adapted by different speakers at the same time, who employ phonetically-, phonologically- as well as orthographically-based strategies of adaptation, depending on a variety of factors such as the channel of borrowing or their proficiency in L2.

In the present monograph, we adopt the phonological input view as proposed by Jacobs and Gussenhoven (2000). The results of online adaptation experiments presented and analysed in Chapters 4 and 5 demonstrate that in the vast majority of cases foreign structures are faithfully perceived, even by monolinguals, and subsequently modified by the native production grammar. This lends support to Jacobs and Gussenhoven's claim that the input to loan adaptation is constructed by the universal segment parser which assigns a phonological representation to borrowed items.

3.2 The channel of borrowing and the influence of spelling

Another factor relevant to the study of phonological loanword assimilation is the channel through which loans enter the target language. As is well-known, the input to loan adaptation may be either spoken or written (or a mixture of both). In the case of the former, the issue of perception and its role assumes primary importance, whereas the latter kind of input raises the question of the possible impact of spelling.

As pointed out by Vendelin and Peperkamp (2006), the influence of orthography on loanword nativisation patterns may be twofold. On the one hand, there exist 'reading' adaptations, i.e. words "pronounced as if they were native words of the borrowing language" (p. 997) thus in accordance with the native grapheme-to-phoneme rules. A representative example is the English adaptation of French *cul-de-sac* [kytsak] as [ˈkʌldəsæk] (p. 997). Also, some English loans in Polish are clearly reading adaptations, e.g. *walkower* [valˈkɔvɛr] 'walkover', *kowboj* [ˈkɔvbɔj] 'cowboy' and *hobby* [ˈxɔbbɨ] 'hobby'. On the other hand, loanword assimilation may be based on between-language grapheme-to-phoneme correspondence rules, i.e. the most frequent ways in which the source language graphemes are pronounced in the target language. For instance, as noted by Vendelin and Peperkamp (2006), French schoolchildren usually pronounce the English graphemes <u> (as in *but*) and <oo> (as in *book*) as [œ] and [u] respectively. It might well be the case that adult French speakers also rely on such correspondence rules when they adapt English loanwords. On the other hand, as pointed out by Szpyra-Kozłowska (2016a), the English grapheme <u> is usually realised by Polish adapters as the vowel [a], e.g. *support* [sə'pɔːt] → ['sapɔrt] and *curling* ['kɜːlɪŋ] → ['karlʲiŋk].

According to Vendelin and Peperkamp (2006), the existence of two kinds of orthographically-based adaptations is one of the factors which make it difficult to assess precisely the influence of spelling on loanword nativisation patterns since both types may be identical in some cases. Secondly, given that between-language grapheme-to-phoneme correspondence rules are based on the perception of L2 sounds, it is frequently difficult to differentiate between orthographically-based and phonetically- or phonologically-based adaptations. Finally, even if borrowers have no access to the written input and non-words are adapted, some orthographic influence may be present as "adapters can construct an orthographic representation of non-words that are phonologically similar to high-frequency real words" (Vendelin and Peperkamp 2006: 1004).

In order to investigate the extent of the influence of orthography on loanword assimilation, Vendelin and Peperkamp (2006) conducted an experiment in which they examined the adaptations of American English non-words by late French-English bilinguals. The forms under discussion were produced in two conditions, namely an oral condition, where the input was exclusively oral, and a mixed condition, where both oral and written inputs were provided. The experiment focused on the adaptations of eight American English vowels in French, four of which belonged to the French phonemic inventory, and examined the impact of between-language grapheme-to-phoneme correspondence rules on the nativisation patterns.[9]

The results of the experiment confirmed that loan assimilation was influenced by orthography as loanwords were adapted in accordance with between-language grapheme-to-phoneme correspondence rules more often in the mixed condition, i.e. when the written input was provided, than in the oral condition, i.e. in the absence of the orthographic representation. The response patterns in both conditions overlapped to a significant degree, which, according to Vendelin and Peperkamp (2006), was not unexpected under the assumption that grapheme-to-phoneme rules are constructed on the basis of the perception of the target language sounds. Furthermore, it is important to note that the predictions based on phonological and phonetic proximity are frequently compatible. While the adaptations produced in the mixed condition followed between-language grapheme-to-phoneme correspondence rules to a considerable extent,

---

9　Vendelin and Peperkamp (2006) assumed that testing proficient French-English bilinguals would significantly decrease the possibility of 'reading' adaptations.

the responses obtained in the oral condition displayed greater variability. As argued by Vendelin and Peperkamp (2006), this indicates that the latter adaptations should be regarded as resulting from the phonetic approximation since the fine-grained phonetic differences among the input stimuli were reflected in the nativisation patterns. Under the phonological approximation view uniform adaptation is predicted.

Dohlus (2005) holds a view that orthography plays a significant role in loanword nativisation in that it facilitates faithful perception and, consequently, phonological adaptation. She argues that written forms provide borrowers with information concerning the phonemes of the donor language. Under this view, perception is of secondary importance since it is possible to identify source segments solely on the basis of spelling. Dohlus, who examines variable treatment of French and German mid front vowels in Japanese, also suggests that the substantial number of phonological approximation cases in this language reflects the importance of written forms in foreign language teaching in Japan (see Crawford 2009 for a similar view).

On the other hand, Paradis and LaCharité (1997), who examine a corpus of 545 French loanwords in Fula, maintain that the influence of orthography is relatively weak since it is responsible for only 4.6 % of adaptations in their corpus. According to Vendelin and Peperkamp (2006), these figures fail to accurately reflect the actual impact of spelling due to the fact that the predictions based on between-language grapheme-to-phoneme correspondence rules and the phonological approximation stance may both yield identical adaptation patterns. In this way, it becomes impossible to distinguish between the two factors and, consequently, to determine precisely the extent of their influence. An example illustrating this point presented by Vendelin and Peperkamp (2006) is the French adaptation of English *brunch* [brʌntʃ] as [bʁœntʃ]. On the one hand, this form may be accounted for on phonological grounds in that the observed pattern may be regarded as the result of a phonological operation mapping English [ʌ] onto French [œ]. On the other hand, it is possible to argue that the adaptation in question is based on a between-language grapheme-to-phoneme correspondence rule according to which English <u> is pronounced as [œ] in French. Similarly, as observed by Szpyra-Kozłowska and Radomski (2016), the adaptation of English [æ] as [a] in Polish, e.g. *slang* → [slaŋk] or *laptop* → ['laptɔp], might be attributed either to the influence of spelling or to the perception of [æ] as [a].

To sum up, it has been demonstrated that various researchers disagree over the extent of the impact of orthography on loanword adaptation. In this monograph, we acknowledge that spelling plays an important role in loan assimilation, particularly when the written input is provided. Furthermore, we accept Dohlus's (2005) and Crawford's (2009) claims that in many cases it is impossible to accurately determine the role of orthography due to the fact that phonologically- and orthographically-based adaptation strategies yield identical loanword assimilation patterns.

3.3 The degree of community bilingualism

Another factor frequently claimed to be at play in borrowing situations is the degree of bilingualism in society and the adapters' proficiency in L2. This issue takes on particular significance in the phonological approach to loanword adaptation, based on the assumption that loan nativisation is performed by competent bilinguals who have access to both L1 and L2 phonology. As noted by Paradis and LaCharité (1997), there is an extensive body of, mainly sociolinguistic, literature (Haugen 1950, Weinreich 1970, Grosjean 1982, Poplack *et al.* 1988) which provides ample evidence in support of the claim that it is bilingual speakers who are chiefly responsible for active borrowing. In this view, loanwords enter the target language as a result of bilinguals incorporating certain foreign words into the target language when communicating with other such speakers. The role of the monolingual community is therefore restricted to using and spreading already adapted loans.

In his seminal paper on borrowing, Haugen (1950) emphasises the importance of bilingual speakers in the process under discussion and identifies three stages of bilingualism in society, adding that they do not necessarily occur in a chronological order. In 'a pre-bilingual period', loanwords are introduced by a small group of bilingual speakers and subsequently spread among the monolingual community. Some characteristic features of borrowings integrated at this stage include a considerable degree of native substitution and irregularity of adaptation as a result of erratic substitution.[10] Thus, for example, the English diphthong [əʊ] in words *road* [rəʊd] and *load* [ləʊd] has been adapted in American Norwegian to two different Norwegian sounds, namely [å] in the former case, i.e. [råd], and [o] in the latter, i.e. [lod].

Another stage is 'a period of adult bilingualism', when loans are adapted in a more regular fashion with a given source phoneme being mapped consistently

---

10 Paradis and LaCharité (1997) maintain that irregularity of adaptation at this stage, referred to as 'low community bilingualism' period in their paper, stems from the fact that sometimes more than one 'minimal' repair is available for a particular structure and none of these options have gained the status of the social convention yet.

onto the same sound in the target language (systematic substitution). Also in this period a phenomenon called phonemic redistribution may take place, i.e. some phonotactic restrictions of the recipient language may be relaxed so that certain native sounds are found in new contexts. Haugen (1950) cites the example of Czech, in which [g] occurs word-initially only in loanwords, whereas in the native vocabulary it is an allophone of /k/. Another example is provided by Szpyra-Kozłowska (2016c), who examines the patterns of adaptation of /ɪ/ in English borrowings into Polish. The vowel in question is mainly substituted with the high front [i] but in some cases with a somewhat lower and centralised [ɨ]. Szpyra-Kozłowska observes that the native phonotactic constraint against sequences of dentals or alveolars and [i] is satisfied in older loans, where [ɪ] → [ɨ] adaptation takes place, e.g. *detective* → *detektyw* [dɛ'tɛktɨf] or *editor* → *edytor* [ɛ'ditɔr]. However, in more recent borrowings this constraint is relaxed and /i/ is tolerated after coronal obstruents, e.g. *lady* → *lady* ['lɛjdʲi] or *tick* → *tik* [tʲik].

In 'a period of childhood bilingualism' importation takes precedence over substitution. This means that, as a result of borrowing, new sounds begin to appear in the target language. For instance, as pointed out by Haugen, the adaptation of English *whip* [wɪp] among American Norwegian speakers changed from the initial [hyppa] to [wippa]. In this way, [w] was introduced into this language.

Thus, according to Haugen, there is a correlation between the degree of bilingualism in a community and the incidence of importation vs. substitution in loanword adaptation. In other words, an increase in the number of proficient bilinguals leads to a greater preference for importation over substitution. Paradis and LaCharité (1997) point out that this correlation has been confirmed by Harriott and Cichocki (1993), who examined how Acadian French listeners with varying degrees of proficiency in English evaluated the accentedness of English loans. The study revealed that the listeners who had a good command of English were more tolerant towards foreign sounds in loanwords than those with low proficiency in L2.

Furthermore, Paradis and LaCharité (1997: 390) claim that "the percentage of non-adaptations is directly proportional to the number of bilinguals in a community." This correlation is corroborated by their analysis of English loanwords corpora in three dialects of French, namely Montreal French, Quebec French and European French. For instance, as indicated by Paradis and LaCharité (1997), English rhotic [ɹ] remains unadapted in 63.1 % of the cases in the Montreal corpus, in 30.1 % of the cases in the Quebec City corpus and in 0 % of the cases in the European French corpus. The percentage of importations in these dialects directly reflects the degree of bilingualism in the communities of Montreal, Quebec City and France respectively.

To sum up, it has been established that the level of bilingualism is a significant factor in loanword adaptation according to phonological approaches to loan nativisation, which rest on the assumption that bilingual speakers, who have access to both L1 and L2 phonology, are primary agents of adaptation. It should also be pointed out that phonetic approaches to loan assimilation, which attach key importance to perceptual mechanisms, assume that borrowers' proficiency in L2 is of limited significance. This is because the native phonetic categories and the phonetic decoder, where foreign sound structures are mapped onto the phonetically closest native ones, are acquired during the first year of life and remain unchanged regardless of the level of proficiency in L2 (Peperkamp and Dupoux 2003).

In the present monograph, we are not concerned with the issue of the influence of community bilingualism on the patterns of loan nativisation. As our main focus is on online adaptations performed by monolingual speakers of English, the adapters' proficiency in L2 plays no role in the study.

3.4 Problematic patterns in phonological loanword adaptation

This Section is devoted to the presentation of several problematic patterns, identified by Kang (2011), which emerge in phonological loanword adaptation. These include the too-many-solutions problem (3.4.1), divergent repair (3.4.2), unnecessary repair (3.4.3), differential importation (3.4.4) and retreat to the unmarked (3.4.5). Since theoretical explanations for some of these phenomena proposed within specific approaches to loanword adaptation will be discussed in Chapter 2, here we restrict ourselves to their brief introduction.

3.4.1 The too-many-solutions problem

The too-many-solutions problem refers to the situation where it is logically possible to apply to an illicit input any of a number of repair strategies, all of which yield well-formed outputs, but only one specific strategy is consistently used. As pointed out by Steriade (2001/2008: 151–152), when a language bans voiced obstruents word-finally (*[+VOICE]/__]WORD), this requirement may be satisfied in a variety of ways, as shown in (2).

(2) Possible reactions to the violation of *[±VOICE]/]WORD in the input /tæb/

(a) devoicing	/tæb/ → [tæp]	(e) vowel insertion	/tæb/ → [tæbə]
(b) nasalisation	/tæb/ → [tæm]	(f) segment reversal	/tæb/ → [bæt]
(c) lenition to glide	/tæb/ → [tæw]	(g) feature reversal	/tæb/ → [dæp]
(d) consonant deletion	/tæb/ → [tæ]		

All these repairs yield well-formed structures with respect to the constraint in question, yet the strategy predominantly applied in such cases is word-final devoicing (/tæb/ → [tæp]).

An examination of loanwords in various languages reveals that in a situation where different adaptation strategies are available and there is no evidence from native phonology as to how a given structure should be handled, borrowers tend to choose one specific repair. Adler (2006) cites the example of Hawaiian, which does not have the bilabial voiced plosive /b/ in its inventory. When words containing /b/ are borrowed from English, the segment in question is invariably mapped onto [p], as exemplified in (3) (p. 1027).

(3) Adaptation of English words containing /b/ in Hawaiian
Colby	[kolopíː]
boulder	[polukáː]
blessing	[pelekíne]

Thus, the illicit phoneme is made to conform to the native sound system through devoicing (/b/ → [p]) rather than nasalisation (/b/ → [m]) or lenition (/b/ → [w]), which would also produce well-formed outputs since both /m/ and /w/ belong to the Hawaiian inventory.

Another important aspect of the too-many-solutions problem is mentioned by Kang (2011), who observes that in a language prohibiting complex onsets, a word-initial cluster of the shape C_1C_2V may be repaired by means of the elision of one of the consonants (C_1V or C_2V) or vowel epenthesis either in front of the cluster (VC_1C_2V) or between the consonants (C_1VC_2V). As noted by Kang (2011), these strategies are consistently employed within specific groups of loanwords in particular languages, for instance consonant deletion applies in French loanwords in Vietnamese (e.g. *crème* → [kem]), whereas vowel epenthesis occurs in English loans in Japanese (e.g. *Christmas* → [kurisumasu]). Since the main focus of the present monograph is on online adaptation of Polish consonant clusters by native speakers of English, the too-many-solutions problem will assume key importance in Chapters 4 and 5, where the patterns of adaptation of CC and CCC consonant sequences are dealt with respectively.

The examples presented in this Section clearly indicate that there is a high degree of convergence among borrowers as to which repair strategy should be used when adapting a loanword. In this light, the question naturally arises regarding the mechanisms governing this process.

3.4.2 Divergent repair

We are dealing with a case of divergent repair when a given constraint is satisfied by means of different repair strategies in the native lexicon and in loanwords. For instance, Kenstowicz and Suchato (2006), who investigate English loanwords in Thai, point out that final syllables in Thai must be heavy. In the native phonology, this requirement is fulfilled by means of the glottal stop epenthesis in the coda position, whereas in loanwords through vowel lengthening, as illustrated in (4) (p. 933).

(4) Divergent repair in Thai

		loanwords from English	
native vocabulary		data	[dāatâa]
/pʰrá/ → [pʰráʔ] 'lord, monk'		auto	[ʔôotôo]
		center	[sēntâə]

A yet different repair is employed word-medially when Thai borrows an English word containing a short vowel. In the majority of such cases, the consonant following the vowel is geminated (e.g. *cookie* → [kúk.kìi]) and the native strategy of the glottal stop insertion is used only when the output of gemination would constitute an ill-formed structure. Thus, English *gorilla* is adapted as [kɔ̄ɔ.ríʔ. lâa], with the glottal stop rather than [l] since Thai bans liquid codas.

Another example of divergent repair is provided by Yip (2002: 5), who notes that in Maori the constraint which prohibits codas is satisfied by different repairs in the native vocabulary and in loanwords from English, as shown in (5).

(5) Divergent repair in Maori

native vocabulary			loanwords from English	
/hopuk/ → [hopu]	'catch'		cream	[kirimi]
/inum/ → [inu]	'drink'		chariot	[ha:riata]
/maatur/ → [maatu]	'know'		wool	[wu:ru]

As can be seen in (5), native stems ending in a consonant at the phonological level delete the final segment so as to conform to the Maori syllable structure. In loanwords, however, the underlying coda consonant is retained and the final vowel epenthesis ensures the satisfaction of the no coda requirement.[11]

The data provided in this Section reveal that in some languages a given underlying ill-formed structure may be repaired in a number of different ways depending on whether it belongs to the native lexicon or comes from a foreign source. This may prove that loanwords hold a special status in grammars of languages.

---

11 Further examples of divergent repair are provided in Peperkamp *et al.* (2008: 156).

In Chapter 3 we will argue that the English phonotactics provides evidence for the core vs. periphery organisation of the lexicon, with certain loanwords being located in the latter. This will be further supported by the results of online adaptation experiments presented and examined in Chapters 4 and 5.

3.4.3 Unnecessary repair

Unnecessary repair takes place when a given source form undergoes some sort of modification even though it contains no structures which are ill-formed in the target language. This phenomenon occurs for instance in White Hmong (Golston and Yang 2001), where although /ʒ/ belongs to the native inventory, in French loanwords it is consistently realised as [j], as demonstrated in (6).[12]

(6) Unnecessary adaptation of French loanwords in White Hmong
    Joel   [ʒɔɛl] → [jɔ̀.ê]
    Jacob   [ʒakɔb] → [jà.kɔ̀]

Another case of unnecessary repair is reported by Peperkamp (2005). Drawing on Shinohara's (1997) findings, she points out that French loanwords in Japanese ending in [n] are adapted with a geminated nasal and a final epenthetic vowel in spite of the fact that [n] is permitted word-finally in Japanese and occurs in this position much more frequently than the sequence [nnu]. Some relevant examples are listed in (7) (p. 344).

(7) Unnecessary adaptation of French loanwords in Japanese
    douane 'customs'   [dwan] → [duannu]
    piscine 'swimming pool'   [pisin] → [pisinnu]

This adaptation strategy becomes even more puzzling when one considers English loanwords with word-final [n] in Japanese, which do not exhibit unnecessary repair and are adapted in accordance with the native pattern, as illustrated in (8) (p. 344).

(8) Adaptation of English loanwords in Japanese
    screen   [sukuriin]
    napkin   [napukin]
    cotton   [koton]

The cases of source items which are well-formed in the target language but are nevertheless adapted seem particularly puzzling in that they run counter to the principle of the economy of language. Therefore, it appears that another challenge

---

12 This might be an instance of an orthographic adaptation.

for any theory of loanword adaptation is to discover the reasons why certain inputs are modified despite their well-formedness in the recipient language. Since the online adaptation experiments reported on in Chapters 4 and 5 focus on the nativisation of the Polish consonant sequences which are ill-formed in English, the issue of unnecessary repair will assume negligible importance in the present study.

3.4.4 Differential importation

Importation, a process whereby a foreign structure enters the target language as a consequence of borrowing, is a common phenomenon in loanword adaptation. However, not all source patterns are imported equally readily and some are never imported. Differential importation refers to the situation in which, given two foreign ill-formed structures, one is allowed in the target language, whereas the other undergoes consistent adaptation.

A representative example is cited by Itô and Mester (1995: 832–833), who point out that there is a constraint *TI in Japanese, prohibiting sequences of coronal consonants and the high front vowel. The constraint is satisfied by means of palatalisation of coronals before /i/, as illustrated in (9).

(9) Palatalisation of coronal consonants in Japanese
/kat/   kat-e   kač-i   'win,' imperative, infinitive
/hanas/   hanas-e   hanaš-i   'talk,' imperative, infinitive

When English words containing coronals followed by /ɪ/ or /iː/ are borrowed into Japanese, the situation becomes fairly complex. Thus, the foreign items which have an underlying sequence of a coronal fricative and the high front vowel, that is either /sɪ(ː)/ or /zɪ(ː)/, follow the native Japanese pattern and surface with the palatalised affricates [š] and [ǰ], respectively. This is demonstrated in (10).

(10) Adaptation of English loanwords containing /sɪ(ː)/ or /zɪ(ː)/ in Japanese
cinema   [šinema]
dressing   [doreššiŋgu]
zigzag   [ǰiguzagu]

As regards the English borrowings with phonological /tɪ(ː)/ or /dɪ(ː)/, the majority are made to conform to *TI by means of either palatalisation of the consonant (11a) or lowering the following vowel to a mid one (11b).

(11) Adaptation of English loanwords containing /tɪ(ː)/ or /dɪ(ː)/ in Japanese
(a) team   [čiimu]   (b) spaghetti   [supagettee]
    ticket   [čiketto]   tissue   [teššu]
    dilemma [ǰiremma]   disco   [desuko]

However, there are cases of English loanwords in which the structures /tɪ(:)/ and /dɪ(:)/ are not modified in any way but surface as such despite being ill-formed with regard to *TI. This is exemplified in (12).

(12) <u>Violation of *TI in English loanwords in Japanese</u>

teen(ager)	[tiin]	*[čiin]
party	[paatii]	*[paačii]
disc jockey	[disuku-jokkii]	*[jisuku-jokkii]
duet	[dʸuetto]	*[juetto]

The cases presented in (10)-(12) clearly indicate that in Japanese the restriction against the sequences of coronal fricatives and the high front vowel is stronger than the ban on coronal stops followed by this vowel. This is corroborated by the fact that loans containing the former structure are always adapted. On the other hand, it is possible for those with coronal stop + the high front vowel sequences to be only partially nativised so that they surface with the illicit structures [ti] and [di].[13]

Yet another case of differential importation is provided by English loanwords in Hawaiian. As argued by Adler (2006), when these are borrowed, certain cases of segmental importation are tolerated, whereas syllabic violations are invariably repaired, as shown in (13) (p. 1043).

(13) <u>Adaptation of English *truck* in Hawaiian</u>

    (a) *truck*   [kəlákə]   fully nativised
    (b) *truck*   [təlákə]   partially nativised
    (c) *truck*   *[krákə]   impossible nativisation

As can be seen in (13), a partially nativised version of *truck* with an illicit segment [t] is acceptable (13b), which proves that some degree of segmental importation is allowed in Hawaiian. However, the form not conforming to the CV syllable structure by virtue of having a complex onset (13c) is prohibited. This indicates that the constraints on syllable structure are more forceful in Hawaiian than the segmental restrictions.

Similarly, some French loanwords in Polish undergo complete phonemic substitution but preserve the original final stress, even though the default stress placement in Polish is on the penultimate syllable (14).

---

13 A similar phenomenon can be observed in Polish where coronals cannot be followed by /i/ in the native vocabulary (Gussmann 2007), however, in some loanwords this constraint is relaxed, e.g. *sinus* ['sʲinus] 'sine,' *tik* [tʲik] 'tic' and *dinozaur* [dʲi'nɔzawr] 'dinosaur' (Szpyra-Kozłowska 2016c).

(14) French loanwords in Polish with final stress

menu	[mɛ̃ˈɲi]	*[ˈmɛ̃ɲi]
attaché	[ataˈʂɛ]	*[aˈtaʂɛ]
rendezvous	[rãndɛˈvu]	*[rãnˈdɛvu]
tête-à-tête	[tɛtaˈtɛt]	*[tɛˈtatɛt]
vis-à-vis	[vʲizaˈvʲi]	*[vʲiˈzavʲi]

As shown in (14), the Polish segmental constraints are satisfied in loanwords from French, whereas the native stress assignment constraints are not.

The question why certain foreign patterns are readily imported into the target language as opposed to others constitutes another significant theoretical challenge. As a result, any valid theory of loanword adaptation should be able to provide a systematic formal account of such cases. The results of online adaptation experiments presented in Chapters 4 and 5 reveal a number of instances of differential importation, where certain consonant sequences are mostly reproduced targetlike by the adapters, whereas others undergo modification, e.g. vowel epenthesis. It will be argued that the phenomenon under discussion is shaped by a number of factors, including the sonority distance between C_1 and C_2 as well as the voicing and place of articulation of individual members of the cluster.

3.4.5 Retreat to the unmarked

When a loanword is adapted to an unmarked form even though a more faithful well-formed structure is available in the target language, we are dealing with a case of retreat to the unmarked or emergence of the unmarked. In other words, as noted by Kang (2011), the constraints imposed on loanwords by L1 grammar are occasionally stricter than those which pertain to the native vocabulary.

Kenstowicz and Suchato (2006) identify two possible instances of such patterns in Thai. The first example concerns the nativisation of English loans containing word-initial voiceless plosives. As is well known, the segments in question are aspirated and the data presented by Kenstowicz and Suchato suggest that Thai borrowers are sensitive to this feature of loans since aspiration is consistently preserved in adaptation, as illustrated in (15) (p. 928).

(15) Adaptation of English word-initial plosives in Thai

English	Thai	English	Thai
[pʰ]enny	[pʰɛ̄nnīi]	[kʰ]one	[khōon]
[tʰ]eam	[tʰiim]	[kʰ]upid	[kʰīwpît]

However, there is a group of English borrowings where aspiration is not retained. This usually takes place when an aspirated voiceless plosive and a following unaspirated one co-occur in the same word, as shown in (16) (p. 931).

(16) Unaspirated initial plosives in English loans in Thai

English	Thai	English	Thai
[pʰ]ark	[páak]	[tʰ]ick	[tík]
[tʰ]axi	[téɛsîi]	[kʰ]ard	[káat]

As suggested by Kang (2011), the cases presented in (16) seem to indicate a tendency for non-aspiration harmony, which may constitute an instance of retreat to the unmarked since no such generalisation holds in the native Thai grammar.

Another example of the phenomenon under discussion is provided by tone assignment to English loanwords in Thai. Kenstowicz and Suchato (2006) point out that every syllable in this language must be assigned one of five tones, namely high (H), mid (M), low (L), rising (R) or falling (F). The selection of tone for a given syllable depends to a considerable extent on its structure, in particular whether it is 'live' or 'dead'. Syllables of the former kind either have no coda or end in a sonorant and may take each of the five tones. 'Dead' syllables, on the other hand, have an obstruent in the coda and take either a H or L tone when a short vowel forms the nucleus and either a L or F tone when they contain a long vowel. As regards tone assignment to English loanwords, Kenstowicz and Suchato (2006) claim that it is carried out in accordance with a default pattern which assigns mid tone (M) to 'live' syllables and high tone (H) to 'dead' syllables.

Yet another potential instance of retreat to the unmarked is provided by Kenstowicz and Sohn (2001), who examine pitch accent assignment to, mainly English, loanwords in the North Kyungsang dialect of Korean. It is pointed out that since pitch accent in this dialect is generally unpredictable and may fall on any syllable in a word, this feature might be expected to be faithfully replicated in loanwords. However, Kenstowicz and Sohn's (2001) analysis of a corpus of 600 loanwords reveals that a default pattern of accenting penultimate syllable emerges in borrowings.

Retreat to the unmarked is a particularly problematic phenomenon, since, as noted by Kang (2011: 2261), frequently "there is no clear evidence for the <<unmarked>> status of the resulting structure in the native data." In consequence, cases such as those presented in this Section pose a considerable challenge to theories of loanword adaptation.

We will present and examine some instances of the emergence of the unmarked in Chapter 4, where we report on the results of an online adaptation experiment on the nativisation of Polish CC consonant clusters by native speakers of English. It will be argued that such phenomena are best accounted for in the Optimality Theory framework (Prince and Smolensky 1993/2004, McCarthy and Prince 1995) by means of faithfulness constraints demotion with respect to markedness constraints.

4 History of borrowings into English

Before we deal with the main focus of the present thesis, i.e. online phonological adaptation of foreign words with consonant clusters in English, let us briefly sketch the history of foreign lexical influence on this language. The present shape of English is, to a significant extent, a result of extensive borrowing from a variety of sources, with this process going on since the beginnings of the language. English seems to have a remarkable capacity for adopting foreign items, which has exerted a powerful influence on its development. As pointed out by Baugh (1957), although English is classified as a member of the Germanic branch of the Indo-European family, more than 50 % of its words came from Latin, either directly or via French, and other Romance languages. Not only did the massive borrowing result in enriching the vocabulary of English but it also had a profound impact on its structure, including the sound system. Therefore, in what follows it seems justified to mention the major changes in the phonology of this language which have taken place under a foreign influence. In this Section, we briefly outline the history of borrowing in the four periods of the development of English, namely Old English (OE) (450–1100), Middle English (ME) (1100–1500), Early Modern English (EME) (1500–1800) and Present-Day English (PDE) (since 1800).[14] We present the major sources of influence as well as provide a description of the changes in the lexicon and the sound system of English which occurred as a result of borrowing. The discussion is not meant to be detailed and exhaustive as its purpose is to serve as a useful background to the analysis offered in the subsequent Chapters.

4.1 Old English (450–1100)

The period of Old English is assumed to have lasted from 450 to 1100, starting with the conquest of Britain by the Germanic tribes of the Angles, the Saxons and the Jutes in the middle of the fifth century, which resulted in the introduction of a new language into the British territory. As observed by Baugh (1957), Old English was derived from a mixture of the dialects spoken by the invaders. It is also important to emphasise that the language in question was not uniform since it comprised four varieties, namely Northumbrian, Mercian, West Saxon and Kentish. The West Saxon dialect gained primary importance and is usually considered the literary standard of Old English. There were three main linguistic sources shaping, to varying degrees, Old English, namely Celtic, Latin and Old Norse.

---

14 The division adopted here is proposed by Millward and Hayes (2011).

As regards the Celtic influence, the least significant of the three, its evidence survived primarily in place names. Examples taken from Baugh (1957: 84–86) include *Kent, London, York, Thames, Avon, Dover* and *Wye*, among others. Apart from these, Old English borrowed only a handful of Celtic words, such as *binn* 'basket, crib,' *luh* 'lake,' *cumb* 'valley,' *ancor* 'hermit' and *cross* 'cross.'[15] The limited scope of the Celtic influence is usually attributed to the low prestige of the culture and language of the Celts, who were a conquered people. However, Millward and Hayes (2011) suggest that such an explanation cannot be regarded as fully satisfactory since the available evidence demonstrates that conquerors usually borrow a significant number of words from the language of the conquered. This was the case with the Romans and the Germanic tribes as well as with the European settlers in America and Native Americans. In both cases, the number of words taken over from the language of the subjugated nation was significantly greater. In this light, the scarcity of Celtic loanwords in Old English seems surprising and no compelling explanation of this puzzle is available.

The language which contributed to the vocabulary of Old English to a much larger extent was Latin. This is not surprising when one takes into consideration the fact that the Germanic tribes which conquered Britain maintained regular and steady contact with the Roman civilisation. Baugh (1957) distinguishes three periods of Latin influence, namely 1) the stage of continental borrowing (the zero period), 2) the stage of Latin through Celtic transmission (the first period) and 3) the stage of Christianizing Britain (the second period).

As regards the zero period, borrowing was a result of the contact of the two cultures on the European mainland. The primary vocabulary areas where the Latin influence is evident include war, trade, domestic life and food. Examples are provided in Tab. 2 (Baugh 1957: 91–92).

Tab. 2: Borrowings from Latin in the zero period

war	trade	domestic life	food
camp 'battle'	*cēap* 'bargain'	*mēse* 'table'	*cīese* 'cheese'
segn 'banner'	*mangian* 'to trade'	*cytel* 'kettle'	*pipor* 'pepper'
pīl 'javelin'	*pund* 'pound'	*scamol* 'bench'	*senep* 'mustard'
weall 'wall'	*mynet* 'coin'	*teped* 'carpet'	*spelt* 'wheat'

---

15 According to Crystal (2003), *ancor* and *cross* were borrowed from Latin through Celtic transmission.

In the next period, i.e. the stage of Latin through Celtic transmission, the number of loanwords is relatively small, most probably due to the minor influence of the Celtic culture on the Anglo-Saxon civilisation. One of the words borrowed at this stage is *ceaster* from Latin *castra* 'camp', which survived in such place names as *Chester, Colchester, Manchester, Lancaster* and *Gloucester*. Other examples include *port* 'harbour, gate, town', *munt* 'mountain' and *torr* 'tower, rock' (Baugh 1957: 93–94).

The most extensive Latin influence was brought about by the introduction of Christianity into the British Isles in 597. This event fundamentally changed the culture of the Anglo-Saxons and exerted a profound influence upon their language. The largest group of new words which came into English at the early stage of this period concern religion and its organisation. Examples taken from Baugh (1957) include *abbot, angel, candle, chalice, deacon, disciple, hymn, litany, mass, nun, pope, priest, psalm, shrine, temple* and many others. Latin also influenced other areas of vocabulary, such as clothes, food, plants and education. This is exemplified in Tab. 3 (Baugh 1957: 99).

Tab. 3: Borrowings from Latin in the early second period

clothes	food	plants	education
cap	beet	pine	school
sock	lentil	lily	master

The second wave of Latin borrowings came as a result of the Benedictine Reform in the late tenth century. The revival of learning in this period facilitated the introduction of words of predominantly scientific and learned character, such as *accent, history, term* or *title*. The major fields where the Latin influence was visible include religion, plants, animals and medical terms, as demonstrated in Tab. 4 (Baugh 1957: 103).

Tab. 4: Borrowings from Latin in the late second period

religion	plants	animals	medical terms
apostle	verbena	aspide 'viper'	cancer
canticle	coriander	camel	paralysis
cloister	ginger	lamprey	scrofula

Baugh (1957) indicates that altogether up to 450 words were borrowed from Latin into Old English, out of which 100 preserved their foreign character and were used only to a limited degree. The extent of the Latin influence may have been even greater since these figures do not include derivatives and proper names.

The third language playing a major part in shaping Old English was Old Norse, spoken by Scandinavian tribes invading Britain from the late eighth century and subsequently settling in a large part of the country. The languages under discussion were very similar, which greatly facilitated borrowing.

As observed by Baugh (1957), the Scandinavian influence can be traced primarily in a large number of place names (over 1400), particularly those ending in -by 'farm', -thorp 'village', -toft 'a piece of ground' and -thwaite 'an isolated piece of land'. Representative examples are presented in Tab. 5 (Baugh 1957: 115).

Tab. 5: Scandinavian place names in English

-by	-thorp	-toft	-thwaite
Grimsby	Althorp	Brimtoft	Applethwaite
Whitby	Bishopsthorpe	Eastoft	Braithwaite
Derby	Gawthorpe	Langtoft	Cowperthwaite

Old Norse also left its mark on personal names, most notably those ending in -son, such as *Johnson* or *Stevenson*.

Other significant areas of the Scandinavian influence include sea-roving, war, law and words generally connected with everyday life. This is exemplified in Tab. 6 (Baugh 1957: 116–117).

Tab. 6: Scandinavian borrowings in Old English

sea-roving	war	law	everyday life
barda 'beaked ship'	dreng 'warrior'	law	bull
cnearr 'small warship'	orrest 'battle'	outlaw	egg
	rān 'robbery'	māl 'action at law'	sister
scegþ 'vessel'	fylcian 'to collect or marshal a force'	wapentake 'an administrative district'	skill
liþ 'fleet'			sky
			window

However, not only nouns were borrowed from Old Norse, but also a number of adjectives, for example *awkward, flat, ill, rotten, sly, tight* and *weak*, as well as verbs, such as *bask, call, cast, die, get, give, raise, scare, take* and *thrust*. The extent of the Scandinavian influence was so considerable that it resulted in the transfer of items hardly ever finding their way into other languages, such as adverbs, pronouns and prepositions, as shown in Tab. 7 (Baugh 1957: 120–121).

adverbs	pronouns	prepositions
aloft	they	till
athwart	their	fro
seemly	them	though

Also, the form *are* of the verb *to be* has the Scandinavian origin, which constitutes yet another piece of evidence for the significance of the Old Norse influence.

Although borrowing exerted a considerable impact on the lexicon of Old English, it had only a limited effect on its sound system. Thus, the basic phonemic inventory was not altered in any way under foreign influence. Nonetheless, certain phonotactic modifications took place as a result of borrowing, the most important probably being the introduction of the cluster /sk/. As pointed out by Millward and Hayes (2011: 88), in Old English words of Germanic origin the sequence /sk/ was palatalised to /ʃ/, e.g. in *fisc* 'fish', *wascan* 'wash' and *scearp* 'sharp' (the graphemes <sc> corresponded to the phoneme /ʃ/). Present-Day English words with the /sk/ cluster, such as *skirt*, *skip* or *skill*, are mostly loanwords from Old Norse, in which the sequence under discussion did not undergo palatalisation. As noted by Gelderen (2006), in some cases a Germanic item which already existed in Old English and had undergone Palatalisation was borrowed from Old Norse in its non-palatalised version. When both words survived, their meanings were differentiated. This resulted in such pairs as *shirt – skirt, ship – skipper* and *shatter – scatter*.

To sum up, the period of Old English marks the beginning of a growing tendency for English to adopt foreign elements. However, the most substantial changes in this respect, determining to a significant degree the shape of Present-Day English, took place in the following period, i.e. Middle English.

4.2 Middle English (1100–1500)

In the period after the Norman Conquest of England in 1066, English underwent far-reaching modifications, both in terms of its grammar and vocabulary. As regards the former, the most profound change was the loss of the majority of inflectional endings and, consequently, the simplification of grammar.[16] As for

---

16 As pointed out by Millward and Hayes (2011), one of the most popular explanations of this phenomenon is a sort of creolisation of English at that time, which could have resulted from the confusion caused by different inflectional systems of Old English and

the latter, the lexicon of English was greatly enriched by extensive borrowing, mainly from French and Latin.

As a matter of fact, the influx of French words in this period constitutes one of the greatest foreign influences in the history of English. It was one of the consequences of the Norman Conquest, which introduced French as the official language of England. The coexistence of both languages, lasting for about three hundred years after the Conquest greatly facilitated borrowing. The extent of the French influence on the Middle English lexicon reflected the profundity of changes in culture and the organisation of society in England brought about by the Norman rule. Therefore, it comes as no surprise that loanwords from French can be found in a wide range of semantic fields, with the most important ones presented in Tab. 8 (Millward and Hayes 2011: 195–196).

Tab. 8: French loanwords in Middle English

relationships and ranks	*parentage, ancestor, aunt, uncle, cousin, gentle, peer, servant, page, madam, sir, princess, duke, count, marquis, baron*
the house and its furnishings	*porch, cellar, pantry, closet, parlour, chimney, arch, pane, chair, table, lamp, couch, cushion, mirror, curtain, quilt*
food and eating	*dinner, supper, taste, broil, fry, plate, goblet, serve, beverage, sauce, salad, gravy, fruit, grape, beef, pork, mutton, salmon*
fashion	*fashion, dress, garment, coat, cloak, boots, serge, cotton, satin, fur, button, ribbon, embroider, pleat, jewel, pearl*
sports and entertainment	*tournament, kennel, scent, terrier, stallion, park, dance, chess, checkers, fool, prize, tennis, racket, audience, entertain*
arts, music, literature	*art, painting, sculpture, portrait, colour, music, melody, lute, carol, poet, story, chapter, title, romance, tragedy, ballad*
education	*study, science, reason, university, college, dean, grammar, noun, subject, test, pupil, copy, pen, pencil, paper, page,*
medicine	*medicine, surgeon, pain, disease, remedy, cure, contagious, plague, pulse, fracture, drug, balm, herb, powder, sulphur*
government	*government, state, country, city, village, office, rule, reign, public, crown, court, police, tyranny, subsidy, tax, counsellor*
law	*judge, jury, appeal, evidence, inquest, accuse, proof, convict, pardon, attorney, heir, statute, broker, fine, punish, prison*

---

the two foreign languages exerting the most powerful influence on it, i.e. Old Norse and French. For the discussion of the problem, see Millward and Hayes (2011: 164–166).

the church	*chapel, choir, cloister, crucifix, religion, clergy, chaplain, sermon, confession, penance, pray, anoint, absolve, trinity, faith, miracle, temptation, heresy, divine, salvation*
the military	*enemy, battle, defence, peace, force, advance, capture, siege, attack, retreat, army, navy, soldier, guard, sergeant, captain*

As can be seen in Tab. 8, French borrowings permeated the vocabulary concerning virtually every aspect of life. This impact becomes even more striking in the light of the fact that many common words widely used in Present-Day English are in fact loanwords from French. Some examples given by Millward and Hayes (2011: 196) include *age, catch, chance, change, close, enter, face, fine, flower, fresh, hello, join, letter, line, move, offer, part, pay, people, piece, place, please, rock, save, search, sign, square, strange, sure, touch, try, turn* and *use*.

It should also be pointed out that a number of Old English words were lost in this period, some of which were replaced by their French equivalents, as illustrated in Tab. 9 (Baugh 1957: 217).

Tab. 9: Old English words replaced by French loanwords

Old English	French loanword
ieldu	*age*
lyft	*air*
earm	*poor*
herian	*praise*

In other cases, both words survived but their meanings underwent differentiation. For instance, the English words *ox, sheep, swine* and *calf* refer to animals whereas their French loan equivalents, i.e. *beef, mutton, pork* and *veal* respectively, denote the meat of those animals (Baugh 1957: 218). Altogether, as claimed by Baugh (1957), over 10,000 words were borrowed from French during the Middle English period, 75 % of which are still in use.

Another important source of new words in Middle English was Latin, the language of the Church. Although a great number of Latin loans entered English via French, some were borrowed directly, primarily through written language. These were usually religious terms as well as less popular words of a learned character, such as *apocalypse, limbo, purgatory, contempt, subjugate, innumerable, incarnate, homicide, reprehend, testimony* and *malefactor* (Baugh 1957: 223, Millward and Hayes 2011: 197). It is important to note that the Latin influence was moderate compared with the French impact of that time as well as with the Latin influence in the Early Modern English period.

Other languages and their contributions to Middle English are presented in Tab. 10 (Millward and Hayes 2011: 197–198). Of these, the most numerous were Dutch and Low German borrowings, mainly due to increased commerce between England and the Low Countries.

Tab. 10: Middle English – other influences

Celtic languages	*bard, clan, crag, glen, loch, bald, bray, bug, gull, hog, loop*
Dutch and Low German	*halibut, pump, shore, skipper, whiting, bundle, bung, cork, dowel, firkin, tub, trade, huckster clock, damp, grime, luck, offal, scour*
Other[17]	<u>Greek</u> (*squirrel, diaper, cinnamon, philosophy, paradigm, phlegm, synod, physic*) <u>Arabic</u> (*azimuth, ream, saffron, cipher, alkali*) <u>Persian</u> (*borax, mummy, musk, spinach, taffeta, lemon*) <u>Hebrew</u> (*jubilee, leviathan, cider*)

Middle English is also a period when profound changes affected the sound system of English, some of which were inspired by foreign sources. With regard to the consonantal inventory, the major development was the emergence of the phonemic voiced fricatives /v, ð, z/. As pointed out by Millward and Hayes (2011), in Old English there existed only voiceless fricative phonemes, i.e. /f, θ, s, ʃ, h/. The sounds [v, ð, z] occurred only as allophones of /f, θ, s/ respectively between two voiced segments. In Middle English /v, ð, z/ gained the phonemic status due to numerous factors, one of which was the influence of loanwords, particularly French ones.[18] Millward and Hayes (2011) note that it is primarily the /f/ - /v/ contrast that was enhanced by French borrowings, in particular by such minimal pairs as *fine* and *vine*. Also, the /f/ - /v/ distinction was crucial in distinguishing between such French loans as *vetch, view* and *vile* and English words *fetch, few* and *file* respectively. Millward and Hayes (2011) also emphasise that in Present-Day English the distribution of /v, ð, z/ is much more limited with regard to other consonants in that, for example, the initial /v/ and /z/ are found only in loanwords (the former in Latin and French, the latter in Greek ones).

---

17 The loanwords listed here were borrowed into English via either Latin or French.

18 /ʃ/ did not develop a corresponding voiced phoneme in Middle English. The phonemic /ʒ/ appeared in the Early Modern English period.

Although foreign influence exerted some impact on English consonants, its effects can be seen primarily in the vocalic inventory of this language. First and foremost, the unprecedented influx of French loanwords introduced two new diphthongs into the English vowel system, namely /ʊɪ/ and /ɔɪ/.[19] The former appeared in such ME words as *boille(n)* 'boil' and *point* (from Old French *bouillir* and *point* respectively), whereas the latter, for instance, in *noise* and *chois* 'choice' (from Old French *noyse* and *choisir* respectively).

Besides adding new diphthongs to the inventory of English, French loans provided secondary sources for the development of other vocalic segments. Thus, /ɛʊ/ developed from Old English [æw] and [æəw], as in OE *fēawe* (ME *fewe* 'few'), as well as from the vowels in Old French loanwords, such as *neveu* (ME *neveu* 'nephew'). Similarly, /aʊ/ had its origins in OE /aw/, /aɣ/ and /ax/, e.g. OE *clawu* (ME *clawe* 'claw') or *awiht* (ME *aught*), as well as in Old French borrowings such as *cause* (ME *cause*).

Foreign words also contributed to the development of some monophthongs in Middle English. For instance, ME /ɪ/ and /ɛ/, originated in both the native sources as well as in Old Norse loans such as *skin* and *egg*. Similarly, Old French borrowings, such as *test* and *part* played some part in the rise of ME /ɛ/ and /a/. Furthermore, loanwords provided secondary sources for certain ME long vowels such as /ā/ (OF *save*), /ō/ (ON *root*), /ī/ (ON *thrive*) and /ē/ (OF *beste* 'beast').

In addition, Millward and Hayes (2011) claim that foreign influence had an effect on the prosody of English in that it contributed to the shift in the rhythm of the language. The rhythm of Old English was primarily trochaic, i.e. words and phrases usually started with a stressed syllable followed by unstressed syllables, as in *fēlă míssĕră* 'for many half-years' or *fólcĕ to frófrĕ* 'as a consolation to the people.' Middle English, on the other hand, had an iambic rhythm, i.e. unstressed syllables tended to be followed by stressed ones, as in *ŏf mȳ gráce* or *whăn thĕ sónne wăs tŏ réste*. One of the causes of this shift was the vast influx of French loanwords, the majority of which retained their native stress pattern and, consequently, carried final stress.

To sum up, Middle English differed to a significant degree from Old English in that it lost most of its inflectional endings and incorporated thousands of loanwords, particularly from French, into its lexicon. In this light, it becomes evident that foreign influence has had an enormous effect on the development of English and has determined its present shape to a considerable extent.

---

19 These diphthongs coalesced into /ɔɪ/ in the Early Modern English period.

4.3 Early Modern English (1500–1800)

The most important non-linguistic factors which influenced the evolution of English in the sixteenth and the following centuries include the invention of print, the spread of popular education, the development of communication as well as the growth of social consciousness (Baugh 1957: 240). All these conditions facilitated rapid progress in virtually every field of learning and, in turn, had some bearing on the shape of English. In the period under discussion, this language underwent relatively slight changes in grammar but much more extensive modifications in terms of the lexicon, mainly due to borrowing (Baugh 1957: 243). Borrowing was facilitated by the need to enrich the vocabulary of English in order to make it adequate to express new concepts and ideas which appeared as a result of scientific progress. In addition, the discovery of new territories and contact with their inhabitants resulted in the adoption of a number of loans from non-European languages.

Nonetheless, the most important sources of borrowings in the period of Early Modern English were Latin and Greek.[20] As observed by Millward and Hayes (2011: 278), these two languages contributed words primarily of a learned character, i.e. scientific, technical, artistic, philosophical, educational and literary terms. Some examples are presented in Tab. 11 (p. 278–279).

Tab. 11: Latin and Greek loans in Early Modern English

Latin	*ambiguous, biceps, census, decorate, emotion, fanatic, gladiator, harmonica, identical, joke, lichen, mandible, navigate, opponent, perfidious, quotation, ratio, scintillate, tangent, ultimate, vacuum*
Greek	*anarchy, aorist, aphrodisiac, autarchy, autochthon, analysis, anathema, angina, anonymous, antidote, archetype, autograph*

Since Latin and Greek were languages of science and education, it comes as no surprise that a great number of classical loans entered English in the period under examination, when rapid scientific progress took place.

It is also important to note that some words from Latin borrowed in Middle English were reintroduced in Early Modern English with a different form and meaning. This phenomenon gave rise to the so-called doublets, that is, according

---

20 Millward and Hayes (2011) point out that in some cases it is impossible to determine whether a given word was borrowed directly from Latin or Greek, or indirectly through one of the Romance languages.

to Millward and Hayes (2011: 278), "two words from the same source that enter a language by different routes." Some examples are given in Tab. 12 (p. 278).

Tab. 12: Latin doublets

Middle English	Early Modern English
jealous	zealous
prove	probe
treasure	thesaurus
frail	fragile
gender	genus

Apart from classical loans, English borrowed numerous terms from contemporary European languages. Of these, French contributed the largest number of loanwords, mainly due to its popularity among the upper classes. The increased cultural, political and commercial relations between England and such countries as Italy or the Low Countries resulted in the introduction of a number of Italian, Dutch and German loans. Furthermore, the colonisation of non-European territories as well as the competition between England and Spain or Portugal in this respect yielded many Spanish and Portuguese terms related to life in the colonies, some of which came indirectly through non-European languages. Examples of loans borrowed from European languages in the Early Modern English period are listed in Tab. 13 (Millward and Hayes 2011: 279–280).

Tab. 13: Loanwords from European languages in Early Modern English

French	*admire, barbarian, compute, density, effigy, formidable, gratitude, hospitable, identity, javelin, liaison, manipulation, notoriety, optic, parade, ramify, sociable*
Italian	*adagio, alto, andante, aria, operetta, oratorio, solo, sonata, balcony, bandit, ghetto, macaroni, motto, regatta, vermicelli, carnival, ditto, malaria, zany, antic, archipelago, arsenal, artichoke, tariff*
Spanish	*cigar, papaya, potato, puma, alpaca, avocado, cannibal, canoe, chilli, maize, tomato, coyote, llama, iguana, hammock, anchovy, breeze, castanet, cockroach, sombrero, tortilla*
Portuguese	*mango, albacore, betel, pagoda, tank, yam, tapioca, cashew, auto-da-fé, palaver, molasses, albino, dodo*
Dutch	*avast, boom, commodore, cruise, deck, reef, scow, sloop, smack, smuggle, splice, stoke, yacht, easel, etch, landscape, sketch, stipple, blunderbuss, brandy, clapboard, drill, foist, gruff, muff, ravel, sleigh, snuff, sputter, uproar*

German	bismuth, cobalt, gneiss, meerschaum, quartz, zinc, carouse, fife, halt, knapsack, noodle, plunder, swindle, veneer, waltz
Celtic languages	banshee, brogue, caber, cairn, galore, hubbub, leprechaun, plaid, ptarmigan, shamrock, shillelagh, slogan, trousers, whiskey
Other	Russian (beluga, kvass, mammoth, steppe) Norwegian (auk, fjord, lemming, troll) Icelandic (eider, geyser) Swedish (tungsten) Hungarian (hussar)

Early Modern English is also a period when for the first time English borrowed a considerable number of words from non-European languages. This was one of the consequences of the discovery of new territories outside Europe and extensive contacts with their inhabitants. The contribution of the languages under discussion to the lexicon of English is presented in Tab. 14 (Millward and Hayes 2011: 281–282).

Tab. 14: Loanwords from non-European languages in Early Modern English

Amerindian languages[21]	**animals:** *moose, muskrat, opossum, raccoon, skunk, terrapin, woodchuck* **plants and food products:** *hickory, hominy, pecan, persimmon, poke(weed), pone, squash, succotash, tamarack* **artefacts:** *moccasin, tomahawk, totem, wampum, wigwam* **cultural relations:** *caucus, manitou, papoose, powwow, sachem, sagamore, squaw*
Asian languages	Hindi: *bandanna, bangle, bungalow, cheetah, cowrie, cummerbund, dungaree, gunny, guru, jungle, myna, nabob, pundit, sari, seersucker, shampoo, toddy, veranda* Tamil: *catamaran, cheroot, corundum, curry, pariah* Bengali: *dinghy, jute* Urdu: *coolie* Malay: *amuck, caddy, cassowary, kapok, orangutan, rattan, sago, teak* Chinese: *ginseng, ketchup, kum-quat, litchi, nankeen, pekoe, pongee, sampan, tea, typhoon* Japanese: *mikado, sake, shogun, soy* Tibetan: *lama, yak*

---

21 The majority of loanwords listed here come from Algonquian languages.

Near and Middle Eastern languages	Turkish: *dervish, divan, jackal, pasha, pilaf, sherbet, turban, vizier, yogurt* Persian: *attar, bazaar, percale, shawl* Arabic: *ghoul, harem, hashish, henna, hookah, sheik*
African languages	*chigger, marimba, okra*

With regard to the foreign-induced sound changes in Early Modern English, they were relatively slight. Thus, as indicated by Millward and Hayes (2011), both the consonantal and the vocalic inventories of Present-Day English were established by the end of this period. The major development in Early Modern English was the emergence of phonemic /ʒ/ and /ŋ/. Both had their origins in the native sources, however, the distribution of /ʒ/, which resulted from the coalescence of /zj/ in words like *pleasure* or *decision*, was extended to the word-final position by French loanwords such as *garage* or *beige*.

In the period under discussion, the vowel inventory of English underwent profound changes known as the Great Vowel Shift. As a result of these modifications, all the Middle English long vowels were raised and those which were already high became diphthongs. As pointed out by Millward and Hayes (2011), some scholars claim that the Great Vowel Shift was brought about by the extensive influx of French loans, whereas others maintain that it was borrowing from all Romance languages that induced the change. Although the cause of the Great Vowel Shift is still debated, it may be safely assumed that foreign influence played some part in this process.

To sum up, foreign sources continued to exert their influence on the shape of English in the Early Modern English period. Although their impact on the sound system was less strong than in Middle English, their contribution to the lexicon was still significant.

4.4 Present-Day English (since 1800)

The primary sources of borrowing in the period of Present-Day English are classical languages, i.e. Latin and Greek, which have been contributing to the English vocabulary since the middle of the fifth century. However, as pointed out by Millward and Hayes (2011: 324), the classical loans in Present-Day English differ from those of earlier periods in several respects.

First of all, although some new words taken over from Latin or Greek, such as *latex, television, antibiotic, electron* or *psychoanalyse* have entered the general English vocabulary, the majority are mainly technical terms. Another difference concerns the fact that a significant number of loanwords in question were not directly borrowed from classical languages, but were created out of Latin and Greek morphemes which had entered English at the earlier stages of development. For example, the word *retrovirus* consists of two Latin items, namely *rētro* 'backward' and *vīrus* 'poison', both borrowed in the sixteenth century. Similarly, the word *phylloclade* is a combination of two Greek nouns, i.e. *phullon* 'leaf' and *klados* 'branch'. Neither *retrovirus* nor *phylloclade* were used in Latin and Greek respectively but were created out of morphemes borrowed from these languages a few centuries earlier. The process of combining Latin and Greek elements in order to form new words has been so productive that, according to Millward and Hayes (2011: 281), "the classical vocabulary of English today is larger than the total known vocabularies of classical Greek and Latin." Two most common ways of forming new words out of classical morphemes include compounding, as in *phylloclade*, and affixation. Affixes taken over from Greek and Latin in the period under discussion include *auto-*, *epi-*, *ex-*, *hypo-*, *intra-*, *meta-*, *micro-*, *mini-*, *multi-*, *neo-*, *para-* and *ultra-*. Yet another characteristic of classical loans in Present-Day English is the fact that the majority of them are found in other European languages. An example given by Millward and Hayes (2011) is English *antitoxin*, French *antitoxine*, Italian *antitossina*, Swedish *antitoxin* and Russian *antitoksin*, all of which have a common classical source.

Apart from Latin and Greek loans, English has borrowed many words from various European languages, as demonstrated in Tab. 15 (Millward and Hayes 2011: 326–328).

Tab. 15: Loanwords from European languages in Present-Day English

French	beige, beret, blouse, crepe, lingerie, negligee, suede, au gratin, chef, éclair, gourmet, margarine, menu, restaurant, sauté, au jus, au pair, brochure, camouflage, chauffeur, cliché, coupon, elite, garage
Italian	lasagna, pasta, radicchio, salami, scaloppine, zucchini, fiasco, inferno, mafia, ocarina, piccolo
Spanish	adobe, alfalfa, bonanza, chaparral, mescal, quinine, silo, vamoose
Dutch[22]	boss, bushwhack, coleslaw, cruller, poppycock, snoop, spook, waffle, aardvark, apartheid, spoor, trek, veldt, wildebeest
German	seminar, semester, kindergarten, gestalt, leitmotif, lager, schnapps, pretzel, strudel, zwieback, accordion, glockenspiel, yodel, zither, dachshund, poodle, ersatz, kaput, strafe, paraffin, stalag, hinterland

---

22 Loanwords from Afrikaans, a South African dialect of Dutch are also included (Millward and Hayes 2011: 326).

Yiddish	*halvah, knish, kvetch, schlep, schlock, tsuris, bagel, chutzpah, kibitzer, kosher, lox, matzo, pastrami*
Irish	*colleen, dolmen, keen 'to lament', phoney, slew, drumlin, smithereens, blarney*
Russian	*babushka, balalaika, borscht, borzoi, intelligentsia, pogrom, samovar, troika, tundra, vodka*
Other	Norwegian (*ski, vole*) Czech (*polka, robot*) Danish (*flense*) Swedish (*rutabaga*) Polish (*mazurka*) Hungarian (*paprika, goulash*)

A variety of non-linguistic factors, such as the development of global communication, wars as well as free exchange of products and information have contributed to the increase in the number of loanwords from non-European languages. Representative examples are provided in Tab. 16 (Millward and Hayes 2011: 328–329).

Tab. 16: Loanwords from non-European languages in Present-Day English

Amerindian languages	Algonquian (*mugwump muskeg, pemmican, quahog, wickiup*) Navaho (*hogan*) Siouan (*tepee*) Eskimo (*anorak, husky, igloo*)
Asian languages	Japanese (*banzai, bonsai, geisha, ginkgo, hara-kiri, hibachi, jinrikisha, judo, jujitsu, kamikaze, karaoke, karate, kimono, obi, origami, samurai, sukiyaki, tempura, tsunami, tycoon*) Chinese (*feng shui, gung-ho, kowtow, mahjong, oolong, shanghai, shantung, tai chi, wok, dim sum*) Hindi (*chutney, loot, puttee, thug*) Urdu (khaki) Hawaiian (*aloha, hula, lei, poi, ukulele*) Australian (boomerang, koala, wallaby)
African languages	*bongo, dashiki, goober, gumbo, hoodoo, impala, safari, banjo, rumba, zombie, apartheid, commando, trek, ewe, gumbo, juke(box), mumbo-jumbo, voodoo, yarn*

It should also be pointed out that borrowing in Present-Day English did not have such a considerable influence on the sound system of English as in earlier periods, especially in Middle English. As noted by Millward and Hayes (2011: 310), the phonemic inventory of Present-Day English was established in Early Modern English and no significant changes in this respect took place in the nineteenth and twentieth century.

4.5 Polish loanwords in English

Since the main focus of the present monograph is on online adaptation of Polish words with consonant clusters by native speakers of English, a question naturally arises concerning the extent of Polish influence on English vocabulary. A survey of the current literature reveals that the number of such loanwords is very low. For example, Durkin (2014: 27), in a monograph on lexical borrowing into English, claims that Polish contributed no more than 20 words to the English lexicon. The following items of Polish origin can be found in Wells (2008).

(17) Polish loanwords in English

grosz	P [grɔʂ] → E [grɒʃ]
kielbasa (kiełbasa)	P [kʲɛw'basa] → E [kiːl'bɑːsə]
mazurka	P *mazurek* [ma'zurɛk] → E [mə'zɜːkə]
ogonek	P [ɔ'ɡɔ̃nɛk] → E [ɒ'ɡɒnek]
zloty (złoty)	P ['zwɔti] → E ['zlɒti]

Moreover, there are several Polish proper names which are used by some speakers of English, as exemplified in (18) (Wells 2008).

(18) Polish proper names

Bialystok (Białystok)	P [bʲja'wistɔk] → E [bi'ælɪstɒk]
Brzezinski (Brzeziński)	P [bʐɛ'ʑij̃skʲi] → E [brə'zɪnski]
Bydgoszcz	P ['bɨdgɔʂt͡ʂ] → E ['bɪdgɒʃ]
Gdansk (Gdańsk)	P [gdãj̃sk] → E [dænsk] / [gə'dænsk]
Gorecki (Górecki)	P [gu'rɛt͡skʲi] → E [gɔː'retski]
Jaruzelski	P [jaru'zɛlskʲi] → E [jæru'zelski]
Kosciusko (Kościuszko)	P [kɔɕ't͡ɕuʂkɔ] → E [kɒsi'ʌskəʊ]
Lodz (Łódź)	P [wut͡ɕ] → E [wʊd͡ʒ] / [loʊdz] (AmE)
Paderewski	P [padɛ'rɛfskʲi] → E [pædə'refski]
Penderecki	P [pɛ̃ndɛ'rɛt͡skʲi] → E [pendə'retski]
Pilsudski (Piłsudski)	P [pʲiw'sufskʲi] → E [pɪl'sʊdski]
Poznan (Poznań)	P ['pɔznãɲ] → E ['pɒznæn]
Pulaski (Pułaski)	P [pu'waskʲi] → E [pə'læski]
Strzelecki	P [stʂɛ'lɛt͡skʲi] → E [strez'leki]
Szczecin	P ['ʂt͡ʂɛt͡ɕin] → E ['ʃtʃetʃiːn]
Wajda	P ['vajda] → E ['vaɪdə]
Walesa (Wałęsa)	P [va'wɛw̃sa] → E [vɑː'wensə]
Wojtyla (Wojtyła)	P [vɔj'tiwa] → E [vɔr'tɪlə]
Wozniak (Woźniak)	P ['vɔʐɲak] → E ['wɒzniæk]
Wroclaw	P ['vrɔt͡swaf] → E ['vrɒtslɑːv]

The number of loanwords in question is too limited to draw any valid conclusions concerning established patterns of nativisation of Polish items by native speakers of English. On the one hand, there are a handful of clearly spelling-based adaptations. For instance, *zloty* is pronounced with the initial cluster [zl] rather than [zw], which reflects the way this word is spelt in English (the Polish grapheme <ł> corresponding to [w] is replaced with <l> in English). Other similar examples include *Kosciusko, Lodz* (in American English) and *Wozniak*, with the initial consonant pronounced according to the native English grapheme-to-phoneme rule, according to which <w> corresponds to [w]. On the other hand, some adaptations are undoubtedly pronunciation-based, e.g. *Walesa, Lodz* (in British English) or *Wajda*. There are also mixed cases, where both orthography and pronunciation play some role, as in *Wojtyla*, with the initial consonant realised as [v], in accordance with the original pronunciation, and the consonant in the final syllable adapted as [l], clearly on the basis of spelling.

The evidence concerning the treatment of Polish consonant clusters is scant. It can be observed that native English phonotactic restrictions are relaxed in some items, as in *zloty, Szczecin* and *Wrocław*, in which the initial CC sequences [zl], [ʃtʃ] and [vr] are tolerated, even though they are not attested in the native vocabulary. In Chapter 3 it will be demonstrated in more detail that such items belong to the peripheral stratum of the English lexicon, where certain native phonological constraints may be deactivated. Other clusters undergo some kind of modification. Thus, we find segment change in the initial cluster [bʑ] in *Brzeziński* ([bʑ] → [br]), deletion of [t͡ʂ] in the final sequence [ʂt͡ʂ] in *Bydgoszcz* as well as variation between vowel epenthesis and consonant deletion in the adaptation of [gd] in *Gdańsk*.

To sum up, given the scarcity of Polish loanwords in English, it may be concluded that there are no established repair strategies which native speakers of English apply in order to nativise Polish lexical items. In this situation, an online adaptation experiment can provide an answer to the question concerning the mechanisms which govern the phonological integration of foreign sound structures into English. Two such experiments will be the major focus of Chapters 4 and 5.

5 Conclusions

This Chapter has dealt with the basic concepts and fundamental issues relevant to the study of phonological loanword adaptation in general and in English in particular. These include the definition and classification of borrowings, the key factors conditioning loanword integration along with some problematic patterns emerging in this process and a history of foreign influence in English.

In Section 2 we defined a loan as a word taken from the source language and incorporated into the discourse of the target language. It was pointed out that loanword adaptation may affect various aspects of phonological organisation, namely the phonemic, phonetic, phonotactic and prosodic levels. Furthermore, the distinction between established or integrated borrowings and online adaptations should be made. The study of loan nativisation has been shown to have a number of benefits, such as providing a unique insight into the native phonology as well as facilitating an inquiry into the interface between phonology and sociolinguistics. Finally, we have found insightful Haugen's (1950) classification of borrowing phenomena based on the degree of morphemic substitution found in various types of loans in which three main groups of borrowings are isolated: loanwords (no morphemic substitution), loanblends (partial morphemic substitution) and loanshifts (complete morphemic substitution).

Contemporary studies on phonological loanword adaptation focus on several controversial issues. These include, on the one hand, the key factors exerting an influence on the process in question, i.e. the nature of the input representation, the role of orthography and the degree of the borrowing community bilingualism. On the other hand, certain puzzling patterns can be found in phonological loan nativisation which are difficult to account for in terms of native processes or constraints. Five such patterns identified by Kang (2011) have been presented and discussed.

As regards the nature of the input, two major approaches are posited in the current literature, i.e. the phonological input view and the phonetic input view, which carry different predictions about loanword nativisation patterns. The possibility of the orthographic input must also be taken into account along with the problems involved in distinguishing between purely phonetically-, phonologically- and orthographically-based adaptations. Loanword integration has been argued not to be a uniform process as a foreign item can be adapted by different speakers by means of different strategies of adaptation, depending on a variety of factors. This issue will be addressed in more detail in Chapters 4 and 5.

An important problem concerns the effect of orthography on loanword nativisation. The results of Vendelin and Peperkamp's (2006) experiment suggest that loan integration is influenced by orthography in that loanwords are adapted in accordance with between-language grapheme-to-phoneme correspondence rules more often when the written input is provided than in the absence of written representation. However, numerous complicating factors make it impossible to precisely determine the influence of spelling. For this reason, various researchers attach different degrees of significance to the role of orthography in borrowing.

The next relevant issue is the role of borrowers' proficiency in L2 in loanword adaptation. This aspect assumes central importance in phonological approaches to loan assimilation, based on the assumption that borrowing is performed by bilinguals who have access to both L1 and L2 phonology. On the other hand, phonetic approaches to loanword adaptation emphasise the role of perceptual factors in this process and tend to minimise the significance of orthographic influence.

Finally, some problematic patterns identified by Kang (2011) emerging in loan integration should be considered. These include the too-many-solutions problem, divergent repair, unnecessary repair, differential importation and retreat to the unmarked. The too-many-solutions problem was described as a situation whereby it is logically possible to apply any of a number of repair strategies to an ill-formed input, all yielding well-formed outputs, but in which adapters consistently employ one specific strategy. Divergent repair takes place when a given constraint is satisfied by means of different repair strategies in the native phonology and in loanwords. Unnecessary repair occurs when a foreign item undergoes some sort of modification in the target language even though it contains no structures which are ill-formed from the point of view of that language. Differential importation refers to the situation whereby, given two foreign ill-formed structures, one is allowed in the recipient language, whereas the other invariably undergoes adaptation. Finally, retreat to the unmarked takes place when a loanword is adapted to an unmarked form even though a more faithful well-formed structure is available in the target language. Many of these issues arise in our analysis of consonant clusters in Chapters 4 and 5. All the problematic patterns pose a considerable challenge to any theory of loanword adaptation.

Section 4 was devoted to a concise presentation of the history of foreign influence in English in four periods of the development of this language, i.e. Old English, Middle English, Early Modern English and Present-Day English. Foreign sources exerted a profound impact on the vocabulary of English in that they contributed numerous borrowings. The languages providing the largest number of loanwords included French (particularly, in the Middle English period) and Latin (throughout the history of English). Furthermore, foreign sources had some effect on the development of the sound system of English in that they occasionally introduced new sounds to the inventory of the language in question (e.g. French diphthongs /ʊɪ/ and /ɔɪ/ in Middle English) or altered the distribution of the already existing ones. The Polish contribution to the English vocabulary can be described as minor, if not negligible.

2 Major theoretical approaches to phonological loanword adaptation

1 Introduction

The issue of phonological loanword nativisation has been a subject of intense debate in the literature in recent years. In this light, it comes as no surprise that a significant number of theoretical approaches accounting for this phenomenon have been developed. These models attach various degrees of importance to different factors, such as phonological production, perception or orthography, in explaining modifications in the sound structure of borrowings which are triggered by the differences between the sound systems of the source and the recipient languages.

This Chapter contains a survey of the most important theoretical models of phonological loanword adaptation. We start with a presentation of selected analyses belonging to the phonological approximation view, where loanword nativisation is claimed to be a function of the phonological production grammar. Next, we focus on the phonetic approaches to the process in question which maintain that loan assimilation originates in perception and that the role of phonology is limited. Finally, some mixed models involving both the perception grammar and the production grammar are examined. It should be noted that, given the abundance of relevant theoretical proposals, the Chapter deals with a selection of the most popular and influential frameworks only.

The approaches discussed in Section 2 assume that loanword adaptation is performed in the phonological component of grammar. In 2.1 we examine the Theory of Constraints and Repair Strategies Loanword Model (TCRS LM) advocated by Paradis (1996) and Paradis and LaCharité (1997). Section 2.2 focuses on Itô and Mester's (1995, 1999, 2001) Optimality Theory account of lexical stratification phenomena in Japanese and its implications for the study of loan nativisation.

Section 3 is devoted to the presentation of selected phonetic approaches to loan assimilation which claim that the process under examination takes place at the perception stage. In 3.1 we discuss the psycholinguistic three-level model of speech processing proposed by Peperkamp and Dupoux (2002, 2003), Peperkamp (2005) and Peperkamp et al. (2008). Section 3.2 deals with Boersma and Hamann's (2009) bidirectional model of L1 speech processing which accounts for both native alternations as well as modifications applying to loanwords.

Next, in Section 4 we review some proposals which postulate that both the perception grammar and the production grammar are involved in computing loanword adaptation. In 4.1 Silverman's (1992) two-tier model of loan assimilation is discussed. Section 4.2 deals with the perceptual similarity approach, advocated by Kang (2003) among others, where perception is encoded into the production grammar in the form of correspondence constraints (Steriade 2001/2008).

Finally, Section 5 concludes the discussion with a summary of the theoretical approaches presented in this Chapter.

2 The phonological approximation view

This Section is devoted to the presentation of theoretical models which claim that loanword adaptation is computed predominantly by the phonological component of grammar. In 2.1 we discuss the Theory of Constraints and Repair Strategies Loanword Model (TCRS LM) proposed by Paradis (1996) and Paradis and LaCharité (1997). Section 2.2 deals with Itô and Mester's (1995, 1999, 2001) account of lexical stratification in Japanese and its implications for phonological loanword adaptation.

2.1 Theory of Constraints and Repair Strategies Loanword Model

As mentioned in Chapter 1, the phonological approximation view, advocated by Paradis (1996), Paradis and LaCharité (1997, 2008) and LaCharité and Paradis (2005), rests on the assumption that loanwords are primarily introduced by proficient bilinguals who have access to both L1 and L2 phonology. As a result, when borrowing a foreign word, they rely on its abstract phonological representation rather than its surface phonetic form. This means that borrowers easily recognise the phonemic categories of the source language and make use of this knowledge when performing adaptations. Since the process of nativisation is to a considerable extent based on phoneme recognition and matching, the phonetic forms of source items as well as the surface variants of phonemes in L2 are of limited significance in loanword adaptation. The fundamental assumptions of the phonological approximation view are outlined in (19) (LaCharité and Paradis 2005: 224).

(19) Central claims of the phonological approximation view
    (a) Loanword adaptation is generally based on the L2- (not the L1-) referenced perception of L2 phoneme categories.
    (b) Phonetic approximation (phoneme mismatching or non-perception of sounds) plays a limited role in loanword adaptation.
    (c) Loanword adaptation is a rich source of information for phonological theory.

One of the most comprehensive phonological analyses of loanword adaptation has been carried out within the Theory of Constraints and Repair Strategies Loanword Model (TCRS LM) (Paradis 1996, Paradis and LaCharité 1997), based on the Theory of Constraints and Repair Strategies (TCRS) framework (Paradis 1988a, Paradis 1988b). The TCRS assumes that the phonological system of a given language consists of universal constraints, called principles, as well as non-universal constraints, that is parameters. The former constitute the common core of all languages, whereas the latter are "<<marked options>> offered by Universal Grammar" (Paradis and LaCharité 1997: 387), which may be either accepted or rejected in particular linguistic systems. Given these assumptions, the similarities between languages result from a common set of universal principles, whereas all the differences are due to the language-specific parameter settings. When a given input violates one or more constraints, repair strategies are used in order to bring this form into conformity to the native phonology. The definition of a repair strategy is provided in (20) (Paradis and LaCharité 1997: 384).

(20) Repair strategy
a universal, non-contextual phonological operation that is triggered by the violation of a phonological constraint, and which inserts or deletes content or structure to ensure conformity to the violated constraint

As pointed out by Paradis and LaCharité (1997), the internal sources of constraint violations are morphological operations, constraint conflicts and underlying ill-formedness, whereas the major external source is provided by loanwords.

Paradis and LaCharité's (1997) examination of five corpora of loanwords, namely French borrowings in Kinyarwanda, Fula and Moroccan Arabic, as well as English loans in Quebec French and Montreal French, reveals a general cross-linguistic tendency to repair illicit structures by means of vowel epenthesis rather than consonant elision. In the corpora under discussion, foreign phonemes are predominantly preserved and adapted (78.5 %), whereas deletion is extremely rare (3.6 %). The remaining cases (17.9 %) are non-adaptations or importations, that is L2 structures which enter L1 unadapted. The figures presented above indicate that languages press for the preservation of phonological information in the input. This is formally expressed as the Preservation Principle in (21) (Paradis and LaCharité 1997: 384).

(21) Preservation Principle
segmental information is maximally preserved within the limits of the Threshold Principle

The Preservation Principle stipulates that as much phonological information in the input as possible should be retained in the output. This accounts for the fact that epenthesis is universally favoured over deletion as a strategy for repairing ill-formed structures since the former satisfies a violated constraint and at the same time maximally preserves the phonological content of the input. However, the Preservation Principle is limited by the Threshold Principle in (22) (Paradis and LaCharité 1997: 385).

(22) Threshold Principle
   (a) All languages have a tolerance threshold to the amount of repair needed to enforce segment preservation.
   (b) This threshold is the same for all languages: two steps (or two repairs) within a given constraint domain.[23]

The Threshold Principle states that a particular segment will be saved unless its rescue requires more than two steps of repair within the scope of a given constraint. If this is the case, that is if the preservation of a segment is too costly, then it is predicted to undergo elision.

The TCRS also postulates that all repairs apply in an economical fashion. This is formally stated as the Minimality Principle in (23) (Paradis and LaCharité 1997: 386).

(23) Minimality Principle
   (a) A repair strategy must apply at the lowest phonological level to which the violated constraint refers.
   (b) Repair must involve as few strategies (steps) as possible.

Part (23a) of the Minimality Principle requires that the input should be modified at the lowest phonological level so that as little phonological information as possible is lost. Part (23b) stipulates that when a given structure may be repaired in more than one way, the repair involving the fewest steps is given priority. The lowest phonological level referred to in (23a) is determined by the Phonological Level Hierarchy presented in (24) (Paradis and LaCharité 1997: 386).

(24) Phonological Level Hierarchy (PLH)
   metrical level > syllabic level > skeletal level > root node > feature with a dependent > feature without a dependent

According to Paradis and LaCharité (1997), the PLH is a hierarchy of phonological organisation required independently of the TCRS.

---

23 Paradis and LaCharité (1997) allow for the possibility of parameterisation of (22b) in different languages.

Another important element of the TCRS is the Precedence Convention (25), which determines priority relationships when two or more constraints make conflicting demands (Paradis and LaCharité 1997: 386).

(25) Precedence Convention
In a situation involving two or more violated constraints, priority is given to that constraint referring to the highest phonological level of the PLH.

Thus, when two or more constraints are violated, the one referring to a higher phonological level, as determined by the PLH, is given priority.

Apart from adopting the TCRS framework, the TCRS LM postulates that the phonological system of each language is organised into the core and the periphery.[24] The former contains all constraints of a language and constitutes its phonology, whereas the latter includes only a subset of core constraints. The majority of native words belong to the core thus they satisfy all requirements included therein. On the other hand, items such as interjections, onomatopoeia as well as some borrowings, remain in the periphery where certain core constraints are relaxed or even completely deactivated. This means that it is possible for these peripheral items to contain structures not found in the native vocabulary. Paradis and LaCharité (1997) claim that the core-periphery distinction accounts for the fact that some segments are invariably modified or deleted in the adaptation process (prohibited segments), whereas others are imported (tolerated segments).[25] Thus, fully nativised borrowings belong to the core and satisfy all the native requirements. On the other hand, words containing ill-formed structures are situated in the periphery and, as a result, conform to a subset of the constraints of a given language. This does not mean, as pointed out by Paradis and LaCharité (1997), that loanword phonology is peripheral phonology since not all loanwords belong to the periphery and the periphery itself also contains other items such as interjections or onomatopoeia.

In order to demonstrate how the TCRS LM accounts for the patterns of segment adaptation, deletion and importation in loanwords, Paradis and LaCharité (1997) carry out an analysis of 545 French loanwords in Fula, a West African language. They observe that illicit segments are in the first place preserved and adapted (91.5 %). The remaining cases, that is, segment deletions and non-adaptations,

---

24 See Itô and Mester (1995, 1999, 2001) for an in-depth discussion of a core-periphery structure of the phonological lexicon.
25 Paradis and LaCharité (1997: 391) suggest that importations provide evidence in support of the phonological approximation view in that they "clearly show that borrowers perceive and properly handle the sounds of the source language."

occur infrequently (6.5 % and 2 % respectively). As regards the former, Paradis and LaCharité maintain that the rate of segment elision may be even lower in that only 3.7 % of cases are phonologically-conditioned segment deletions, whereas the rest are influenced by extra-linguistic factors, such as orthography or analogy.

Let us now present an example of how the TCRS LM deals with phonotactic adaptations. Fula prohibits both complex onsets and codas therefore French loanwords with such structures are ill-formed from the point of view of this language. There are basically two strategies by means of which consonant clusters may be repaired in Fula, namely deletion of one of the consonants or vowel insertion. As demonstrated by Paradis and LaCharité (1997: 405–407), the repair most frequently applied to both complex onsets and codas is vowel epenthesis. As regards onsets, the vowel is inserted between the consonants (C_1VC_2) if sonority is rising or in front of the cluster (VC_1C_2) if sonority is falling. The relevant examples are presented in (26a) and (26b) respectively.

(26) Adaptation of complex onsets in French loanwords in Fula

		French		Fula	
(a)	*briquet*	[brikɛ]	→	[birikɛt]	'lighter'
	classe	[klas]	→	[kalaːs]	'class'
(b)	*statue*	[staty]	→	[istati]	'statue'

In the case of complex codas, the vowel is inserted between the consonants (C_1VC_2) if sonority is rising or after the cluster (C_1C_2V) if sonority is falling. This is exemplified in (27a) and (27b) respectively.

(27) Adaptation of complex codas in French loanwords in Fula

		French		Fula	
(a)	*filtre*	[filtr]	→	[filtir]	'filter'
	table	[tabl]	→	[taabal]	'table'
(b)	*carde*	[kard]	→	[karda]	'card'
	force	[fɔrs]	→	[fɔrsɔ]	'force'

The data in (26) and (27) indicate that consonant clusters in French loanwords in Fula are mainly adapted through vowel epenthesis rather than consonant deletion, a pattern in accordance with the Preservation Principle.

Nonetheless, Paradis and LaCharité (1997: 408) observe that elision is preferred to insertion in certain borrowings, as illustrated in (28).

(28) Consonant deletion in French loanwords in Fula

	French		Fula	
voyage	[vwajaʒ]	→	[wajaːs]	'trip'
voitur	[vwatyr]	→	[watiːri]	'car'
cuivre	[kɥivr]	→	[kiri]	'copper'
chewing gum	[ʃwiŋgɔm]	→	[siŋgɔm]	'chewing gum'

The French loanwords presented in (28) contain consonants clusters in which one of the segments is ill-formed in Fula (*[v, ɥ, ʃ]). This means that these structures violate two constraints, namely the phonotactic requirement militating against complex onsets and codas as well as the segmental one prohibiting [v, ɥ, ʃ]. In this situation, the former is given priority over the latter in accordance with the Precedence Convention and, in consequence, the illicit syllable structure is repaired in the first place. Paradis and LaCharité argue that deletion is selected rather than insertion since the latter option would require more than two modifications. Thus, a repair through vowel epenthesis would entail 1) insertion of a nucleus between the consonants, 2) supplying the nucleus with segmental content via vowel or glide spreading and 3) adaptation of the illicit segment. Such a solution involves three steps of repair and is too costly in terms of the Threshold Principle. As a result, although not favoured by the Preservation Principle, deletion applies in the cases listed in (28).

In spite of the fact that the TCRS LM provides a satisfactory account of the patterns of segment preservation vs. deletion in a corpus of French loanwords in Fula, it fails to do so when some other datasets are taken into consideration, as argued by Brasington (1997) and Ulrich (1997) among others.

According to Brasington (1997), the datasets examined by Paradis and LaCharité (1997), where French is either the source or the target language, are biased in favour of the TCRS LM in that they include a limited range of borrowing situations and exclude those which could pose a challenge to the model in question. Brasington (1997), who investigates English loanwords in Marshallese, maintains that the cost of repair is only one of a series of factors governing the choice between epenthesis and deletion in loan adaptation. Thus, when Marshallese borrows English words containing complex onsets or codas, both prohibited in the target language, the selection of a repair strategy depends to a large extent on the position of the cluster within a word. The relevant figures provided by Brasington (1997: 3) are presented in Tab. 17.

Tab. 17: Epenthesis vs. deletion in English loanwords in Marshallese

	epenthesis	deletion	total
initial position	101	5	106
final position	12	56	68
total	113	61	174

As evidenced in Tab. 17, initial clusters are predominantly adapted via epenthesis (101 cases out of 106), whereas elision is a preferred strategy in adapting complex codas (56 cases out of 68). This indicates that the position of a consonant cluster within a word is a significant variable influencing the selection of a repair strategy. Brasington (1997: 2) suggests that "initial position is both perceptually and productively (…) strong or salient" therefore epenthesis, which preserves phonological information, seems more suitable. On the other hand, "final position is (…) both perceptually and productively weak or non-salient" thus the choice of deletion.

Another factor affecting the selection of a repair strategy is the structure of a cluster. The data analysed by Brasington (1997) indicate that elision is much more frequent in the final clusters consisting of a nasal and a homorganic stop (30 cases out of 32) than in the lateral + obstruent codas, where the relationship between deletion and epenthesis is more balanced (3 cases of both repairs).

Similarly, Ulrich (1997), who analyses French and English loanwords in Lama, argues that the TCRS LM fails to account for both segmental and phonotactic adaptations in the examined data. For instance, he demonstrates that the limit of two steps of repair imposed by the Threshold Principle cannot be maintained in Lama where some structures (e.g. French /ʒ/ in coda position) are repaired through vowel epenthesis, even though it requires three steps of repair.

Given Brasington's (1997) as well as Ulrich's (1997) findings, it is reasonable to assume that the choice between consonant deletion and vowel insertion in phonotactic adaptations is determined by a number of factors, including the cost of repair as well as the structure of a cluster and its position in a word.

2.2 Itô and Mester's (1995, 1999, 2001) Optimality Theory account of lexical stratification in Japanese

One of the most comprehensive phonological accounts of loanword adaptation within the Optimality Theory framework (Prince and Smolensky 1993/2004) was proposed by Itô and Mester (1995, 1999, 2001), whose analysis of lexical stratification in Japanese is based on the assumption that lexicons of natural languages are organised into a core-periphery structure. In other words, they consist of a number of strata or subdomains, centred on the unmarked core, in which all phonological constraints of a language are satisfied. Items located in the peripheral strata satisfy fewer and fewer constraints, with some fulfilling only a subset of the fundamental well-formedness requirements, such as basic syllable structure restrictions. The core stratum of the lexicon includes the native vocabulary, whereas peripheral subdomains contain, among others, onomatopoeia as well as loanwords with different degrees of nativisation. Itô and Mester (1995: 183–184) illustrate their claims with an analysis of syllable-related constraints in Japanese and their domains of application. The relevant constraints are provided in (29).

(29) Syllable-related constraints in Japanese
SYLLSTRUC: Constraints defining the basic syllable canons of Japanese, including NOCOMPLEXONSET, NOCOMPLEXCODA, CODACOND.
NOVOIGEM: No voiced obstruent geminates.
NO-[P]: No (single) [p].
POSTNASVOI: Post-nasal obstruents must be voiced.

According to Itô and Mester (p. 184), the Japanese lexicon consists of four strata, each with its own subgrammar, as demonstrated in Tab. 18.

Tab. 18: The domains of syllable-related constraints in the Japanese lexicon

	SYLLSTRUC	NOVOIGEM	NO-[P]	POSTNASVOI
Yamato	✓	✓	✓	✓
Sino-Japanese	✓	✓	✓	n.a.
Foreign	✓	✓	n.a.	n.a.
Unassimilated Foreign	✓	n.a.	n.a.	n.a.

As shown in Tab. 18, constraint domains are organised hierarchically, with SYLLSTRUC active in all strata of the Japanese lexicon and the remaining constraints gradually deactivated in its less central areas. This means that only native Japanese words invariably respect all syllable-related constraints, whereas items belonging to subsequent peripheral strata of the Japanese lexicon fulfil fewer and fewer syllable-related requirements. Thus, NOVOIGEM may be violated in some unassimilated foreign words (e.g. *roddo* 'rod') and NO-[P] is frequently disobeyed in all items of foreign origin, both unassimilated and nativised (e.g. *peepaa* 'paper' and *sepaado* 'German shepherd dog'). POSTNASVOI, which is satisfied in the native Yamato vocabulary, may be violated in Sino-Japanese items (e.g. *sampo* 'walk' and *hantai* 'opposite') as well as in all loanwords (e.g. *kompyuutaa* 'computer' and *santa* 'Santa') (Itô and Mester 1999: 69).

Itô and Mester (1995, 1999) argue that the facts about lexical stratification in Japanese are best accounted for within the Optimality Theory framework through reranking of faithfulness constraints with respect to an invariant hierarchy of markedness constraints. The syllable-related well-formedness requirements in Japanese are ranked as in (30) (Itô and Mester 1995: 186).

(30) The ranking of syllable-related constraints in Japanese
    SYLLSTRUC >> NOVOIGEM >> NO-[P] >> POSTNASVOI

The hierarchy in (30) is identical for all strata of the Japanese lexicon. The gradual deactivation of subsequent constraints in the periphery results from different rankings of FAITH with respect to the markedness constraints in (30),[26] as
shown in (31) (Itô and Mester 1995: 187).

(31) Constraint rankings for different strata of the Japanese lexicon
    Yamato
    SYLLSTRUC >> NOVOIGEM >> NO-[P] >> POSTNASVOI >> FAITH
    Sino-Japanese
    SYLLSTRUC >> NOVOIGEM >> NO-[P] >> FAITH >> POSTNASVOI
    Foreign
    SYLLSTRUC >> NOVOIGEM >> FAITH >> NO-[P] >> POSTNASVOI
    Unassimilated Foreign
    SYLLSTRUC >> FAITH >> NOVOIGEM >> NO-[P] >> POSTNASVOI

The rankings in (31), which differ only with respect to the location of FAITH,
produce correct results for items belonging to different strata of the Japanese
lexicon. This is demonstrated in Tableau 1 (Itô and Mester 1999: 15–17).

Tableau 1: Constraint interaction in different strata of the Japanese lexicon

Yamato: *šiɴ-de* 'die-GERUND'					
/šiɴ-te/	SYLLSTRUC	NOVOIGEM	NO-[P]	POSTNASVOI	FAITH
☞ [šiɴde]					*
[šiɴte]				*!	

Sino-Japanese: *šiɴ-tai* 'body'					
/šiɴ-tai/	SYLLSTRUC	NOVOIGEM	NO-[P]	FAITH	POSTNASVOI
☞ [šiɴtai]					*
[šiɴdai]				*!	

26 Itô and Mester (1995) maintain that FAITH is a single group of constraints ranked
    differently with respect to markedness requirements in each part of the lexicon. As
    a result, each stratum has a slightly different grammar. On the other hand, Itô and
    Mester (1999) adopt the Correspondence Theory approach to faithfulness (McCarthy
    and Prince 1995) and account for lexical stratification within a single grammar by
    postulating stratally-indexed replicas of IO-FAITH located at different points with
    regard to markedness constraints.

Foreign: *(hando)bakku* 'handbag'					
/baggu/	SYLLSTRUC	NOVOIGEM	FAITH	NO-[P]	POSTNASVOI
☞ [bakku]			* (IDENT-F)		
[baggu]		*!			

Unassimilated Foreign: *beddo* 'bed'					
/beddo/	SYLLSTRUC	FAITH	NOVOIGEM	NO-[P]	POSTNASVOI
☞ [beddo]			*		
[betto]		*! (IDENT-F)			

As illustrated in Tableau 1, reranking of FAITH with respect to a uniform set of markedness constraints accounts for lexical stratification in Japanese as well as for the different degrees of nativisation found in loanwords.

Furthermore, Itô and Mester (1999, 2001) argue that the model under discussion makes accurate predictions concerning possible and impossible nativisations. As an example, they discuss the German adaptation of English word-initial [sC] clusters as well as [r]. The former are usually realised as [ʃC] in German whereas the latter is adapted as the uvular [ʀ]. Taking into consideration the word *story*, which contains both structures in question, Itô and Mester (2001: 10) observe that three nativisations are possible.

(32) Possible and impossible nativisations of *story* in German
(a) [ʃtɔʀi] (fully nativised) (c) [stɔri] (least nativised)
(b) [stɔʀi] (partially nativised) (d) [ʃtɔri] (impossible nativisation)

As demonstrated in (32), the English word *story* may be fully nativised (32a), ʷⁱᵗʰ both [st] and [r] replaced with native German structures or it may undergo ⵑportation (32c). As regards partial nativisations, only the form where [r] is ⵑapted but [sC] cluster remains unchanged is allowed (32b). The other logically ɔssible option (32d), with the reverse pattern of nativisation, is unattested.

Itô and Mester (2001) hold a view that this puzzling pattern may be accounted ⵑor by reranking of FAITH in relation to relevant markedness constraints, i.e. *r, prohibiting rhotics, and *[sC, which militates against the syllable-initial sequences of [s] and a consonant. Assuming the ranking *r >> *[sC, there are three possible locations of FAITH with respect to these well-formedness requirements (33) (Itô and Mester 2001: 11).

(33) Reranking of FAITH in relation to *r and *[sC
(a) *r >> *[sC >> FAITH (c) FAITH >> *r >> *[sC
(b) *r >> FAITH >> *[sC

As illustrated in Tableau 2, the rankings in (33) correctly predict the possible nativisation patterns of *story* in German (Itô and Mester 2001: 12).

Tableau 2: Evaluation of the input /stɔri/ in German

		FAITH-C	*r	FAITH-B	*[sC	FAITH-A
a. /stɔri/ A fully nativised	☞[ʃtɔri]	n.a.		n.a.		**
	[stɔri]				*!	*
	[stɔri]		*!		*	
	[ʃtɔri]		*!			*
b. /stɔri/ B partially nativised	[ʃtɔri]	n.a.		**!		n.a.
	☞[stɔri]			*	*	
	[stɔri]		*!		*	
	[ʃtɔri]		*!	*		
c. /stɔri/ C least nativised	[ʃtɔri]	**!			n.a.	n.a.
	[stɔri]	*!			*	
	☞[stɔri]		*		*	
	[ʃtɔri]	*!	*			

As pointed out by Itô and Mester (2001), the item *[ʃtɔri] is unattested as there is no possible ranking of FAITH with respect to *r >> *[sC that would yield such a form.[27]

The approach advocated by Itô and Mester (1995, 1999, 2001) has also been adopted by Davidson and Noyer (1997) in their production-oriented analysis of stress adaptation in Spanish loans in Huave. According to Davidson and Noyer, the relevant data can be accounted for by reranking of MAX, which prohibits deletion, with respect to a constant hierarchy of markedness constraints. In both analyses, the major advantage of the approach under discussion is that it provides an explanation of differential importation, i.e. a phenomenon whereby, given two ill-formed structures, one is allowed in the recipient language, whereas the other is invariably adapted. However, some constraint rankings proposed by Davidson and Noyer raise questions regarding their motivation and learnability.

---

27 See Itô and Mester (1999) for a discussion of possible and impossible nativisations in Japanese.

3 The phonetic approximation view

In this Section we present the major approaches in which loanword adaptation is viewed as a process taking place in perception. In 3.1 we discuss the psycholinguistic three-level model of speech processing advocated by Peperkamp and Dupoux (2002, 2003), Peperkamp (2005) and Peperkamp et al. (2008). Section 3.2 deals with Boersma and Hamann's (2009) bidirectional model of L1 speech processing which accounts for both native alternations as well as loanword adaptation phenomena.

3.1 The psycholinguistic three-level model of speech processing

The phonetic approximation view, advocated by Peperkamp and Dupoux (2002, 2003), Peperkamp (2005) and Peperkamp et al. (2008), challenges the idea that L2 words are faithfully perceived and mapped onto L1 underlying forms which are subsequently computed by the native phonological grammar. Instead, this approach assumes that the vast majority of loanword adaptations are "phonetically minimal transformations" (Peperkamp and Dupoux 2003: 367) taking place in perception.

One of the fundamental assumptions underlying the view in question is the central role of perception in loanword integration. This hypothesis is based on the experimental studies which demonstrate that non-native sound structures, including segments, suprasegments and syllable phonotactics, are distorted in speech perception (Massaro and Cohen 1983, Werker and Tees 1984, Dupoux et al. 1997, 1999). In other words, when foreign structures are mapped onto the native ones, a great deal of phonetic information is lost. This is a natural consequence of the fact that phonetic categories vary across languages. Perception is also influenced to some extent by the native phonological grammar, which determines the range of native structures available for loan adaptation.

Peperkamp and Dupoux (2003) point out that unfaithful perception is the source of L1 speakers' inability to distinguish between some non-native contrasts, a phenomenon called phonological 'deafness.' Some representative examples are presented in (34) (p. 367).

(34) Examples of phonological 'deafness'
[liːd] – [riːd]	Korean listeners
[vásuma] – [vasúma]	French listeners
[ebzo] – [ebuɯzo]	Japanese listeners

As exemplified in (34), Korean listeners have difficulty distinguishing between [r] and [l] (Ingram and See-Gyoon 1998), French listeners find it extremely hard to discriminate stress contrasts (Dupoux *et al.* 1997) and Japanese listeners have major problems with perceiving the difference between CC and CVC sequences (Dupoux *et al.* 1999).

Phonological 'deafness' is mirrored in loanword adaptation data provided in (35) (Peperkamp and Dupoux 2003: 367).

(35) Phonological 'deafness' reflected in loanword adaptation

London	[lʌndən] > [rəntən]	Korean
walkman	[wɔːkmən] > [wɔkmán]	French
sphinx	[sfɪŋks]> [suɸiŋkɯsɯ]	Japanese

The data in (35) demonstrate that the inability to perceive certain non-native contrasts is reflected in repair strategies applied to loanwords. This similarity between speech perception patterns and loanword adaptation data leads Peperkamp and Dupoux (2002, 2003) to conclude that the process of loanword nativisation takes place in perception and is phonetic rather than phonological in nature.

Drawing on these assumptions, Peperkamp and Dupoux (2002, 2003) and Peperkamp *et al.* (2008) analyse loanword adaptation in terms of the psycholinguistic three-level model of speech processing presented in Fig. 1.

Fig. 1: Psycholinguistic three-level model of speech processing

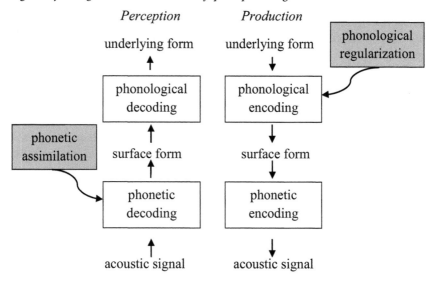

The model in Fig. 1 accounts for both speech perception and production. The input to the former consists of a continuous acoustic signal mapped onto a series of discrete segments, i.e. the phonetic surface form, by the phonetic decoder. The output of this process is the input to the phonological decoder, which transforms the phonetic surface form into the underlying representation. On the other hand, speech production is computed by the phonological encoder, whose function is to map the underlying form onto the phonetic surface form, as well as by the phonetic encoder, where the surface form is realised as a series of fine-grained articulatory gestures.

With regard to loanword adaptation, the crucial element of the model in Fig. 1 is the phonetic decoder, responsible for mapping foreign sound structures onto the phonetically closest native ones in the process called phonetic (or perceptual) assimilation. Phonetic closeness is defined as similarity in terms of either acoustic distance (Kuhl 2000) or articulatory gestures (Best and Strange 1992). This means that the underlying feature matrix specification of a structure involved in the phonetic decoding is irrelevant. As a result, phonology plays a limited role in the process of perceptual assimilation in that it only determines the range of native sound structures onto which the foreign ones can be mapped. Since not only segments but also suprasegments and phonotactic structures are subject to perceptual assimilation, the input to the phonetic decoder must be a chunk of an acoustic signal with the size of a syllable rather than a single segment.

According to the model under discussion, the vast majority of loanword adaptations are computed by the phonetic decoding module in the process of perceptual assimilation. This module is claimed to be responsible for the phonological 'deafness' and, in consequence, for transforming illicit segmental, suprasegmental and phonotactic structures in loanwords. Therefore, speakers who perform borrowing depend to a large extent on fine-grained phonetic details rather than phonological information. In fact, they may have no access to the source language phonology at all. However, even highly proficient bilinguals with near-native phonological knowledge of the donor language, are claimed to perform loanword adaptation in perception. This is because, as pointed out by Peperkamp and Dupoux (2003), native phonetic categories and the phonetic decoder are acquired during the first year of life and remain virtually unchanged, regardless of the level of bilingualism. As a result, it is concluded that both monolinguals and bilinguals perform loanword adaptation via perceptual assimilation.

Although most loanwords are argued to be assimilated in perception, Peperkamp et al. (2008) acknowledge that there exist two groups of adaptations determined by other factors. The first group under discussion are orthographic adaptations, based on the spelling of a source word. Such forms are not accounted for within the model in question. The other group is called 'generalisations' or 'regularisations' and these are words which, despite being well-formed in the recipient language, are nevertheless adapted since they do not conform to some default pattern. For example, Kenstowicz and Sohn (2001) argue that English loanwords in Kyungsang Korean are assigned pitch accent in accordance with the default accent assignment pattern. Such cases are argued to be computed by the phonological encoder in the process of phonological regularisation. Peperkamp and Dupoux (2002) maintain that the module under investigation has a regularizing tendency, the evidence for which is supplied by overgeneralisation errors made by children. Phonological regularisation is assumed to apply gradually through several generations and to affect both native as well as foreign forms.

To provide evidence for perceptual assimilation as the main locus of loanword adaptation, Peperkamp *et al.* (2008) examine the case of word-final [n] in French and English loanwords in Japanese. The segment in question is adapted in two different ways, depending on the source language. Thus, English loans emerge with a final moraic nasal, whereas in French borrowings [n] is always followed by an epenthetic vowel, as exemplified in (36) (Peperkamp *et al.* 2008: 130).

(36) Adaptation of [n] in English and French loanwords in Japanese
  (a) English loanwords

pen	[pen]	> pen
walkman	[wɔːkmən]	> wōkuman
monsoon	[mɒnsuːn]	> monsūn

  (b) French loanwords

Cannes	[kan]	> kannu
parisienne	[paʁizjɛn]	> parijennu	'Parisian-FEM'
terrine	[tɛʁin]	> terīnu	'pâté, terrine'

Peperkamp *et al.* (2008) argue that the asymmetry in the adaptation patterns illustrated in (36) is due to the fine-grained phonetic differences in the realisation of the English and French [n]. Thus, the French [n] is typically accompanied by a strong release as opposed to the English [n]. The experiments conducted by Peperkamp *et al.* (2008) demonstrate that Japanese listeners are indeed sensitive to these differences since they perceive the English [n] as closest to the Japanese moraic nasal consonant and the French [n] as a sequence of a nasal and the vowel [ɯ]. This is mirrored in the loanword adaptation data in (36). The experiments also show that even bilingual Japanese speakers find it hard to distinguish between the French forms with word-final [n] and those ending in [nɯ].

According to Peperkamp (2005), the hypothesis that loanword adaptation originates in perceptual assimilation accounts for two sets of loans which are problematic for phonological analyses. The first group comprises adaptations conflicting with native alternations, i.e. cases of divergent repair. For instance, in Korean [s] cannot occur in the syllable coda. In native forms, an underlying /s/ in coda position surfaces as [t], whereas in English loanwords /s/ is realised as a sequence of [s] and the epenthetic vowel [ɪ]. Examples are provided in (37) (Peperkamp 2005: 343).

(37) Divergent repair in Korean
   (a) native alternations
      /nas/   [nat]   'sickle-NOM'
      /nas+ɪl/   [nasɪl]   'sickle-ACC'
   (b) loanwords from English
      boss [bɒs]   >   [posɪ]
      charisma [kə'rɪzmə]   >   [kʰarɪsɪma]

According to Peperkamp, this asymmetry is a natural consequence of the fact that native alternations and loanword adaptations are computed by two separate systems, the former by the phonological grammar in production, whereas the latter by the phonetic decoder in perception.

The other problematic group of loanwords consists of 'unnecessary adaptations,' that is cases where a given source form undergoes modification despite being licit in the borrowing language. An example is provided by Kang (2003: 223), who points out that although native Korean words may end in a voiceless stop, English word-final stops are adapted as a sequence of an aspirated plosive and the epenthetic vowel [ɪ], as shown in (38).

(38) Unnecessary repair in Korean
   (a) native Korean words   (b) English loanwords
      [pat]   'field'   *bat* [bæt] > [pætʰɪ]
      [kæk]   'guest'   *deck* [dek] > [tɛkʰɪ]
      [ʧip]   'house'   *hip* [hɪp] > [hipʰɪ]

Peperkamp (2005) argues that, under the phonetic approximation view, a given source form may have a corresponding form in the borrowing language which is faithful but not phonetically closest. If this is the case, the source item will undergo adaptation in spite of its being acceptable in the recipient language.

3.2 The bidirectional three-level model for L1 processing and loanword adaptation

The idea that loanword adaptation originates in perception has been taken up by Boersma and Hamann (2009), who hold a view that both native alternations and modifications applied to loanwords can be adequately described in terms of a single model of L1 speech processing. The model under discussion is bidirectional, i.e. it accounts for the processing on the part of the listener (speech comprehension) as well as the speaker (speech production). All mappings are formalised in terms of the interaction of Optimality Theory constraints. The model under discussion is presented in Fig. 2 (Boersma and Hamann 2009: 12).

Fig. 2: Three-level model for L1 processing and loanword adaptation

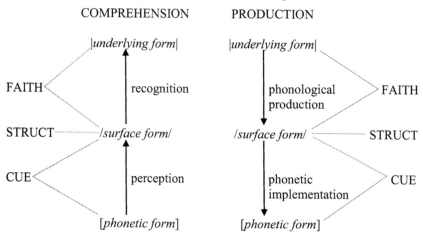

On the comprehension side, the model provides an explanation for two processes, namely speech perception and word recognition. The input to the former is a continuous auditory-phonetic signal, which is transformed into a more abstract discrete representation, i.e. the phonological surface form. This is formalised in terms of the interaction between cue constraints, evaluating the relationship between the input to the perception and its output, and structural constraints, evaluating only the output of this process. Word recognition, i.e. mapping the phonological surface form onto the underlying representation, is handled by a single set of faithfulness constraints.

On the production side, the model provides an account of phonological production and phonetic implementation. The former consists in mapping the underlying form onto the phonological surface form. This is formally expressed as the interaction between faithfulness constraints, evaluating the relation between the input and the output of the process under discussion, and structural constraints, i.e. constraints on the well-formedness of the output. Phonetic implementation, i.e. mapping the phonological surface form onto the detailed phonetic form is handled exclusively by cue constraints.

In order to demonstrate how the model in question works, Boersma and Hamann (2009) examine vowel insertion in English loanwords in Korean. This process is a case of divergent repair since it is never applied in Korean as a way of repairing illicit structures. These are made well-formed by means of one of three processes, namely neutralisation, assimilation or deletion. Several examples illustrating this point are provided in (39) (Boersma and Hamann 2009: 13).

(39) Native repair strategies of Korean

	pat^h	- /pat/	'field'	coda neutralisation
	os	- /ot/	'clothes'	strident neutralisation
	kaps	- /kap/	'price'	deletion
	kuk+min	- /kuŋmin/	'nation'	assimilation

As noted by Boersma and Hamann (2009: 13), these forms supply evidence that the following markedness constraints are active in Korean:

(40) Active markedness constraints in Korean

*/+asp./: assign one violation mark for every aspirated consonant in coda position
*/+stri./: assign one violation mark for every strident consonant in coda position
*/CC./: assign one violation mark for every complex coda
SYLLCON: assign one violation mark for every segment in coda position which is less sonorous than the following onset

When loanwords from English are adapted, the constraints in (40) are satisfied by vowel insertion, as demonstrated in (41) (p. 13).

(41) Vowel epenthesis in English loanwords in Korean

| *deck* → /tɛkʰɪ/ | *false* → /pʰolsɪ/ |
| *mass* → /mæsɪ/ | *picnic* → /pʰikʰɪnik/ |

Boersma and Hamann argue that this discrepancy between native alternations and loanword adaptations is due to the fact that the former are computed in production as opposed to the latter, which take place in perception.

As regards native alternations, the constraint against vowel insertion, that is DEP-V, is ranked high hence the relevant markedness constraints are satisfied by neutralisation, assimilation or deletion, as shown in Tableau 3 (Boersma and Hamann 2009: 15).

Tableau 3: L1 Korean production: strident neutralisation

|os|	*/+stri./	DEP-V	MAX-C	IDENT(stri)
a. /.os./	*!			
☞ b. /.ot./				*
c. /.o.sɪ./		*!		
d. /.o./			*!	

Tableau 3 is a production tableau where the native Korean underlying form /os/ is evaluated. Candidate (a) is immediately ruled out since it violates the top-ranked constraint against strident coda consonants. Candidates (c) and (d) are also eliminated, the former because of its epenthetic vowel, the latter due to the deleted final consonant. As a result, candidate (c) emerges as optimal despite its violation of IDENT(stri).

On the other hand, loanwords are claimed to be adapted in perception. This means that the markedness constraints in (40) interact with cue rather than faithfulness constraints. In consequence, the Korean structural restrictions are satisfied in a different way than in L1 phonology, namely by vowel insertion. This is illustrated in Tableau 4 (Boersma and Hamann 2009: 28).

Tableau 4: Korean perception of the English word mass

[mæs]	*/+stri./	*[friction] /-stri/	*[] /ɪ/
a. /.mæs./	*!		
b. /.mæt./		*!	
☞ c. /.mæ.s'ɪ./			*

Tableau 4 is a perception tableau in which the auditory-phonetic form [mæs] is evaluated. The constraint *[friction] /-stri/ stipulates that friction noise should not be perceived as the phonological feature [-strident] and *[] /ɪ/ states that the absence of auditory signal should not be interpreted as the vowel [ɪ]. The markedness constraint */+stri./ plays a crucial role in the perception of the form [mæs] in that it rules out the most faithful candidate (a). The cue constraint *[friction] /-stri/ eliminates candidate (b), therefore candidate (c) becomes the winner.

To sum up, conflicts between loanword adaptations and native alternations stem from the fact that the former are computed in perception, whereas the latter in production. In consequence, the inputs to both processes are evaluated by different sets of constraints, with structural constraints being a common element. However, this does not mean that perception and production are separate systems as the same structural constraints are employed in both modules. Therefore, perception is not regarded as an extra-grammatical passive module. On the contrary, it is to a large extent phonological in that it is heavily influenced by the native structural restrictions.

4 The phonetic-phonological approximation view

This Section is devoted to the presentation of selected approaches in which loanword adaptation is computed by both the phonetic and the phonological component. In 4.1 we discuss Silverman's (1992) two-tier model of loanword assimilation couched in the classical generative framework (Chomsky and Halle 1968). In 4.2 we present the perceptual similarity approach, advocated by Kang (2003) among others, in which perception is built into the production grammar in the form of faithfulness constraints (Steriade 2001/2008).

4.1 Silverman's (1992) two-tier model of loanword adaptation

Silverman's (1992) two-tier model of loanword adaptation is based on the assumption that borrowers have no access to the phonological structure of L2 items and the input to loan phonology is "merely a superficial non-linguistic acoustic signal" (p. 289). In the process of adaptation, borrowers analyse this raw acoustic signal in accordance with their native phonological system and map the input onto an L1 phonological representation. Since speakers of different languages have different phonological systems, a single input may be parsed in a variety of ways, depending on the range of structures available in a given language. As noted by Silverman (1992), this is a source of variation in adaptation patterns in various languages.

The model under discussion is presented in Fig. 3 (Silverman 1992: 293).

Fig. 3: Silverman's (1992) two-tier model of loanword phonology

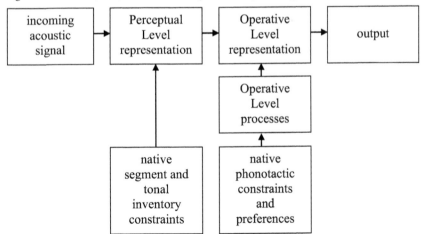

According to the model, both perception and production are involved in computing loanword adaptation. The incoming non-linguistic acoustic signal is first parsed into segment-sized elements at the Perceptual Level (Scansion One), where they are provided with the closest native phonological representations on the basis of their articulatory and/or acoustic properties. This process is subject to native segment and tonal inventory constraints which determine the range of possible feature configurations for the input mapping. Drawing on the experimental evidence which demonstrates that perception is dependent on the language set (e.g. Elman *et al.* 1977), Silverman argues that bilinguals' perception of foreign items is also constrained by their L1 phonology since they speak their L1 and, consequently, they are in their L1 mode when performing loanword adaptation. The mapping at the Perceptual Level is generally context-free, as phonotactic restrictions play no role at this stage in accordance with the Perceptual Uniformity Hypothesis which states that "[a]t the Perceptual Level, the native segment inventory constrains segmental representation in a uniform fashion, regardless of string position" (Silverman 1992: 297). However, some input segments may be found in a context which renders them phonetically non-salient, with the context established on a language-specific basis. Such parts of the input may be unperceived and not represented at the Perceptual Level. According to Silverman (1992), this is the reason why in loanwords from English into Cantonese obstruents are deleted in coda clusters, e.g. *band* → [pɛn] or *lift* → [lip]. Under this view, English word-final post-consonantal obstruents, frequently unreleased, are not perceived by Cantonese speakers and, consequently, not included in the Perceptual Level representation. Thus, deletion is not due to production grammar processes but takes place in perception.

Silverman (1992) illustrates Perceptual Level processes with a number of examples from Cantonese loanword phonology, e.g. the adaptation of English stops (42) (p. 297–298).

(42) Adaptation of English stops in Cantonese

	(a) input	Perceptual Level		(b) input	Perceptual Level
	ball	[pɔ]		*pie*	[pʰay]
	game	[kɛm]		*tie*	[tʰay]
	salad	[saløt]		*cut*	[kʰɐt]
	stick	[sitik]			
	motor	[mɔta]			

As shown in (42a), both English voiced as well as unaspirated voiceless plosives are adapted in Cantonese as unaspirated voiceless stops. Since Cantonese lacks underlying [±voice] distinctions, speakers of this language cannot perceive a voicing contrast and realise both kinds of English plosives as respective L1 un-aspirated voiceless stops. In other words, the closest matches available to Cantonese borrowers for pairs of the English segments [p, b], [t, d] and [k, g] are [p], [t] and [k] respectively. On the other hand, English aspirated [pʰ, tʰ, kʰ] are realised as such (42b). This is because aspiration is contrastive in Cantonese and the presence or lack thereof is correctly perceived and identified by speakers of this language, which is reflected in the patterns of adaptation.

The output of the Perceptual Level is the input to the Operative Level (Scansion Two), where a string of segments formed at Scansion One undergoes phonological processes which bring it into conformity to the native syllable structure constraints (SSCs) and prosodic constraints. Based on evidence from Cantonese, Silverman (1992) concludes that native phonology and loanword phonology constitute separate components. This is because the processes applying to loanwords, e.g. vowel epenthesis, are not attested in the native Cantonese vocabulary.

An example of an Operative Level process in this language is the occlusivisation of coda fricatives. In English, fricatives appear in both onset and coda positions, whereas in Cantonese these segments occur only in the former context. At the Perceptual Level, English fricatives may be represented in the coda, however, at the Operative Level they are occlusivised in order to satisfy the native Cantonese SSCs, as shown in (43) (Silverman 1992: 300).

(43) Occlusivisation of coda fricatives in English loanwords in Cantonese

input	*shaft*	*lift*
Perceptual Level	[sɐf]	[lif]
Operative Level	[sɐp]	[lip]

First, the English inputs *shaft* and *lift* are mapped onto native Cantonese sequences of segments at the Perceptual Level. The English fricative [ʃ] in *shaft* is analysed as [s] and the word-final [t] in the [-ft] cluster in both words is not perceived due to its lack of phonetic salience. Thus, after the perceptual scan both items contain a structure illicit from the point of view of the native Cantonese SSCs, namely the coda fricative [f]. This phonotactic violation is repaired at the Operative Level by the process of occlusivisation of [f] to [p].

Silverman's (1992) two-tier model of loanword phonology has been heavily criticised, particularly by Paradis and LaCharité (1997), who advance four major arguments against the model in question.

First of all, they argue that Silverman's (1992) approach faces a redundancy problem. Thus, the Perceptual Level is redundant as both non-phonological Perceptual Level processes as well as phonological Operative Level processes work towards the same goal, namely the satisfaction of native phonological (segmental and sequential) constraints. Furthermore, the separation of native and loan phonology is unnecessary since all surface requirements that loanwords are made to satisfy also hold in the native phonology. The fact that in Silverman's (1992) study some processes seem to be specific to borrowings is due to the lack of native Cantonese inputs containing structures which mirror those found in loanwords. In other words, for some constraints there are considerably more instances of external violations (i.e. loanwords) than internal ones (e.g. native morphological operations), which creates the impression of loanword-specific processes. However, if it is assumed that repairs found in borrowings are different responses to violations of native phonological constraints, then the need for a separate loanword phonology component disappears. Such a position is also adopted by Yip (1993), who analyses the Cantonese data in terms of Optimality Theory.

Another objection to Silverman's (1992) model is that it contains contradictions. For instance, it is assumed that the input to loanword adaptation is non-linguistic and borrowers have no access to L2 phonology, but at the same time Cantonese speakers are said to have a command of English and to rely on knowledge of English morphology when assigning tone to compounds at the Perceptual Level.[28] Moreover, if borrowers can access English morphology, then they must know that a word like *print* ends in [t], even if it is unreleased, since they know a morphologically related word *printer*, adapted as [pʰɛntʰa] (Silverman 1992: 318). This means that although final obstruents in coda clusters may be perceptually non-salient, they are still recoverable. If this is the case, deletion of [t] in *print* → [pilin] cannot be due to the low perceptibility or lack of salience of this segment, but rather constitutes a response to the violation of the native Cantonese phonological constraint prohibiting consonant clusters.

Next, Paradis and LaCharité (1997) argue that the assumption that borrowing is mainly carried out by monolinguals who do not have access to L2 phonology is incompatible with the results of numerous sociolinguistic and psycholinguistic studies (e.g. Grosjean 1982 and Poplack and Sankoff 1984) demonstrating that bilinguals are the primary performers of adaptation. Furthermore, a body of literature (e.g. Soares and Grosjean 1984) suggests that in language contact situations both L1 and L2 phonological systems are activated in bilinguals, which contradicts Silverman's (1992) claim, based on Elman *et al.* (1977), that bilinguals' perception of the foreign input is constrained by L1 phonology because they are in their L1 language mode when performing adaptation.

---

28 See Silverman (1992: 305) for details of tone assignment to compounds.

Finally, according to Paradis and LaCharité (1997), the fact that nativisation patterns vary across language communities and display stability within communities indicates that loanword adaptation is primarily a phonological rather than a phonetic process. This claim is illustrated with an example of the adaptation of the English interdental [θ] in Quebec French and European French. In the former case, [θ] is systematically realised as [t], whereas in the latter as [s]. Since both dialects have the same consonantal inventory, there is a single sound representing the closest perceptual match in both cases. Thus, a loanword adaptation model based on phonetic proximity, such as Silverman's (1992), predicts identical adaptations in Quebec French and European French, which is not the case. Paradis and LaCharité (1997) mention the possibility of the two sounds in question, i.e. [t] and [s], being phonetically equidistant with respect to [θ]. Nonetheless, they argue that such a hypothesis is implausible for two reasons. First, the acoustic properties of plosives and fricatives differ significantly and thus it is highly unlikely for [t] and [s] to be equally distant to [θ]. Secondly, given the assumption of equal distance between [t] and [θ] as well as [s] and [θ], a considerable variation in the adaptation patterns within a single community is expected. However, the available data demonstrate that such patterns are remarkably constant. According to Paradis and LaCharité (1997), this suggests that loanword adaptation operates on a stable phonological representation rather than on a variable acoustic signal. The cross-linguistic variation may be accounted for by the availability of alternative minimal phonological modifications as well as by the culturally-determined choices of a given community.

Yip (1993) proposes a reanalysis of English borrowings in Cantonese within the framework of Optimality Theory. In this study, loanword adaptation results from subjecting foreign inputs to the hierarchy of native phonological constraints, which makes a separate loan phonology component advocated by Silverman (1992) redundant. Nevertheless, some processes found in borrowings, e.g. vowel epenthesis, have no precedence in Cantonese phonology. As pointed out by Yip (1993), all such repairs are simply different responses to violations of native phonological constraints and the impression that they are loanword-specific stems from the fact that there are no native inputs containing structures such as those in borrowings.

Yip (1993) follows Silverman (1992) in assuming that loanword adaptation proceeds in two phases, i.e. the perceptual stage and the phonological stage, however, she is primarily interested in the latter. Her assumptions are based on the central claim of Optimality Theory that all attested surface forms are the result of the interaction between universal, yet ranked on a language-specific basis, markedness and faithfulness constraints. Thus, in loanword adaptation the phonological component attempts to satisfy two conflicting demands. On the one hand, it aims to select the output well-formed from the point of view of native structural constraints and, on the other hand, to select the output as similar as possible to the input. In the mapping of foreign inputs, frequently containing structures illicit in terms of L1 phonology, this can be achieved by a range of phonological modifications, such as feature change, vowel epenthesis or consonant deletion, all of which are different possible responses to violations of native constraints.

Yip (1993: 280–281) claims that the following constraints are of crucial importance in the phonological system of Cantonese:

(44) <u>Cantonese phonological constraints</u>
   OK-σ: the output is a well-formed Cantonese syllable; a set of four constraints on syllable structure
   – ONSET: avoid σ[V and avoid σ[CC = onsets consist of exactly one consonant
   – NUCLEUS: nuclei may always be vocalic; word-finally, nuclei may be any [+son]
   – CODA: coda licenses Place, [sonorant], [consonantal] = the set of possible codas is [p, t, k, m, n, ŋ, w, y]
   – MINSYLL: [μμ]MINσ = the bimoraic syllable requirement
   FAITHFULNESS: do not alter underlying form
   MINWD: [σσ]MINWD = outputs should be minimally bisyllabic
   PARSE: parse (salient) segments = no deletion
   FILL: avoid unfilled nodes = no epenthesis understood as the insertion of an empty node

PARSE and FAITHFULNESS constraints require some additional explanation. As regards PARSE, Yip (1993) maintains that it is sensitive to the perceptual salience of input segments. This assumption is adopted in order to account for the occurrence of deletion vs. epenthesis in certain cases. Thus, highly salient segments, such as [s] in *spanner* → [sipala], are never deleted as this would constitute a PARSE violation. However, elision of less salient (but still perceived) sounds, such as liquids in initial [Cl] and [Cr] clusters (e.g. *freezer* → [fisa] or *place* → [pheysi]), is not treated by Yip (1993) as a PARSE violation.[29] FAITHFULNESS is understood as a cover term for PARSE and FILL. Yip (1993: 281) argues that the three constraints should be treated separately, as they function in a slightly different way. Thus, FAITHFULNESS penalises all empty nodes, like

---

29 As pointed out by Yip (1993), some words with initial [Cl] or [Cr] clusters undergo epenthesis, e.g. *plum* → [powlam] and *cream* → [keylim]. This is because in such items liquid deletion yields monosyllabic outputs, which results in MINWD violation.

FILL, and all unparsed segments (both salient and non-salient), unlike PARSE, which is violated only when salient segments are deleted.

Yip (1993: 281) argues that the following rankings of constraints can be established on the basis of the native and loanword data in Cantonese:

(45) Rankings of Cantonese phonological constraints
   (a) native phonology
       OK-σ >> FAITHFULNESS >> MINWD >> FILL
       PARSE >> FILL
   (b) loanword phonology
       OK-σ >> FAITHFULNESS >> MINWD >> FILL
       OK-σ >> PARSE >> FILL

As shown in (45), there are no significant differences between the rankings in (45a) and (45b), which indicates that the separation between native and loanword phonology is redundant. Both native and foreign inputs are evaluated by the same language-specific hierarchy of markedness and faithfulness constraints. According to Yip (1993), given this hypothesis, all repairs found in the Cantonese loanword vocabulary, i.e. feature change, deletion and epenthesis, can be accounted for in a straightforward manner.

4.2 Perceptual similarity approach

The perceptual similarity approach to loanword adaptation, advocated by Yip (2002) Kang (2003), Fleischhacker (2005) and Miao (2006) among others, rests crucially on Steriade's (2001/2008) P-Map theory. The starting point for Steriade's (2001/2008) proposal is the too-many-solutions problem, i.e. the situation in which several logically possible repairs are available for a given ill-formed input, but only one specific strategy is consistently used. For instance, when voiced obstruents are prohibited word-finally in a given language (*[+VOICE]/__] WORD), this requirement may be satisfied in a variety of ways. For convenience, we repeat (2) from Chapter 1 in (46), adding to each repair a faithfulness constraint that it violates (Steriade 2001/2008: 151–152).

(46) Possible reactions to the violation of *[±VOICE/   ]WORD in the input /tæb/
   (a) devoicing   /tæb/ → [tæp]   IDENT[±voice]
   (b) nasalisation   /tæb/ → [tæm]   IDENT[±nasal]
   (c) lenition to glide   /tæb/ → [tæw]   IDENT[±consonantal]
   (d) consonant deletion   /tæb/ → [tæ]   MAX-C
   (e) vowel insertion   /tæb/ → [tæbə]   DEP-V
   (f) segment reversal   /tæb/ → [bæt]   LINEARITY(segments)
   (g) feature reversal   /tæb/ → [dæp]   LINEARITY(features)

Of all logically possible repairs listed in (46) only devoicing is cross-linguistically attested as a response to the violation of *[+VOICE]/__]WORD. From an Optimality Theory perspective, all strategies in (46) are equally minimal modifications of the input /tæb/ as each potential output incurs the violation of a single yet different faithfulness constraint. However, the fact that devoicing is a cross-linguistically preferred strategy of dealing with *[+VOICE]/__]WORD violations means in Optimality Theory terms that IDENT[voice] is the lowest-ranked of all faithfulness constraints in (46). This situation poses a challenge to the standard version of the model in question as there is no independent principle which would account for the constraint rankings emerging from the data. According to Steriade (2001/2008), only one strategy is consistently used because the output [tæp] is more similar to the input /tæb/ than any other possible output. If it is assumed that the output should depart from the input minimally, then of all pairs, /tæb/ → [tæp] constitutes the least perceptible modification. Since other mappings are examples of more serious deviations from the source, they are avoided cross-linguistically.

Steriade (2001/2008) provides a formal account of this view by invoking the concept of the P-Map, defined as "a mental representation of the degree of distinctiveness of contrasts in various positions [in the form of] (...) a set of statements about relative similarity between sounds or other phonological properties" (p. 156). In other words, the P-Map hypothesis claims that speakers possess knowledge of the degree of similarity between pairs of phonological structures in particular contexts. Drawing on a number of experimental studies focusing on imperfect rhyming and eliciting similarity judgements, Steriade (p. 163) establishes the following hierarchy of the distinctiveness of contrasts relevant to (46).

(47) A hierarchy of distinctiveness of contrasts
$\Delta(C_1VC_2\text{-}C_2VC_1)$, $\Delta([\vartheta]\text{-}[\emptyset]) > \Delta(C\text{-}\emptyset) > ([\pm son]/\_\_]) > \Delta([\pm voice]/\_\_])$

As evidenced in (47), the least distinctive difference in the word-final position concerns voicing. The P-Map hypothesis assumes that each contrast is mapped onto a respective correspondence constraint, either an input-output or output-output constraint, prohibiting contrast neutralisation, e.g. IDENT[±voice] or IDENT[±son]. Their ranking is determined by the P-Map component in that the constraints corresponding to more distinctive contrasts are higher-ranked than those referring to less distinctive differences. In this way, the perceptual knowledge of relative similarity between pairs of structures in a given context is encoded in the production grammar.

Steriade's proposal has been adopted by Kang (2003) in her analysis of the patterns of adaptation of English word-final postvocalic stops in Korean. The central problem posed by the data is the variable occurrence of epenthesis after the segments in question, as shown in (48) (Kang 2003: 223).

(48) The adaptation of English word-final postvocalic stops in Korean
vowel epenthesis after postvocalic word-final stops

bat → [pæ.tʰɨ]	*hip* → [hi.pʰɨ]
deck → [tɛ.kʰɨ]	*pad* → [pʰæ.ti]

no vowel epenthesis after postvocalic word-final stops

flat → [pʰɨʟ.ʟæt]	*bag* → [pæk]
pack → [pʰæk]	*club* → [kʰɨʟ.ʟʌp]

variable vowel epenthesis after postvocalic word-final stops

cut	→	[kʰʌ.tʰɨ]	~ [kʰʌt]
cake	→	[kʰɛ.i.kʰɨ]	~ [kʰɛ.ik]

Apart from the variability of vowel epenthesis after postvocalic word-final stops, there is an additional complicating factor, namely the lack of motivation for the repair under discussion in native Korean phonology. As regards English voiceless stops, usually realised as aspirated stops in Korean, it may be argued that a vowel is inserted after these segments in order to avoid the violation of the constraint prohibiting aspirated consonants in the coda. Nonetheless, native Korean phonology employs deaspiration rather than vowel insertion to satisfy this requirement, e.g. /patʰ/ 'field' → [pat] (Kang 2003: 224), an example of a divergent repair. The situation is even more puzzling with regard to English voiced stops, which are generally adapted as Korean plain stops. In this case, epenthesis is an instance of an unnecessary repair, as plain stops are acceptable codas in Korean.

The available literature (e.g. Hirano 1994, Broselow and Park 1995) as well as Kang's (2003) survey of a corpus of English loanwords in Korean reveals three main phonological factors co-determining the probability of vowel epenthesis after postvocalic word-final stops (49) (Kang 2003: 233).

(49) Factors which determine vowel epenthesis after postvocalic word-final stops
1. Tenseness of the pre-final vowel: tense > lax
   vowel epenthesis is more frequent when the pre-final vowel is tense (89 %) than when it is lax (28 %)
2. Voicing of the final stop: voiced > voiceless
   vowel epenthesis is more frequent when the final stop is voiced (88 %) than when it is voiceless (39 %)
3. Place of articulation of the final stop: coronal > dorsal = labial
   vowel epenthesis is more frequent when the final stop is coronal (72 %) than when it is dorsal (34 %) and the least frequent when it is labial (21 %)

According to Kang, the first two patterns result from borrowers' maximisation of the perceptual similarity between the foreign input and the native output. As regards the place of articulation effect, the factors related to perceptual similarity are coupled with the influence of some morphophonemic restrictions.

Let us now discuss briefly each pattern in turn. Kang's explanation of the vowel-tenseness effect is based on the assumption that English released stops are acoustically very similar to Korean stop + [ɨ] sequences, as suggested in a number of experimental studies (e.g. Parker 1977). Since coda stops in Korean are invariably unreleased, Korean listeners are likely to perceive a release burst in the input as a weak devoiced vowel, similar to [ɨ]. This is corroborated by the relevant loanword literature (e.g. Sohn 2001) suggesting that there is a correlation between the presence of stop release in English and vowel epenthesis in borrowings into Korean. Based on Parker and Walsh (1981) and her survey of the TIMIT corpus, Kang points out that word-final stops in English are released more frequently when the pre-final vowel is tense rather than when it is lax. If stop release in English correlates with vowel epenthesis in Korean, then a high rate of released stops after tense vowels explains the vowel-tenseness effect.

On the other hand, the voicing effect is unrelated to the presence or absence of stop release since there are no statistically significant differences between the frequency of release of final voiced vs. voiceless stops in the corpus examined by Kang. Instead, she suggests that the high rate of epenthesis after English postvocalic voiced stops is due to their perceptual similarity to Korean postvocalic plain stops followed by [ɨ]. When an English final voiced stop is adapted via vowel insertion, it is put in an intervocalic context and surfaces as a voiced stop, e.g. gag → [kægi], which would not be the case if no epenthesis took place (gag → *[kækʼ]) (Kang 2003: 247). Since Korean plain stops are invariably voiced when they occur between sonorant sounds, vowel insertion maximises the perceptual similarity between the Korean output and the English input. Furthermore, as pointed out by Kang, this similarity is enhanced in yet another way. English vowels are longer when they occur before voiced obstruents than before their voiceless counterparts. When epenthesis applies to a final voiced stop in an English loan, the penultimate syllable becomes open. Since vowels in Korean are longer in open syllables than in closed syllables, epenthesis makes the output of adaptation similar to the input with respect to pre-final vowel length.

Kang formalises the vowel tenseness effect and the voicing effect in terms of the interaction of the Optimality Theory constraints maximizing the perceptual similarity between the input and the output (50) with DEP(V), which prohibits vowel epenthesis (p. 252–253).

(50) <u>Perceptual similarity constraints</u>
BESIMILAR[release]: Strings of sounds in correspondence should be similar in the release characteristics of their stops.
BESIMILAR[voice]: Strings of sounds in correspondence should be similar in stop voicing and vowel length

Tableau 5 accounts for the variable adaptation of *jeep* [tsi.pʰɨ] ~ [tsip] (Kang 2003: 253).

Tableau 5: Adaptation of jeep → *[tsi.phɨ] ~ [tsip]*

A. tsijpʳ	BeSimilar[release]	BeSimilar[voice]	Dep(V)
☞a. tsipʰɨ [...pʰʳɨ]			*
b. tsip [...p˺]	*!		
B. tsijp˺			
a. tsipʰɨ [...pʰʳɨ]	*!		*
☞b. tsip [...p˺]			

When the final stop in the English input is released (A), the high ranked BESIMILAR[release] eliminates the candidate with an unreleased stop (A.b.) and selects the form with an epenthetic vowel as the optimal output (A.a.). On the other hand, when the final plosive in the input is unreleased (B), the same constraint forces the selection of the candidate with no release (B.b.). Since final stops in English are released more frequently when the preceding vowel is tense than when it is lax, the rate of epenthesis is accordingly higher in the former case than in the latter.

Tableau 6 demonstrates the variable adaptation of *zigzag* → [tsi.kɨ.tsæ.kɨ] ~ [tsi.kɨ.tsæk] (Kang 2003: 254).

Tableau 6: Adaptation of zigzag → *[tsi.kɨ.tsæ.kɨ] ~ [tsi.kɨ.tsæk]*

A. zɪgzægʳ	BeSimilar[release]	BeSimilar[voice]	Dep(V)
☞a. tsikɨtsæki [...æːgʳɨ]			*
b. tsikɨtsæk [...æk˺]	*!	*!	
B. zɪgzæg˺			
☞a. tsikɨtsæki [...æːgʳɨ]	*		*
☞b. tsikɨtsæk [...æk˺]		*	

Again, when the final stop in the input is released (A), the candidate with an epenthetic vowel emerges as optimal (A.a.). However, when the segment in question is unreleased (B), two outcomes are possible. Given the assumption that BESIMILAR[release] and BESIMILAR[voice] are equally ranked, the optimal output may be either the candidate with an epenthetic vowel (B.a.) or without it (B.b.).

As regards the place of articulation effect, Kang argues that the vowel epenthesis asymmetry between dorsal stops and labial stops (34 % vs. 21 % of epenthesis cases respectively) may be explained in a similar manner to the vowel-tenseness effect. Thus, Kang's (p. 249–250) survey of the TIMIT corpus reveals that labial stops in sentence-final postvocalic position in English are released less frequently than dorsal stops in the same context (52 % vs. 83 %, respectively), which is reflected in the lower rate of vowel insertion after the former segments. However, this hypothesis fails to account for the high frequency of epenthesis after coronal stops, as they are released even less often than labial stops in the TIMIT corpus (37 %). According to Kang, the problematic data may be explained by reference to the Korean morphophonemic constraint against non-uniform realisations of a morpheme. In Korean, all coronal obstruents are neutralised to [t] in coda position. However, when vowel-initial suffixes are added, the final [t] is realised as [s], giving rise to an alternation between [t] in citation forms and [s] before vowels in inflected forms, e.g. [pɑt] 'to receive' ~ [pɑsɨʟ] 'to receive ACC' ~ [pɑsɛ] 'to receive LOC.' This regularity, producing a non-uniform paradigm, also holds in the adaptation of some loanwords, e.g. cut → [kʰʌt] ~ [kʰʌsɨʟ] ~ [kʰʌsɛ]. However, [t]-final loanwords may be alternatively adapted with an epenthetic vowel, e.g. cut → [kʰʌtʰɨ] ~ [kʰʌtʰɨʟiʟ] ~ [kʰʌtʰiɛ]. In such a case, the [t] ~ [s] alternation does not take place and paradigm uniformity is satisfied, as the relevant form is invariably realised as [kʰʌtʰɨ].

5 Conclusions

This Chapter presented an overview of the major approaches to loanword adaptation put forward within the last 30 years. The proposals were arranged into three major groups based on the degree of importance they attach to the role of phonetics vs. phonology in the process under discussion. We started with the models which view loanword nativisation as a function of the phonological production grammar. Next, we examined the phonetic approaches claiming that loan assimilation takes place in perception. Finally, a variety of mixed models involving both the perception grammar and the production grammar were discussed.

The phonological approximation view maintains that loanword adaptation is computed by the phonological component of grammar. The Theory of Constraints and Repair Strategies Loanword Model advocated by Paradis (1996) and Paradis and LaCharité (1997) claims that loanword adaptation is governed by a set of universal inviolable principles. The most important of these is the Preservation Principle which stipulates that as much phonological information in the input as possible should be retained in the output. The Preservation Principle is limited by the Threshold Principle stating that a particular segment will be saved unless its rescue requires more than two steps of repair. If this is the case, that is, if the preservation of a segment is too costly, then it is predicted to undergo elision. As a result, epenthesis is universally favoured over deletion as a strategy of repairing ill-formed structures since it maximally preserves the phonological content of the input.

Itô and Mester's (1995, 1999, 2001) Optimality Theory analysis of lexical stratification phenomena in Japanese also represents a phonological approach to loanword adaptation. According to this analysis, the core-periphery structure of the Japanese lexicon may be best accounted for within the Optimality Theory framework through reranking of faithfulness constraints with respect to an invariant hierarchy of markedness constraints. The model under discussion also makes accurate predictions concerning possible and impossible nativisations as well as provides an explanation of differential importation.

Section 3 dealt with the phonetic approaches to loan assimilation which assume that this process takes place in perception. The psycholinguistic three-level model of speech processing proposed by Peperkamp and Dupoux (2002, 2003), Peperkamp (2005) and Peperkamp et al. (2008) is based on the assumption that the input to speech perception consists of a continuous acoustic signal mapped by the phonetic decoder onto the phonetically closest native structures in the process called perceptual assimilation. Perceptual assimilation takes place before production grammar applies, which means that the output of perception is already well-formed in the recipient language. The model in question also explains two puzzling patterns found in loan adaptation, namely divergent repair and unnecessary repair.

Boersma and Hamann's (2009) bidirectional model of L1 speech processing postulates that divergent repair, i.e. the asymmetry between loanword repair strategies and native alternations, results from the fact that the former are computed by the perception grammar, whereas the latter by the production grammar. This means that the inputs to both processes are evaluated by different kinds of constraints, with structural constraints being a common element. Perception is not regarded as an extra-grammatical passive module, but it is to a large extent phonological, i.e. heavily influenced by native structural restrictions.

An overview of selected proposals claiming that both the perception grammar and the production grammar are involved in computing loanword adaptation was presented in Section 4. Silverman's (1992) two-tier model of loan assimilation assumes that the incoming non-linguistic acoustic signal is first parsed into segment-sized elements at the Perceptual Level (Scansion One). At this stage, the foreign input is provided with the closest native phonological representation on the basis of its articulatory and/or acoustic properties. This process is subject to native segment and tonal inventory constraints determining the range of available feature configurations for the input mapping. The output of the Perceptual Level is the input to the Operative Level (Scansion Two), where a string of segments formed at Scansion One undergoes phonological processes bringing it into conformity to the native syllable structure constraints (SSCs) and prosodic constraints. Based on evidence from Cantonese, Silverman (1992) concludes that native phonology and loanword phonology constitute separate components. This is because the processes applying to loanwords have no precedence in Cantonese.

The perceptual similarity approach is based on the concept of the P-Map proposed by Steriade (2001/2008). The fundamental assumption underlying the P-Map is that speakers possess the knowledge of perceptual similarity between certain pairs of structures in particular contexts. This knowledge is encoded in the production grammar in the form of correspondence constraints exerting pressure towards perceptually minimal repairs. In loanword adaptation this means that borrowers aim to maximise the perceptual similarity between source items and the output of adaptation in that they employ strategies which result in the least perceptible deviations from the source as possible. The approach in question was adopted by Kang (2003) among others, who argues that considerations of perceptual similarity underlie the patterns of adaptation of English word-final postvocalic stops in Korean.

In the following Chapters, the predictions made by the major approaches to loan nativisation will be verified against the experimental data. We will focus on repair strategies applied by native speakers of English in online adaptation of Polish words with CC and CCC consonant clusters. Our main goal is to contribute to the ongoing debate concerning the phonetic vs. phonological nature of loan assimilation by verifying the validity of various loan adaptation models.

3 Consonant clusters in English and Polish. A sonority-based and optimality theoretic perspective

1 Introduction

This Chapter focuses on the major aspects of English and Polish phonotactics relevant to the experiments on the adaptation of Polish CC and CCC consonant clusters by native speakers of English reported in Chapters 4 and 5. Its fundamental aim is to place the experiments in a broader theoretical perspective by examining previous research on the subject as well as various sonority-based interpretations of the phonotactics and syllable structure of the languages in question. The second goal is to provide a brief introduction to Optimality Theory – the framework within which the analysis of the experimental data will be carried out.

Sections 2 and 3 contain an overview of the phonotactic restrictions on initial and final CC and CCC consonant clusters in English and Polish respectively. The relevant sequences are enumerated and classified according to their segmental composition. The data presented in these Sections provide the basis for a sonority-based discussion of co-occurrence restrictions holding in both languages in Section 5.

The main focus of Section 4 is on the notion of sonority and on several sonority-based cross-linguistic principles. First, we discuss briefly the physical correlates of sonority and various sonority hierarchies proposed in the literature. Next, we focus on the most frequently invoked universal sonority-based generalisations, including the Sonority Sequencing Principle (e.g. Selkirk 1984), the Minimum Sonority Distance (e.g. Steriade 1982), the Syllable Contact Law (e.g. Murray and Vennemann 1983) and the Sonority Dispersion Principle (e.g. Clements 1990).

Section 5 is devoted to a sonority-based comparison of English and Polish CC and CCC clusters in initial and final positions. It is argued that English branching onsets and codas conform to the Sonority Sequencing Principle. Any surface violations of this generalisation are assumed to contain a syllable appendix. Furthermore, evidence is presented for the core-periphery organisation of the English lexicon, with items located in the latter satisfying only a subset of the structural constraints which hold in the core. Finally, various interpretations of the Polish phonotactic restrictions on consonant clusters are briefly examined.

Section 6 contains a presentation of selected frameworks in which the notion of sonority is criticised, rejected or modified. We discuss briefly various alternative approaches to sonority adopted in Government Phonology, Onset Prominence Phonology and Beats-and-Binding Phonology.

Section 7 provides a theoretical background for a formal analysis of the experimental results carried out within the framework of Optimality Theory (OT) (Prince and Smolensky 1993/2004, McCarthy and Prince 1995) in Chapters 4 and 5. First, we outline the basic assumptions of OT as well as the central tenets of the syllable theory developed within this model. Next, we establish the ranking of universal syllable structure constraints as well as relevant faithfulness constraints and sonority-based constraints for English.

Section 8 contains a concise report on previous research on online loanword adaptation. More specifically, studies by Davidson (2001), Davidson *et al.* (2004) and Haunz (2007) are examined. We present their major findings as well as point out their limitations. The conclusions are presented in Section 9.

2 CC and CCC consonant clusters in English

According to Cruttenden (2014: 261), 56 initial CC sequences can be found in Standard British English, including 40 core clusters, i.e. those occurring freely, and 16 peripheral ones, i.e. those appearing in a limited number of items, mostly borrowings. The former structures are listed in (51).

(51)		Core initial CC clusters in Standard British English			
	/pl/	please, plan		/tr/	try, trust
	/pr/	pray, proud		/tj/	tune, tutor
	/pj/	puke, pure		/tw/	twin, twist
	/bl/	blood, black		/dr/	drum, draw
	/br/	brown, break		/dj/	dune, dew
	/bj/	beauty, bugle		/dw/	dwell, dwarf
	/kl/	clean, close		/vj/	view
	/kr/	cry, creep		/θr/	throne, through
	/kj/	cute, cube		/θj/	thew, thuja
	/kw/	quick, quest		/θw/	thwack, thwart
	/gl/	glow, glad		/sl/	slow, slay
	/gr/	greed, grow		/sj/	sue, pseudo
	/gj/	gular, gules		/sw/	swan, sweet
	/gw/	Gwen, guano		/sp/	spit, sport
	/mj/	music, mule		/st/	stop, start
	/nj/	new, nude		/sk/	school, sky
	/lj/	lurid, lure		/sm/	smoke, smell
	/fl/	flow, fly		/sn/	snow, sneeze
	/fr/	frown, fresh		/ʃr/	shroud, shrink
	/fj/	few, future		/hj/	huge, human

The vast majority of initial CC clusters in English are obstruent + sonorant sequences (34 out of 40). There are only three obstruent + obstruent structures, i.e. /sp/, /st/ and /sk/, and three sonorant + sonorant clusters, i.e. /mj/, /nj/ and /lj/. The peripheral initial CC sequences are provided in (52) (Cruttenden 2014: 261).

(52) Peripheral initial CC clusters in Standard British English

/pw/	*pueblo* (Spanish), *puissance* (French)
/bw/	*Buenos Aires* (Spanish), *boite* (French)
/mw/	*moi, moire* (French)
/nw/	*noir, noisette* (French)
/vl/	*Vladimir, Vladivostok* (Russian)
/vr/	*Wrocław* (Polish), *vroom*
/vw/	*voila, voyeur* (French)
/sr/	*Sri Lanka, Srebrenica, Srinagar*
/sf/	*sphere, sphinx*
/sv/	*Svalbard* (Norwegian), *svelte*
/ʃl/	*schlep* (Yiddish), *Schleswig* (German)
/ʃw/	*schwa, Schwartz* (German)
/ʃp/	*spiel* (German)
/ʃt/	*schtick, shtetl* (Yiddish)
/ʃm/	*schmaltz, schmuck* (Yiddish)
/ʃn/	*schnapps, schnitzel* (German)

The clusters listed in (52) are found only in words of foreign origin and in onomatopoeic *vroom*. In Section 5, it will be argued that the sequences under discussion provide evidence for the core-periphery organisation of the English lexicon, with items located in the periphery satisfying only a subset of the structural constraints which hold in the core.

Let us now turn to the initial CCC clusters presented in (53) (Cruttenden 2014: 261).

(53) Initial CCC clusters in Standard British English

/spl/	*split, splash*	/skl/	*sclaff, sclerosis*
/spr/	*spray, spread*	/skr/	*screen, script*
/spj/	*spew, spume*	/skj/	*skew, skewer*
/str/	*street, stress*	/skw/	*square, squash*
/stj/	*stew, stupid*		

As demonstrated in (53), the only segment which can occur in C_1 position is /s/. C_2 is occupied by a voiceless plosive and C_3 contains an approximant, i.e. /l/, /r/, /j/ or /w/. Initial CCC structures in English are therefore sequences of /s/ + one of the core CC clusters with a voiceless plosive as C_1. Since /pw/ and /tl/ are not attested, neither are /spw/ and /stl/ (note an exception: /tw/ vs. */stw/).

Let us now examine final consonant clusters in English. As observed by Cruttenden (2014: 260), a wider range of CC sequences is allowed in final position than initially (60 vs. 40), especially obstruent + obstruent structures, as evidenced in (54).

(54) <u>Final CC clusters in Standard British English</u>

/pt/	stopped, apt	/ŋk/	blink, thank
/pθ/	depth	/ŋz/	lungs, strings
/ps/	caps, corpse	/lp/	help, gulp
/tθ/	eighth	/lb/	bulb, alb
/ts/	gets, bats	/lt/	melt, fault
/kt/	act, backed	/ld/	build, filled
/ks/	box, nicks	/lk/	milk, bulk
/bd/	rubbed, curbed	/ltʃ/	belch, zilch
/bz/	robs, labs	/ldʒ/	bulge, indulge
/dθ/	breadth, width	/lm/	film, realm
/dz/	adze, cods	/ln/	kiln
/gd/	begged, mugged	/lf/	golf, wolf
/gz/	rags, wigs	/lv/	solve, twelve
/tʃt/	stretched, matched	/lθ/	health, filth
/dʒd/	aged, judged	/ls/	pulse, else
/mp/	lamp, damp	/lz/	hills, malls
/md/	harmed, deemed	/lʃ/	Welsh
/mf/	bumph, nymph	/ft/	draft, cuffed
/mθ/	warmth	/fθ/	fifth
/mz/	arms, hums	/fs/	roofs, laughs
/nt/	bent, mint	/vd/	loved, moved
/nd/	band, fund	/vz/	waves, lives
/ntʃ/	bench, clinch	/θt/	breathed, toothed
/ndʒ/	binge, strange	/θs/	maths, paths
/nθ/	labyrinth, tenth	/ðd/	clothed, bathed
/ns/	absence, finance	/ðz/	mouths, clothes
/nz/	bronze, pens	/sp/	clasp, lisp
/ŋd/	winged, prolonged	/st/	cost, passed
/sk/	mask, risk	/ʃt/	washed, brushed
/zd/	used, closed	/ʒd/	garaged

The clusters in (54) can be divided into two main groups in terms of their segmental makeup, namely 1) sonorant + obstruent (28 sequences) and 2) obstruent + obstruent (30 sequences). In addition, there are two sonorant + sonorant clusters, i.e. /lm/ and /ln/. As regards obstruent + obstruent structures, the vast majority of them arise as a result of suffixation and have a coronal obstruent, i.e. /t, d, s, z, θ/, as C_2, which represents the past tense morpheme <-ed>, the plural or third person singular ending <-s> or the ordinal number suffix <-th>. As pointed out by Cruttenden (p. 262), there is only a small group of monomorphemic items with such clusters, e.g. *act, axe, adze, fact, lapse* and *ox*.

Final CCC sequences are provided in (55) (Cruttenden 2014: 263).

(55)   Final CCC clusters in Standard British English

/pts/	*adopts, concepts*	/nst/	*against, balanced*
/pθs/	*depths*	/nzd/	*cleansed, bronzed*
/pst/	*lapsed, eclipsed*	/ŋkt/	*instinct, ranked*
/tθs/	*eighths*	/ŋkθ/	*length, strength*
/dst/	*midst*	/ŋks/	*thanks, banks*
/kts/	*acts, affects*	/ŋst/	*angst, amongst*
/kst/	*mixed, text*	/lpt/	*sculpt, helped*
/ksθ/	*sixth*	/lps/	*helps, yelps*
/mpt/	*attempt, bumped*	/lbz/	*bulbs, albs*
/mps/	*jumps, glimpse*	/lts/	*belts, faults*
/mfs/	*nymphs*	/ldz/	*fields, builds*
/nts/	*ants, taunts*	/lkt/	*mulct, milked*
/ndz/	*bands, tends*	/lks/	*calx, elks*
/ntʃt/	*branched, pinched*	/lʃt/	*squelched, welched*
/ndʒd/	*changed, ranged*	/ldʒd/	*indulged, bilged*
/nθs/	*tenths, synths*	/lmz/	*films, realms*
/lnz/	*kilns*	/fts/	*drafts, lifts*
/lfθ/	*twelfth*	/fθs/	*fifths*
/lfs/	*gulfs*	/spt/	*rasped, gasped*
/lvd/	*solved, delved*	/sps/	*grasps, clasps*
/lvz/	*involves, elves*	/sts/	*artists, lists*
/lθs/	*twelfths*	/skt/	*asked, risked*
/lst/	*whilst, pulsed*	/sks/	*whisks, tasks*

The clusters in (55) can be divided into two groups. The first one comprises the sequences of /mC, nC, ŋC, lC, sC/ + /t, d, s, z, θ/, with C_3 representing a suffix, e.g. *lamps, pants, camped, length* and *twelfth*. Monomorphemic words of this structure are very rare, e.g. *mulct, calx* and *sculpt*. The other group includes the items with the double occurrence of /t, d, s, z, θ/, which usually correspond to suffixes, e.g. *depths, fifths* and *lapsed* (monomorphemic exceptions are e.g. *text* and *next*).

The data presented above will be examined from a sonority-based perspective in Section 5. In particular, it will be argued that both initial as well as final CC and CCC clusters attested in English conform to universal sonority sequencing laws despite a number of apparent counterexamples.

3 CC and CCC consonant clusters in Polish

According to Zydorowicz *et al.* (2016), 218 initial CC clusters can be found in Polish. Some representative examples of cluster types are presented in (56).

(56) Initial CC clusters in Polish
    obstruent + obstruent (103 clusters)

/bz̧/	*brzuch* [bz̧ux] 'a stomach'	/kṣ/	*krzew* [kṣɛf] 'a shrub'
/db/	*dbać* [dbaʨ] 'to care'	/pt/	*ptak* [ptak] 'a bird'
/fk/	*wkoło* ['fkɔwɔ] 'around'	/sp/	*spać* [spaʨ] 'to sleep'
/gb/	*gbur* [gbur] 'a boor'	/ṣk/	*szkoła* ['ṣkɔwa] 'a school'
/ɕf/	*świt* [ɕfʲit] 'dawn'	/gd͡ʑ/	*gdzie* [gd͡ʑɛ] 'where'
/kt/	*kto* [ktɔ] 'who'	/tx/	*tchórz* [txuṣ] 'a coward'

    obstruent + sonorant (88 clusters)

/bl/	*blady* ['bladi] 'pale'	/sm/	*smak* [smak] 'taste'
/dj/	*diabeł* ['dʲjabɛw] 'the devil'	/ṣr/	*szron* [ṣrɔn] 'frost'
/gɲ/	*gniew* [gɲɛf] 'anger'	/ʨm/	*ćma* [ʨma] 'a moth'
/dn/	*dno* [dnɔ] 'a bottom'	/xj/	*hiena* [xʲjɛna] 'a hyena'

    sonorant + obstruent (17 clusters)

/lv/	*lwica* ['lvʲit͡sa] 'a lioness'	/rt/	*rtęć* [rtɛ̃ɲʨ] 'mercury'
/mṣ/	*msza* [mṣa] 'a mass'	/rv/	*rwać* [rvaʨ] 'to tear'
/mx/	*mchowy* ['mxɔvi] 'mossy'	/wz/	*łza* [wza] 'a tear'
/rd/	*rdest* [rdɛst] 'a knotweed'	/wk/	*łkać* [wkaʨ] 'to sob'

    sonorant + sonorant (10 clusters)

/lj/	*liana* ['lʲjana] 'a liana'	/mn/	*mnogi* ['mnɔgʲi] 'numerous'
/lɲ/	*lniany* ['lʲɲani] 'linen'	/mɲ/	*mnich* [mʲɲix] 'a monk'
/mj/	*mieć* [mʲjeʨ] 'to have'	/mr/	*mrok* [mrɔk] 'gloom'
/ml/	*mleko* ['mlɛkɔ] 'milk'	/mw/	*młody* ['mwɔdi] 'young'

The largest groups of initial CC consonant sequences allowed in Polish are obstruent + obstruent clusters, which account for almost half of all the structures under discussion, and obstruent + sonorant clusters. The number of attested sonorant + obstruent and sonorant + sonorant sequences is relatively low in comparison with the former types.

A comparison of the initial CC clusters in English and Polish reveals some striking differences in terms of the number of possible sequences as well as their segmental makeup. One of the most noticeable differences concerns obstruent +

obstruent clusters, which abound in Polish, but are disallowed in English, except for the /sC/ clusters. Furthermore, Polish permits more obstruent + sonorant and sonorant + sonorant sequences than English as well as some initial sonorant + obstruent clusters, which are unattested in English.

As regards the initial CCC clusters, 207 such structures can be found in Polish (Zydorowicz *et al.* 2016). Some examples are provided in (57).

(57) Initial CCC clusters in Polish

obstruent + obstruent + obstruent (50 clusters)

/bzd/	*bzdura* ['bzdura] 'nonsense'	/skʂ/	*skrzydła* ['skʂɨdwa] 'wings'
/fsp/	*wspak* [fspak] 'backwards'	/tkf/	*tkwić* [tkfʲiʨ] 'to be stuck'
/fsx/	*wschód* [fsxut] 'east'	/vzd/	*wzdychać* ['vzdɨxaʨ] 'to sigh'
/kʂt/	*krzta* [kʂta] 'a whit'	/zdv/	*zdwoić* ['zdvɔʲiʨ] 'to redouble'

obstruent + obstruent + sonorant (105 clusters)

/fɕr/	*wśród* [fɕrut] 'among'	/gʐm/	*grzmot* [gʐmɔt] 'thunder'
/ɕfj/	*świat* [ɕfʲjat] 'the world'	/skl/	*sklep* [sklɛp] 'a shop'
/fkr/	*wkrótce* ['fkrutʦɛ] 'soon'	/tkn/	*tknąć* [tknɔ̃ɲʨ] 'to touch'
/gvj/	*gwiazda* ['gvʲjazda] 'a star'	/vbr/	*wbrew* [vbrɛf] 'against'

obstruent + sonorant + obstruent (13 clusters)

/brv/	*brwi* [brvʲi] 'eyebrows'	/trf/	*trwać* [trfaʨ] 'to last'
/drg/	*drgać* [drgaʨ] 'to twitch'	/krf/	*krwi* [krfʲi] 'blood, Gen.'
/drv/	*drwić* [drvʲiʨ] 'to mock'	/krt/	*krtań* [krtaɲ] 'the larynx'
/drʐ/	*drżeć* [drʐɛʨ] 'to tremble'	/plv/	*plwać* [plvaʨ] 'to spit'

obstruent + sonorant + sonorant (20 clusters)

/brn/	*brnąć* [brnɔ̃ɲʨ] 'to wade'	/prj/	*priorytet* [prʲjɔˈrit̪ɛt] 'a priority'
/ɕmj/	*śmierć* [ɕmʲjerʲʨ] 'death'	/smr/	*smród* [smrut] 'stench'
/drj/	*driada* ['drʲjada] 'a dryad'	/trj/	*triumf* [trʲjũw̃f] 'a triumph'
/kmj/	*kmieć* [kmʲjeʨ] 'a serf'	/zmr/	*zmrok* [zmrɔk] 'dusk'

sonorant + obstruent + obstruent (3 clusters)

/mɕʨ/	*mścić* [mʲɕʨiʨ] 'to avenge'	/mʂʈʂ/	*Mszczonów* ['mʂʈʂɔnuf]
/mst/	*Mstów* [mstuf] 'a place name'		'a place name'

sonorant + obstruent + sonorant (16 clusters)

/lgn/	*lgnąć* [lgnɔ̃ɲʨ] 'to cling'	/mgɲ/	*mgnienie* ['mgʲɲɛɲɛ] 'a blink'

/mdl/	mdleć [mdlɛt͡ɕ] 'to faint'	/mgw/	mgła [mgwa] 'fog'
/mdw/	mdły [mdwɨ] 'insipid'	/mkn/	mknąć [mknɔ̃ɲt͡ɕ] 'to rush'
/mgl/	mglisty ['mglʲistɨ] 'foggy'	/rʐn/	rżnąć [rʐnɔ̃ɲt͡ɕ] 'to saw'

The data in (57) demonstrate that the largest group of the items under examination are obstruent + obstruent + sonorant sequences, followed by clusters of three obstruents. The remaining cluster types, i.e. obstruent + sonorant + obstruent, obstruent + sonorant + sonorant, sonorant + obstruent + obstruent and sonorant + obstruent + sonorant, are less numerous.

Again, as in the case of the initial CC sequences, substantial differences may be observed between English and Polish concerning the number and the segmental structure of the initial CCC clusters. While English allows only obstruent + obstruent + sonorant clusters, where C_1 is occupied by /s/, C_2 by /p, t, k/ and C_3 by /l, r, j, w/, Polish permits a considerably wider range of CCC sequences of a different segmental makeup.

Let us now examine final CC consonant clusters in Polish. According to Zydorowicz *et al.* (2016), there are 145 such sequences, as exemplified in (58).

(58) Final CC clusters in Polish

obstruent + obstruent (32 clusters)

/ft͡ʃ/	szewc [ʂɛft͡ʃ] 'a shoemaker'	/sf/	nazw [nasf] 'a name, Gen. pl.'
/ks/	indeks ['indɛks] 'an index'	/ʂt/	koszt [kɔʂt] 'a cost'
/kt/	projekt ['prɔjekt] 'a project'	/t͡ʂp/	liczb [lʲit͡ʂp] 'a number, Gen. pl.'
/ps/	gips [gʲips] 'plaster'	/xt/	jacht [jaxt] 'a yacht'

obstruent + sonorant (35 clusters)

/dl/	módl [mudl] 'to pray, imp.'	/ɕl/	myśl [mɨɕl] 'a thought'
/dm/	kadm [kadm] 'cadmium'	/tr/	łotr [wɔtr] 'a rascal'
/ɕɲ/	baśń [baɕɲ] 'a fairy tale'	/fl/	trefl [trɛfl] 'club'
/pɲ/	wapń [vapʲɲ] 'calcium'	/fr/	gofr [gɔfr] 'a waffle'

sonorant + obstruent (60 clusters)

/rf/	torf [tɔrf] 'peat'	/jt͡ɕ/	pójdź [pujt͡ɕ] 'to go, imp.'
/mʂ/	zamsz [zamʂ] 'suede'	/rt͡ʂ/	skurcz [skurt͡ʂ] 'a cramp'
/wʂ/	fałsz [fawʂ] 'falsehood'	/nt͡s/	glanc [glãnt͡s] 'lustre'
/rt/	tort [tɔrt] 'a cream cake'	/lt͡s/	walc [walt͡s] 'waltz'

sonorant + sonorant (18 clusters)

/jm/	Sejm [sɛjm] 'Parliament'	/rn/	koncern ['kɔnt͡sɛrn] 'a company'
/lm/	film [fʲilm] 'a film'	/rɲ/	czerń [t͡ʂɛrɲ] 'blackness'

/mn/	*hymn* [hɨmn] 'an anthem'	/wm/	*hełm* [xɛwm] 'a helmet'
/rm/	*karm* [karm] 'to feed, imp.'	/wr/	*laur* [lawr] 'a laurel'

As demonstrated in (58), sonorant + obstruent sequences are the most numerous CC structures in the final position in Polish. The number of obstruent + obstruent and obstruent + sonorant clusters is similar (around 30 items). In addition, 18 sonorant + sonorant sequences are attested.

The most significant difference between the final CC clusters in English and Polish concerns obstruent + sonorant sequences, which are attested in Polish but not in English. Moreover, Polish permits a larger number of sonorant + obstruent and sonorant + sonorant clusters than English. The number of obstruent + obstruent sequences is similar in both languages, however, in Polish the C_2 position is not restricted to coronal obstruents as is the case with English.

As regards the final CCC sequences in Polish, Zydorowicz *et al.* (2016) enumerate 53 such structures. Representative examples are provided in (59).

(59) <u>Final CCC clusters in Polish</u>
<u>obstruent + obstruent + obstruent (6 clusters)</u>

/fsk/	*Pietrowsk* ['pʲjetrɔfsk] 'Petrovsk'	/stf/	*bóstw* [bustf] 'a deity, Gen. pl.'
/kst/	*tekst* [tɛkst] 'a text'	/stʂ/	*mistrz* [mʲistʂ] 'a master'
/psk/	*Lipsk* [lʲipsk] 'Leipzig'	/t͡stf/	*śledztw* [ɕlɛt͡stf] 'a probe, Gen. pl.'

<u>obstruent + obstruent + sonorant (3 clusters)</u>

/xtr/	*blichtr* [blʲixtr] 'tinsel'	/stm/	*astm* [astm] 'asthma, Gen. pl.'
/str/	*rejestr* ['rɛjɛstr] 'a register'		

<u>sonorant + obstruent + obstruent (31 clusters)</u>

/jɕt͡ɕ/	*dojść* [dɔjɕt͡ɕ] 'to reach'	/nt͡ʂ/	*zewnątrz* ['zɛvnɔ̃nt͡ʂ] 'outside'
/mst/	*zemst* [zɛmst] 'revenge, Gen. pl.'	/rɕt͡ɕ/	*garść* [garɕt͡ɕ] 'a handful'
/nʂt/	*kunszt* [kũnʂt] 'craft'	/ntp/	*wątp* [vɔ̃ntp] 'to doubt, imp.'
/ŋkt/	*punkt* [pũŋkt] 'a point'	/rʂt/	*herszt* [hɛrʂt] 'a ringleader'

<u>sonorant + obstruent + sonorant (15 clusters)</u>

/ltr/	*filtr* [fʲiltr] 'a filter'	/mbl/	*ansambl* ['ãnsãmbl] 'an ensemble'
/mbr/	*tembr* [tɛ̃mbr] 'a timbre'	/ntn/	*tętn* [tɛ̃ntn] 'a pulse, Gen. pl.'

More than half of all the attested final CCC clusters in Polish have the structure sonorant + obstruent + obstruent. There are also over a dozen instances of sonorant + obstruent + sonorant sequences and a few clusters composed of three obstruents. The clusters /xtr/, /str/ and /stm/ are the only examples of obstruent + obstruent + sonorant sequences.

The number of final CCC sequences in English and Polish is similar (46 vs. 53). In both languages, sonorant + obstruent + obstruent clusters constitute the largest group of the structures under examination. Nevertheless, English allows more obstruent + obstruent + obstruent clusters than Polish (15 vs. 6), whereas Polish permits sonorant + obstruent + sonorant sequences, which are unattested in English.

It should be added that sequences of four consonants can also be found in Polish, both in word-initial and word-final position, as exemplified in (60) (Zydorowicz *et al.* 2016).

(60) CCCC clusters in Polish

word-initial (30 clusters)		word-final (9 clusters)	
/brvj/	*brwiowy* ['brvʲjɔvɨ] 'superciliary'	/fstf/	*ustawodawstw* [ustaˈvɔdafsts] 'legislation, Gen. pl.'
/fskr/	*wskroś* [fskrɔɕ] 'right across'	/jstf/	*zabójstw* ['zabujstf] 'a homicide, Gen. pl.'
/gʐbj/	*grzbiet* [gʐbjɛt] 'a back'	/lstf/	*poselstw* ['pɔsɛlstf] 'legation, Gen. pl.'
/pstr/	*pstrąg* [pstrɔ̃ŋk] 'trout'	/mstf/	*kłamstw* [kwãmstf] 'a lie, Gen. pl.'
/stʧ/	*stwierdzić* ['stfʲjɛrˈd͡ʑiʨ] 'to claim'	/pstf/	*głupstw* [gwupstf] 'nonsense, Gen. pl.'
/vzbr/	*wzbroniony* [vzbrɔ̃'ɲɔ̃nɨ] 'prohibited'	/rstf/	*warstw* [varstf] 'a layer, Gen. pl.'

In terms of the segmental composition, the most common types of CCCC clusters include obstruent + obstruent + obstruent + sonorant sequences in the initial position (18 clusters out of 30) and sonorant + obstruent + obstruent + obstruent sequences in the final position (7 clusters out of 9). Consonant clusters consisting of four segments are unattested in English word-initially, however, a few such structures can be found word-finally, e.g. /mpst/ as in *glimpsed*, /lpts/ as in *sculpts* and /ksts/ as in *texts*. Their characteristic property is that C_3 and C_4 are always coronal obstruents representing various suffixes.

On the whole, a comparison of English and Polish initial and final consonant clusters reveals that their range in Polish is considerably wider than in English for CC, CCC and CCCC sequences. This suggests that native speakers of English are highly likely to find it difficult to reproduce some Polish consonant clusters faithfully. However, it is by no means obvious which sequences will prove particularly problematic and how they will be repaired. The experiments on online adaptation of Polish initial and final CC and CCC consonant clusters will enable us to provide answers to these questions.[30] The data presented above will be analysed in sonority-based terms in Section 5.

4 The concept of sonority and cross-linguistic sonority-based generalisations

This Section deals with sonority, a concept which has traditionally assumed central importance in accounting for a variety of cross-linguistic phonotactic generalisations. We start with a brief examination of the phonetic correlates of sonority (4.1.) as well as various sonority scales proposed in the literature (4.2.). Next, several cross-linguistic sonority-based principles are discussed, including the Sonority Sequencing Principle (4.3.), the Minimum Sonority Distance (4.4.), the Syllable Contact Law (4.5.) and the Sonority Dispersion Principle (4.6.).

4.1 Phonetic correlates of sonority

Sonority is one of the most elusive concepts in phonological theory. Its definition has long been a subject of controversy, with various scholars attempting to identify its acoustic and/or auditory correlate(s). Parker (2002) enumerates as many as 98 characteristics used to define sonority that appear in the literature (some of which are clearly synonymous). Selected examples are presented in (61) (pp. 44–48).

(61) Correlates of sonority
openness of the vocal tract (e.g. Goldsmith 1990)
periodicity (e.g. Puppel 1992)
intrinsic perceptual prominence (e.g. Anderson 1986)
relative loudness (e.g. Giegerich 1992)
continuance (e.g. Donegan 1978)
resonance (e.g. Heselwood 1998)
glottal vibration (e.g. Ladefoged 1997)
vowel affinity (e.g. Fujimura and Erickson 1997)
formant amplitudes (e.g. Howe and Pulleyblank 2001)

Some researchers argue that sonority is not based on a single physical parameter, but rather has multiple phonetic correlates, e.g. duration, amplitude and voicing (e.g. Price 1980). Others put forward phonological definitions, e.g. Clements

---

30 The nativisation of Polish CCCC sequences has not been investigated in our experiments as this would require including a significant number of additional items into the body of experimental stimuli. We therefore leave this matter for future research.

(1990) approaches the concept in question in terms of the binary major class features, such as [syllabic], [vocoid], [approximant] and [sonorant].

The difficulty in defining sonority and establishing its physical parameter(s) made some scholars, e.g. Ohala (1990), Scheer (2004) and Harris (2006), question its status as a formal phonological entity. This criticism of sonority will be briefly examined in Section 6. For the time being, let us emphasise that, as noted by Clements (1990), other concepts, e.g. the phoneme or the syllable, have not been clearly defined in phonetic terms either, yet they are widely accepted and used in phonological theory due to their explanatory power. Sonority has been successfully applied to account for a number of syllable-related phenomena, such as a general syllable structure or permissible consonant clusters in onset and coda positions. For this reason, in the present monograph we assume that the concept in question should be regarded as an important element of phonological theory.

4.2 Sonority scales

Since the concept of sonority is so difficult to define, it comes as no surprise that there is no agreement among researchers as to how segment classes should be arranged in a sonority hierarchy. Parker (2002) claims to have found in the literature more than 100 sonority scales differing in at least one detail. Some of the most frequently used hierarchies are presented in (62).

(62) Sonority scales
Jespersen (1904)
low vowels > mid vowels > high vowels > rhotics > laterals & nasals > voiced fricatives > voiced stops > voiceless fricatives & voiceless stops
Hooper (1976)
vowels > glides > liquids > nasals > voiced fricatives > voiceless fricatives and voiced stops > voiceless stops
Steriade (1982)
vowels > glides > liquids > nasals > fricatives > stops (plosives & affricates)
Selkirk (1984)
vowels > /r/ > /l/ > nasals > /s/ > voiced fricatives > voiceless fricatives > voiced stops > voiceless stops
Goldsmith (1990)
vowels > glides > liquids > nasals > fricatives > affricates > stops
Clements (1990)
vowels > glides > liquids > nasals > obstruents

The scales in (62) vary to a significant extent in terms of both the number and the kinds of distinctions they make. One of the most controversial issues concerning the shape of a sonority hierarchy is related to the need for introducing sonority distinctions among obstruents. As demonstrated in (62), some researchers treat all obstruents as equal in terms of sonority, while others introduce two or more additional distinctions based on voicing or manner of articulation. Other contentious issues include, for instance, the relative sonority of /r/, /l/ and glottal consonants. As noted by Parker (2002: 64), despite all these differences, the majority of scholars agree on the general sonority hierarchy of the following shape,

vowels > liquids > nasals > obstruents.

In the present monograph, Steriade's (1982) hierarchy is employed,

vowels > glides > liquids > nasals > fricatives > stops (plosives & affricates),

in order to make our findings directly comparable to the results of the studies on the adaptation of consonant clusters by Haunz (2007) and Davidson (2001), in which stops and fricatives are assigned different sonority values (see Section 8 for a brief discussion of these works).

4.3 Sonority Sequencing Principle

One of the most frequently invoked sonority-related cross-linguistic generalisations is the Sonority Sequencing Principle (SSP), which expresses the preference for a sonority rise from the syllable margins towards the nucleus. The definition of the SSP formulated by Selkirk (1984: 116) is presented in (63).

(63) Sonority Sequencing Principle (SSP)
In any syllable, there is a segment constituting a sonority peak that is preceded and/or followed by a sequence of segments with progressively decreasing sonority values.

The tendency expressed by the SSP can be observed in a number of languages, including English, in which clusters of rising sonority can be found in many items in word-initial position, e.g. *play*, *grow* and *tune*, and numerous sequences of falling sonority occur word-finally, e.g. *lamp*, *must* and *cold*. Yet the SSP is not without exceptions, at least in surface representations. For instance, English initial /sC/ clusters, such as /sp/, /st/ or /sk/, apparently violate the principle in question, as they constitute sonority reversals or plateaus, depending on whether or not fricatives are assumed to differ from plosives in terms of sonority (see Section 5 for a more detailed sonority-based discussion of English phonotactic restrictions).

Furthermore, some languages abound in consonant sequences that do not conform to the SSP. For example, Polish initial clusters permit sonority falls, e.g. /rt/ as in *rtęć* [rtɛ̃ɲʨ] 'mercury' and /wk/ as in *łkać* [wkaʨ] 'to weep,' as well as sonority plateaus, e.g. /pt/ as in *ptak* [ptak] 'a bird' and /gd/ as in *gdy* [gdɨ] 'when.'

Moreover, final clusters permit sonority rises, e.g. /tr/ as in *wiatr* [vʲjatr] 'wind' and /kl/ as in *cykl* [tʂikl] 'cycle,' as well as sonority plateaus, e.g. /kt/ as in *fakt* [fakt] 'fact' and /mn/ as in *hymn* [hĩmn] 'anthem.'

At first sight, it might seem that, given such a large number of exceptions, the SSP does not hold in Polish and presumably in many other languages permitting consonant sequences disallowed by this principle (see Clements 1990: 288 for examples). However, as noted by Cho and King (2003), a number of explanations of surface exceptions to the SSP have been put forward, such as making a distinction between the syllable core and affix (e.g. Fujimura and Lovins 1978), introducing a notion of a syllable appendix (e.g. Halle and Vergnaud 1980, Giegerich 1992) or treating clusters as single complex segments (e.g. Selkirk 1982). Other scholars make some language-particular stipulations, e.g. Rubach and Booij (1990) argue that in Polish the SSP is generally observed, with the exception of obstruent clusters, where it does not hold. The purpose of all these proposals is to uphold the validity of the SSP despite its apparent violations in many languages.

4.4 Minimum Sonority Distance

The SSP alone cannot account for the observed patterns of permissible onset and coda consonant clusters. In numerous cases, it is not enough for sonority to rise in the onset and to fall in the coda, but some minimum degree of the sonority distance between segments in syllable constituents is required in order for the cluster to be well-formed. This cross-linguistic tendency is expressed as the Minimum Sonority Distance Principle (MSD) (e.g. Steriade 1982). In English, for example, the initial plosive + liquid and plosive + glide clusters are permitted, as liquids and glides are sufficiently distant from plosives in terms of sonority, but plosive + nasal sequences, although well-formed with respect to the SSP, are not acceptable due to an insufficient degree of sonority rise. The minimum sonority distance threshold for English branching onsets is usually set at 2 points (Haunz 2007: 41), however, as noted by Baertsch (2012), this is entirely dependent on the adopted sonority scale. Thus, the assumption that the minimum sonority distance threshold is 2 points for English initial clusters is based on a five-level sonority hierarchy proposed by Clements (1990), i.e. vowel > glide > liquid > nasal > obstruent. This means that permissible onsets may consist of an obstruent and a liquid or a glide (e.g. *glow*, *queen* and *free*). As regards English final sequences, the minimum sonority distance of 2 points is not required as the segments in such clusters can be neighbours on the sonority scale, e.g. /lm/ as in *film* or /mp/ as in *lamp* (Clements 1990: 318).

4.5 Syllable Contact Law

Another cross-linguistic sonority-related generalisation is the Syllable Contact Law (SCL), provided in (64) (Murray and Vennemann 1983, Vennemann 1988: 40).

(64) Syllable Contact Law (SCL) (consonantal strength version)
A syllable contact A.B is the more preferred, the less the consonantal strength of the offset A and the greater the consonantal strength of the onset B.

Vennemann's (1988) version of the principle is formulated in terms of consonantal strength. Nonetheless, in the current phonological literature, the sonority-based formulation of the SCL is more commonly used (65) (Davis and Shin 1999: 286).

(65) Syllable Contact Law (SCL) (sonority version)
A syllable contact A.B is the more preferred, the greater the sonority of the offset A and the less the sonority of the onset B.

The principle thus refers to the sonority distance between the heterosyllabic coda and onset segments and expresses the preference for a sonority drop between them.

The SCL effects can be observed in a number of languages (see Seo 2011 for a concise overview of the SCL phenomena in the world's languages). For instance, in Kazakh if there is no sonority fall across syllable boundaries, onset consonants undergo desonorisation so as to create a syllable contact consistent with the SCL (66) (Davis 1998 after Seo 2011).

(66) Syllable contact in Kazakh
No onset desonorisation
/alma-lar/   [al.ma.lar]   'apples'
/kijar-lar/   [kijar.lar]   'cucumbers'
Onset desonorisation
/kol-lar/   [kol.dar]   'hands'
/murin-lar/   [mu.rin.dar]   'noses'

As demonstrated in (66), neither a flat sonority [l.l] nor a rising sonority [n.l] syllable contact is allowed in Kazakh.

As noted by Seo (2011: 1255), a cross-linguistic variation may be observed regarding the treatment of a flat sonority heterosyllabic coda-onset contact. Some languages respecting the SCL, like Korean, tolerate such structures (e.g. /sal.lim/ → [sal.lim] 'housekeeping'), while others, like Kazakh, invariably repair them. As a result, the SCL has been formulated in two different versions (67).

(67) Two versions of the Syllable Contact Law
Syllable Contact Law (strict) (Rose 2000: 401)
The first segment of the onset of a syllable must be lower in sonority than the last segment in the immediately preceding syllable.
Syllable Contact Law (loose) (Bat-El 1996; Davis and Shin 1999)
The first segment of the onset of a syllable must not be of greater sonority than the last segment of the immediately preceding syllable.

The strict version prohibits a flat sonority syllable contact, whereas the loose version allows it. The SCL will be employed in our analysis of the nativisation patterns of CCC clusters in Chapter 5.

4.6 Sonority Dispersion Principle

Another sonority-based generalisation is the Sonority Dispersion Principle (SDP), proposed by Clements (1990). It states that the sonority rise between the onset and the nucleus should be maximised and the sonority fall between the nucleus and the coda minimised. This means that obstruents make the best onsets in a CV syllable as they are maximally distant from vowels in terms of sonority. On the other hand, sonorants are better codas than obstruents because the sonority drop between vowels and sonorants is lower than between vowels and obstruents. According to Clements (1990), it follows from these assumptions that a maximal sonority fall between heterosyllabic coda-onset sequences is preferred, as predicted by the SCL. As a result, the SCL is no longer necessary as an independent principle because it simply follows from the SDP. In Clements's (1990) proposal, the syllable is divided into two elements, called demisyllables. The first demisyllable consists of the onset and the nucleus, whereas the other one comprises the nucleus and the coda. Thus, the nucleus belongs to both demisyllables. The relative well-formedness of demisyllables depends upon the value of the D coefficient, calculated on the basis of the sonority distance between pairs of segments and the number of pairs of segments.

As pointed out by Parker (2002), the SDP correctly predicts that obstruents constitute the best simple onsets in CV syllables, a prediction that fails to be expressed by the MSD, evaluating complex onsets only. However, according to Parker (2002), the SDP has several drawbacks, all of which stem from the fact that the nucleus is included in the calculation of the D coefficient value in addition to the syllable margins. Thus, for example, Clements's (1990) proposal predicts that an obstruent + glide + vowel demisyllable is more marked than an obstruent + liquid + vowel demisyllable, as the latter is optimally dispersed in terms of the adopted sonority scale where obstruents and vowels are at both extremes, and liquids are exactly in the middle. As observed by Parker (2002), this is rather unlikely as a cross-linguistic implicational universal can be observed whereby if obstruent + liquid clusters are permitted, so are obstruent + glide sequences. Another problematic prediction of the SDP is that obstruent + nasal + vowel demisyllables are considered as well-formed as obstruent + glide + vowel demisyllables since both have the same D coefficient value. Again, as noted by Parker (2002), this prediction is incorrect because there are no languages where the former but not the latter is permitted, so the presence of obstruent + nasal + vowel entails the presence of obstruent + glide + vowel, but the opposite is not attested.

In spite of the problematic issues inherent in the SDP, its basic insight, i.e. that obstruents make the best onsets in CV syllables and sonorants constitute better codas than obstruents, will turn out useful in our analysis of some puzzling patterns of adaptation of initial CC clusters in Chapter 4.

5 Sonority-based comparison of English and Polish CC and CCC consonant clusters

A comparison of English and Polish CC and CCC clusters in initial and final positions reveals considerable differences between these languages concerning both the number as well as the structure of the permitted consonant sequences. As demonstrated in Sections 2 and 3, Polish abounds in various clusters, whereas the English phonotactics is significantly more restricted in this respect. A question naturally arises whether the supposedly universal sonority-based generalisations, e.g. the SSP, can account for the well-formed clusters in languages like English and Polish, whose surface phonotactic patterns differ to such a remarkable degree.

An examination of the core initial CC clusters in English demonstrates that the vast majority of them conform to the SSP, i.e. they are rising sonority sequences. The only exceptions are /sp, st, sk/, which involve a sonority fall. It should be noted that not all logically possible initial CC sequences of rising sonority are found in English, e.g. obstruent + nasal clusters, such as */pm, tn, fm/, are unattested (the only exceptions being /sm/ and /sn/). This might be accounted for by the MSD principle which requires a minimum sonority distance of 2 points between C_1 and C_2 in English branching onsets. In addition, a number of place restrictions must be invoked in order to explain certain gaps in the cluster inventory, e.g. the lack of structures with labial C_1 and C_2, such as /pw/ or /bw/, or the lack of /tl, dl/, all of which are well formed with respect to both the SSP and the MSD. The crucial claim for the purpose of our analyses in Chapters 4 and 5 is that English initial clusters satisfy both the SSP and the MSD (the exceptions will be discussed shortly).

As regards the peripheral initial CC clusters in English, most of them conform to the SSP and the MSD, the only exceptions being /ʃp, ʃt, sf, sv/. Thus, in terms of sonority both the core and peripheral clusters are alike. However, the latter frequently violate the core place restrictions, e.g. in /pw/, /bw/, /mw/ and /vw/ C_1 and C_2 are labial. Therefore, it can be argued that the sequences under discussion provide evidence for the core-periphery organisation of the English lexicon. Items located in the periphery satisfy only a subset of the structural constraints which hold in the core. This insight will assume crucial significance in our analysis of the experimental data in Chapters 4 and 5.

In order to uphold the validity of the claim that English branching onsets conform to the SSP, it is necessary to account for /s/ + obstruent CC clusters as well as for CCC sequences, where the principle in question is apparently violated. In the present monograph we adopt the view that the initial /s/ in both CC and CCC clusters does not belong to the onset constituent. As noted by Goad (2012), there have been numerous proposals concerning the prosodic status of /s/, e.g. it is represented as a syllable appendix linked to a higher level prosodic structure (e.g. Hulst 1984, Levin 1985, Goldsmith 1990, Giegerich 1992, Fikkert 1994, Goad and Rose 2004) or as a coda segment (e.g. Kaye 1992). Since the representational nature of /sC/ clusters is not directly relevant to the analysis of the experimental data in Chapters 4 and 5, a detailed examination of various approaches to their structure is beyond the scope of the present monograph (see e.g. Goad 2011 and Stangel 2013 for an overview of the issue). For our purposes, the crucial claim is that /s/ is not part of the onset. Given this assumption, neither the /sp, st, sk/ clusters nor English CCC sequences violate the SSP.

As far as the final CC and CCC clusters in English are concerned, at first glance it seems that the SSP is of limited validity in accounting for their structure. This is because a considerable number of the sequences under examination constitute surface violations of the relevant principle, i.e. they are clusters of flat (e.g. /bd, kt, vz/) or rising sonority (e.g. /ps, bz/). However, as noted by Giegerich (1992), these violations of the SSP arise mainly due to the final coronal obstruents. In the present monograph we adopt the view that final coronals are not part of the coda constituent (e.g. Fujimura and Lovins 1978, Selkirk 1982, Goldsmith 1990, Giegerich 1992). Instead, they constitute a syllable appendix. The representational details of the prosodic status of these segments, e.g. whether they are linked directly to the syllable or the prosodic word, will not concern us here as they are largely irrelevant to the issue of cluster adaptation. The essential claim relevant to our purposes is that they do not belong to the coda.

To sum up, our assumption is that the SSP remains a valid generalisation for English which holds in the core syllabification. Any surface exceptions to the

SSP, such as /s/ + obstruent initial clusters or final CC and CCC sequences with coronal obstruents, are understood as containing a syllable appendix attached to the core syllable. The class of segments that may function as appendices is limited to coronal obstruents, i.e. [-sonorant, + coronal] segments (Giegerich 1992: 149). While all the sounds in question can follow a coda, it is only /s/ (and /ʃ/ in peripheral clusters) that can precede an onset. Given the core vs. appendix distinction, it may be argued that the segmental structure of English branching onsets and codas is governed crucially by the SSP (and the MSD in the case of onsets).

As for Polish consonant clusters, the attested surface phonotactic patterns seem to indicate that the SSP is not a valid generalisation in this language. This is because the principle in question is frequently violated in both initial and final positions, as exemplified in (68).

(68) SSP violations in Polish

initial position		final position	
sonority fall		sonority rise	
/mʂ/	msza [mʂa] 'a mass'	/çɲ/	baśń [baçɲ] 'a fairy tale'
/rv/	rwać [rvaʨ] 'to tear'	/tr/	łotr [wɔtr] 'a rascal'
/wk/	łkać [wkaʨ] 'to sob'	/dl/	módl [mudl] 'to pray, imp.'

sonority plateau		sonority plateau	
/db/	dbać [dbaʨ] 'to care'	/mn/	hymn [hɨmn] 'an anthem'
/mɲ/	mnich [mjɲix] 'a monk'	/sf/	nazw [nasf] 'a name, Gen. pl.'
/kt/	kto [ktɔ] 'who'	/kt/	projekt ['prɔjɛkt] 'a project'

The data in (68) demonstrate that clusters of various offending sonority profiles are permitted word-initially and word-finally in Polish.

Given the richness of Polish phonotactics, it might be argued that universal sonority sequencing laws, such as the SSP, do not hold in this language. This is indeed a stance adopted by some researchers, e.g. Sawicka (1974, 1985, 1995) and Dukiewicz (1995). For instance, Sawicka (1985: 4) claims that the SSP is generally satisfied in Slavic languages, except for Polish. On the other hand, a number of studies on the structure of the phonological syllable in Polish, e.g. Rubach and Booij (1990), Bethin (1992) and Szpyra-Kozłowska (1998), maintain that the SSP is a valid generalisation in Polish which holds at some lower level of representation than the surface. On the other hand, Kuryłowicz (1952) maintains that some complex consonant clusters which violate the SSP might be interpreted as double onsets where this principle is satisfied, e.g. the initial cluster /drgn/ in drgnąć [drgnɔ̃ɲʨ] 'budge' is assumed to be composed of two well-formed onsets /dr/ and /gn/. This concept reappears in some interpretations of the issue couched in the framework of Government Phonology, where certain clusters are viewed as sequences of two onsets separated by an empty nucleus (see e.g. Gussmann and Kaye 1993, Gussmann 1997, Cyran and Gussmann 1999, Rowicka 1999 and Scheer 2004 for GP accounts of Polish consonant clusters).

Since the present monograph deals with the linguistic competence of native speakers of English rather than Polish, a detailed discussion of the representational status of Polish consonant clusters remains beyond the scope of our analysis. What is crucial for our purposes is that numerous Polish CC and CCC sequences violate the SSP on the surface. Given the assumption that English phonotactics is governed by sonority, it might be expected that the ill-formedness of the Polish stimuli in this respect will trigger various repair strategies aimed at bringing the foreign inputs into conformity with native English patterns. This issue will be examined more thoroughly in Chapters 4 and 5.

6 Other approaches to sonority

In this Section we sketch the selected theoretical models which reject the concept of sonority presented in Section 4 and propose alternative approaches to this issue, including Government Phonology (6.1.), Onset Prominence Phonology (6.2.) and Beats-and-Binding Phonology (6.3.). As they will not be adopted in our analysis, the discussion is going to be brief.

6.1 Sonority in Government Phonology

Let us now briefly address some criticism levelled at the traditional notion of sonority. On the one hand, the opponents of this concept generally admit that various sonority-related effects can be observed in a number of languages, but they usually argue against its theoretical status as a formal phonological concept. The major objection to sonority is its unclear representational character (e.g. Harris 1994, 2006) manifested in the fact that it is not directly encoded in the feature matrix of a segment (see, however, Clements 1990, Dogil and Luschützky 1990 and Rice 1992 for attempts to integrate sonority into the internal structure of a segment), but requires a reference to an external sonority scale. Another objection is based on the claim of circularity inherent in the traditional approach to sonority (e.g. Scheer 1999, 2004, Harris 2006). For instance, as noted by Scheer (1999), the statement that sonority rises in the onset is not an explanation but rather an observation. As a result, the argument behind the claim that sonority must increase in the onset is circular in that it boils down to "X is the way it is because it is the way it is" (Scheer 1999: 291). In this light, sonority effects are viewed as epiphenomena which fall out from the representational environment adopted in a given theoretical framework.

Such an approach is advocated, for example, in the model of Government Phonology (e.g. Kaye *et al.* 1985, 1990, Harris 1990, 1994 and Cyran 2010), in which sonority is derived from the internal structure of a segment. According to this theory, there is a limited number of universal single-valued 'elements' which constitute basic units of segmental structure. Sonority is argued to be directly related to the relative melodic complexity of a sound "defined in terms of the number of privative elements in a segment" (Cyran 2010: 72). The more phonological primes a segment is composed of, the more complex it is. An increase in the complexity of a sound corresponds to a decrease in sonority. In this way, sonority effects can be accounted for without any reference to an external scale as they simply follow from the independent principles of the theory.

6.2 Sonority in Onset Prominence Phonology

Another framework in which sonority is understood as a derived phenomenon is the Onset Prominence (OP) representational environment (Schwartz 2010, 2012, 2013, 2015). A basic unit of phonological structure assumed in the model under discussion is provided in Fig. 4 (Schwartz 2015: 249).

Fig. 4: Onset Prominence representational hierarchy

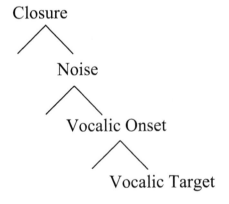

The structure in Fig. 4 is used in the construction of both prosodic constituents and segmental representations. Each level of the hierarchy corresponds to a particular phonetic event related to a stop-vowel sequence. Thus, Closure refers to the closure of the stop, Noise to the noise component produced by the stop release, Vocalic Onset to the CV transition and Vocalic Target to the steady state of the vowel. The manner of articulation is directly encoded in the structure of a particular segment by means of structural nodes, as illustrated in Fig. 5 (Schwartz 2015: 253).

Fig. 5: Manner of articulation in the OP environment

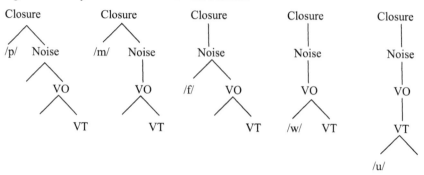

Binary and unary nodes correspond to active and inactive nodes respectively. The segmental symbols stand for the place of articulation and laryngeal specifications, which are assigned at the highest active node. Thus, for example, in /p/ all nodes are active because stops contain Closure, Noise and Vocalic Onset. In /m/ the Noise node is inactive due to the lack of aperiodic noise element in nasals. Since fricatives are pronounced without the complete closure, the Closure node is missing in /f/. Semi-vowels lack both closure and noise component so they contain only the Vocalic Onset node. Finally, the only active node in vowels is the Vocalic Target node.

According to the framework in question, sonority is an epiphenomenon which can be derived in a non-arbitrary fashion from the structural representations such as those in Fig. 5. To be more specific, sonority is directly related to the position of a given segment in the assumed representational hierarchy in that sounds assigned at higher levels are less sonorous than those at lower levels. Thus, stops, assigned at the Closure node, constitute the least sonorous segments, whereas vowels, which occupy the lowest level of the hierarchy, are the most sonorous. As a result, an explanation of sonority effects does not require any reference to an external scale.

6.3 Sonority in Beats-and-Binding Phonology

Beats-and-Binding Phonology (B&B) (Dziubalska-Kołaczyk 2002, 2009, 2014) is a theory developed within the framework of Natural Phonology (e.g. Donegan and Stampe 1979). The model in question rejects the traditional notion of the syllable as a phonological unit and replaces it with the principle of alternation of beats (more prominent, usually realised as vowels) and non-beats (less prominent, always realised as consonants). These units are arranged in a sequence by means of binary relations called bindings (n→B and B←n). According to Dziubalska-Kołaczyk (2002), the concepts of beats, non-beats and bindings make it possible to capture the functions of the syllable without maintaining its existence as a phonological primitive (see Dziubalska-Kołaczyk 2002 for detailed arguments).

The phonotactic restrictions governing consonant clusters are accounted for within the B&B phonology in terms of the Net Auditory Distance Principle (NAD) (e.g. Dziubalska-Kołaczyk 2002, Dressler and Dziubalska-Kołaczyk 2006), which takes into consideration the sonority of the segments in a cluster (corresponding to their manner of articulation, MOA) as well as their place of articulation (POA) and voicing (Lx).[31] The value of the NAD is calculated by adding the absolute values of the differences in MOA, POA and Lx between the segments in a sequence, as demonstrated in (69) (Dziubalska-Kołaczyk 2009: 60).

(69) Net Auditory Distance
$$NAD = |MOA| + |POA| + |Lx|$$

The relative markedness of consonant clusters in particular word positions (initial, medial and final) is governed by universal NAD conditions. For example, the condition relevant to initial CC sequences is as follows (Zydorowicz 2010: 570–571):

(70) NAD condition for initial CC clusters
C_1C_2V NAD $(C_1,C_2) \geq$ NAD (C_2,V)

In word-initial double clusters, the Net Auditory Distance (NAD) between the two consonants should be greater than or equal to the Net Auditory Distance between a vowel and a consonant neighbouring on it.

The NAD condition in (70) expresses the preference for initial CC clusters with a greater perceptual distance between C_1 and C_2 measured in terms of the manner of articulation, the place of articulation and voicing.

---

31 Zydorowicz & Orzechowska (2017) replace the voicing criterion with the sonorant-obstruent contrast.

As argued by Dziubalska-Kołaczyk (2009), a model which takes into account all three criteria is superior to the traditional approach to sonority based on a single parameter of the manner of articulation. For instance, according to the latter view, clusters /pw/ and /pj/ are equally well-formed. However, as demonstrated in Section 2, evidence from English suggests that /pj/ is less marked than /pw/, the former occurring freely in the native vocabulary and the latter only in a handful of loanwords. The NAD Principle is able to capture this difference by incorporating the place of articulation as a significant factor contributing to the relative markedness of a consonant cluster. Thus, /pj/ is preferred to /pw/ due to a greater auditory distance between C_1 and C_2 in terms of the place of articulation. In this light, the B&B phonotactic model is argued to make more accurate predictions concerning the universally preferred phonotactic patterns than the traditional sonority approach.

7 Sonority and syllable structure in Optimality Theory

Since our formal account of the experimental data in Chapters 4 and 5 is couched in the framework of Optimality Theory (Prince and Smolensky 1993/2004, McCarthy and Prince 1995), it is necessary to outline its fundamental aspects relevant to our analysis. In this Section, we briefly examine the basic assumptions of OT (7.1.) as well as the syllable theory developed within this framework (7.2.).

7.1 Basic assumptions of Optimality Theory

Optimality Theory (Prince and Smolensky 1993/2004) is a non-derivational theory of grammar whose central claim is that grammatical structures attested in the world's languages result from an interaction of universal output constraints. These can be classified into two major types, namely markedness constraints and faithfulness constraints. The former express preferences for unmarked structures and can be formulated as negative or positive requirements, e.g. 'vowels must not be nasal' or 'syllables must have onsets' (Kager 1999: 9). The latter exert pressure towards the preservation of lexical contrast, i.e. they militate against any differences between the input and the output, e.g. 'output segments and input segments must share values for [voice]' (Kager 1999: 10). While markedness constraints refer solely to the output, faithfulness constraints take into consideration both the input and the output.

The most important properties of constraints in OT are their universality and violability. The former refers to an assumption that all languages have the same set of constraints and any differences in their grammars are due to language-specific constraint rankings. For instance, a language with final ob-struent devoicing gives priority to the markedness constraint 'obstruents must not be voiced word-finally' at the expense of the faithfulness constraint 'output segments and input segments must share values for [voice].' The ranking in question is reversed in a language where voicing is contrastive for obstruents in the final position. This example demonstrates that certain pairs of markedness and faithfulness constraints make conflicting demands so that the satisfaction of one entails the violation of the other. Constraints in OT are therefore vio-lable, however, violation must be minimal and it must take place in order to avoid the violation of some higher-ranked constraint. As a result, the fact that a given output violates some constraint(s) does not automatically lead to its ill-formedness.

The core components of the OT grammar include the Lexicon, the Genera-tor (GEN) and the Evaluator (EVAL). The Lexicon contains a set of underly-ing forms of morphemes which constitute inputs to the grammar. Since OT assumes no morpheme structure constraints similar to the ones proposed in classical generative phonology (Chomsky and Halle 1968), there are no lan-guage-specific restrictions on the input. This property of the Lexicon in OT is called the Richness of the Base. Inputs from the Lexicon are submitted to the Generator (GEN) whose function is to generate a set of output candidates for a particular input. This set comprises all logically possible renderings of the input and is in principle infinite. The output candidates generated by GEN are next fed into the Evaluator (EVAL). Its central component is *Con*, which consists of a set of universal constraints ranked on a language-specific basis. The function of EVAL is to select the optimal output from among the output candidates gener-ated by GEN.

It should be noted that although the basic mechanism of OT, i.e. constraint in-teraction, has remained unchanged since the inception of the theory in the early 1990s, there have been numerous developments concerning some of its other el-ements. One of the most significant modifications affected the theory of faithful-ness. In the original version of OT, Prince and Smolensky (1993/2004) adopted the Containment Theory, according to which all segments present in the input are contained in each output candidate. For instance, under this view, a deleted segment is not removed from the output, but it is not parsed by some higher pro-sodic structure, such as the syllable, hence it cannot be phonetically interpreted. This concept has been challenged by the Correspondence Theory (McCarthy and Prince 1995), which no longer maintains that each output candidate contains all elements of the input. According to the Correspondence Theory, if a segment is deleted, it is not part of the output.[32] This is the theory of faithfulness adopted in the present monograph.

Since OT is a surface-oriented model, it faces difficulties in accounting for phonological phenomena which seem to require a reference to intermediate levels of representation, especially cases of opacity. For this reason, certain researchers have proposed a number of modifications to the OT framework by including some derivational elements. For instance, Stratal Optimality Theory (e.g. Kiparsky 2000, Rubach 2000, Bermúdez-Otero, forthcoming) combines some fundamental assumptions of Lexical Phonology (e.g. Kiparsky 1982, Halle and Mohanan 1985, Mohanan 1987) with the OT architecture. In general, it is based on a concept of a series of derivationally related parallel OT grammars, where the optimal output of one level serves as the input to another level. Another model based on OT is Harmonic Serialism (McCarthy 2010, McCarthy and Pater 2016). The fundamental aspect in which it deviates from the standard OT is an assumption of serial derivations with intermediate steps. In the model under discussion, GEN is allowed to carry out a single modification of the input when constructing a set of candidates. The optimal output of each round of evaluation is submitted back to GEN as the input. The loop continues until the optimal output is no different than the most recent input to GEN.

In the present monograph, we adopt the standard parallel version of OT which requires neither derivations nor intermediate representations. In Chapters 4 and 5 we will demonstrate that a substantial part of our experimental data can be accounted for in an adequate manner by means of a ranking of universal constraints which is independently needed for the native English phonology.

7.2 Syllable structure in Optimality Theory

Given an ill-formed $/\#C_1C_2/$ or $/C_1C_2\#/$ sequence, native speakers of English usually modify it in some way so as to make it conform to the syllable structure of their native language. This can be achieved by applying various repair strategies, such as inserting an epenthetic vowel before $(/\#(V)C_1C_2/)$ or inside the cluster $(/\#C_1(V)C_2/)$, deleting C_1 or C_2, or changing some feature value(s) in C_1 or C_2. In Optimality Theory, the selection of a repair strategy provides information as to which faithfulness constraint is low-ranked and therefore can be violated in order to ensure the satisfaction of some higher-ranked requirement, e.g. a sonority-related constraint. In general, all the potential modifications affecting foreign

---

32 See Kager (1999: 98–104) for a concise discussion of the main differences between the Containment Theory and the Correspondence Theory versions of faithfulness.

inputs serve the same surface goal, i.e. to create outputs well-formed in terms of the English syllable structure.

According to Optimality Theory, syllable types found in natural languages result from an interaction of the universal basic syllable structure constraints (Prince and Smolensky 1993/2004: 106–109). As mentioned in Section 7.1, these can be divided into markedness and faithfulness constraints, with the former expressing preferences for universally unmarked structures and the latter exerting pressure on the output to be as similar to the input as possible. The relevant constraints are presented in (71).

(71) Basic syllable structure constraints
Markedness constraints
NUC: A syllable must have a nucleus.
ONS: A syllable must have an onset.
*CODA: A syllable must not have a coda.
*COMPLEX: No more than one C or V may associate to any syllable position node.
Faithfulness constraints (McCarthy and Prince 1995: 16)[33]
MAX-IO: Every segment of the input has a correspondent in the output. (No phonological deletion.)
DEP-IO: Every segment of the output has a correspondent in the input. (No phonological epenthesis.)

All the differences among languages concerning permitted syllable types arise due to different rankings of the same set of the basic syllable structure constraints. A CV syllable is universally optimal as it satisfies all the structural requirements, i.e. it has a consonantal onset and a vocalic nucleus as well as no coda and no branching constituents. All other syllable types, e.g. CVC or CCV, are more marked by virtue of incurring violation of one or more basic syllable structure constraints. If a language permits only CV syllables, the relevant markedness requirements dominate faithfulness so that even if, for instance, CC is found in the input, it will be repaired at the expense of a faithfulness violation. On the other hand, if a language permits other, more marked, syllable types, faithfulness is higher-ranked with respect to one or more structural requirements.

Let us now establish the ranking of the universal basic syllable structure constraints in English. In general, English allows quite a wide range of syllable types. The only basic requirement invariably satisfied is that each syllable must have a

---

33 The faithfulness constraints originally proposed by Prince and Smolensky (1993/2004) are PARSE (no deletion) and FILL (no epenthesis). In this monograph, we adopt the Correspondence Theory version of faithfulness (McCarthy and Prince 1995).

nucleus. This means that NUC is higher ranked than faithfulness to the input (NUC >> FAITH).

On the other hand, onsets are not obligatory, as evidenced in (72).

(72) Onsetless syllables in English (violation of ONS)

add /æd/	*about* /ə.baʊt/
odd /ɒd/	*other* /ʌ.ðə/
egg /eg/	*author* /ɔː.θə/

Since onsetless syllables are permitted in English, FAITH dominates ONS (FAITH >> ONS) in accordance with the Onset Theorem (Prince and Smolensky 1993/2004: 113).

Syllables with codas are allowed in English, as demonstrated in (73).

(73) Syllables with codas in English (violation of *CODA)

ill /ɪl/	*arrive* /ə.raɪv/
back /bæk/	*south* /saʊθ/
then /ðen/	*owl* /aʊl/

As English does not prohibit codas, FAITH dominates *CODA (FAITH >> *CODA) in accordance with the Coda Theorem (Prince and Smolensky 1993/2004: 114).

Finally, English tolerates both complex onsets and codas, as shown in (74).

(74) Syllables with complex onsets or codas in English (violation of *COMPLEX)

bride /braɪd/	*monk* /mʌŋk/
glad /glæd/	*pulse* /pʌls/
track /træk/	*lamp* /læmp/

The data in (74) indicate that FAITH is higher-ranked with respect to *COMPLEX (FAITH >> *COMPLEX). To sum up, the hierarchy of the universal basic syllable structure constraints in English is as follows:

(75) Ranking of the universal basic syllable structure constraints in English

NUC >> FAITH (MAX-IO, DEP-IO) >> ONS, *CODA, *COMPLEX

Furthermore, as argued in Section 5, both English branching onsets and codas satisfy the SSP (the former also the MSD), so well-formedness with respect to sonority must be ranked higher than FAITH and, by transitivity, than ONS, *CODA and *COMPLEX. The SSP and the MSD can be expressed in optimality-theoretic terms as the SON-SEQ and SONDIST2 constraints respectively (76).

(76) Sonority well-formedness constraints

SON-SEQ: Complex onsets rise in sonority, and complex codas fall in sonority.
(Kager 1999: 267)

SONDIST2: Minimal sonority distance between consonants in a complex onset is 2 points.[34] (Yildiz 2010: 40)

For the sake of brevity, we will refer to both constraints using a cover term SONORITY. The final ranking for English is presented in (77).

(77) Constraint ranking in English
SONORITY, NUC >> FAITH (MAX-IO, DEP-IO) >> ONS, *CODA, *COMPLEX

If native phonology plays a crucial role in loanword nativisation, then it might be expected that the outputs of the adaptation of Polish CC consonant clusters will be consistent with this ranking. This issue will be examined in more detail in Chapters 4 and 5.

8 Previous research on online adaptation

Our experiments are modelled on the studies by Davidson (2001) (also reported in Davidson *et al.* 2004) and Haunz (2007), both of which examine online phonotactic adaptations. The former focuses on English native speakers' adaptation of Polish pseudo-words containing initial CC clusters that are prohibited in English. The stimuli included 15 such sequences, 10 of which were ill-formed in English, e.g. /kt/, /tf/ or /vn/. Four bisyllabic target words were created for each cluster and these were embedded in 30 carrier sentences (each used twice). The orthographic representation of the stimuli was also provided in addition to the aural input. The participants were 16 monolingual adult native speakers of English, who were asked to perform the repetition task. The results of the experiment demonstrate that the rates of successful reproduction of different ill-formed structures vary considerably. Thus, certain CC sequences are easily imitated (e.g. /zm/ and /zr/ – 63 % of targetlike responses in both cases), whereas others pose greater difficulty (e.g. /vn/ – 11 % of correct reproductions). The most frequent repair strategy is vowel epenthesis (31 %). Consonant deletion and segment change occur marginally (7 % and 2 % respectively).

Davidson (2001) and Davidson *et al.* (2004) focus mainly on the variation in the rate of targetlike reproduction of foreign CC sequences, arguing that they fall into three categories, i.e. 'easy,' 'intermediate,' and 'difficult.' It is argued that these categories correspond to the hidden strata in the phonology of English. This insight is formally expressed in terms of Optimality Theory, where each stratum is defined by the same hierarchy of markedness constraints with a respective

---

34 This constraint is based on a five-point sonority scale, i.e. vowels > glides > liquids > nasals > obstruents (Clements 1990).

faithfulness constraint (FAITH) located at different positions in the ranking. Thus, in the base English grammar, which produces only clusters appearing in the native vocabulary, FAITH is low-ranked. The gradual elevation of FAITH gives rise to an increasingly faithful reproduction of foreign clusters. This proposal is similar to the one advocated by Itô and Mester (1995, 1999) in their analysis of lexical stratification in Japanese and it will assume central importance in our analysis of the experimental data in Chapters 4 and 5. The difficulty in the accurate reproduction of a CC sequence is claimed not to be related to its sonority profile but rather to the markedness of different feature combinations in C_1 and/or C_2. Under the markedness approach, a cluster such as [dv] is predicted to pose more difficulty than [tf], because it contains a marked feature specification of [voice] for obstruents, i.e. [+voice]. This concept will also be employed in our analysis of targetlike responses in Chapters 4 and 5.

Haunz (2007) reports on a similar experiment where native speakers of English were asked to reproduce Russian pseudo-words containing initial CC sequences. The experimental materials included 22 such clusters, 17 of which were illicit in English, e.g. /dv/, /ps/ or /pn/. Five target items were created for each sequence. The participants were 10 native speakers of British English, aged 18–24, recruited at the University of Edinburgh. The stimuli were presented auditorily in two conditions, first within an English carrier sentence, and then in isolation. The main difference between Haunz's (2007) experiment and Davidson's (2001) study is that in the former no orthographic representation of the stimuli was provided. In addition, Haunz (2007) carried out a separate orthographic task where the participants were asked to provide orthographic representations of words that were presented to them auditorily. The study shows higher correct reproduction rate in the isolated word condition than in the carrier sentence condition. No significant relationship has been found between the sonority profile and the rate of targetlike responses as well as the choice of an adaptation strategy. The obtained results exhibit considerable variation, both in terms of reproduction accuracy as well as the selection of repairs. Haunz (2007) provides no formal account of the experimental data.

Both studies under discussion have several drawbacks. First of all, they focus on a small number of ill-formed structures (Davidson 2001 – 10, Haunz 2007 – 17). Secondly, they examine only initial clusters. Finally, the experimental materials contain a limited range of segmental combinations, i.e. only obstruent + obstruent and obstruent + sonorant sequences. Therefore, in order to verify the validity of the conclusions reached by Davidson (2001) and Haunz (2007), it seems necessary to conduct a study which employs a greater number of experimental stimuli, in both the initial and final position, representing a wider range of segmental sequences. We attempt to do so in our experiments on online adaptation of Polish consonant clusters by native speakers of English.

9 Conclusions

The primary goal of this Chapter has been to provide a necessary theoretical background for an analysis of the data obtained in two experiments on the nativisation of Polish CC and CCC consonant clusters by native speakers of English. To this end, we have investigated relevant aspects of the English and Polish phonotactics and syllable structure as well as previous research on online loan adaptation. The other aim has been to introduce the framework of Optimality Theory, within which the experimental data will be analysed in Chapters 4 and 5.

A comparison of the CC and CCC consonant clusters attested in English and Polish reveals considerable differences in terms of both the number of permitted sequences as well as their segmental composition. On the whole, the range of the structures in question is significantly wider in Polish than in English. For instance, Polish allows initial sonorant + obstruent clusters and final obstruent + sonorant sequences, both of which are unattested in English. In this light, English phonotactics seems to be significantly more restricted as far as well-formed consonant clusters are concerned.

A concept which traditionally assumes crucial importance in accounting for phonotactic patterns is sonority. It is widely used in phonological theory despite difficulties in establishing its physical parameter(s) and formulating its definition. A variety of sonority hierarchies have been put forward, varying to a significant degree in terms of both the number and the types of distinctions they make. Moreover, several sonority-based cross-linguistic generalisations are frequently invoked in the relevant literature, the most common being the Sonority Sequencing Principle, which expresses the preference for a sonority rise from the syllable margins towards the nucleus. The Minimum Sonority Distance Principle requires a particular degree of the sonority distance between segments in a well-formed cluster. The Syllable Contact Law expresses the preference for a sonority drop between the heterosyllabic coda and onset segments. The Sonority Dispersion Principle states that the sonority rise between the onset and the nucleus should be maximised and the sonority fall between the nucleus and the coda minimised. For the purposes of our analysis, sonority distance is calculated on the basis of Steriade's (1982) scale so as to make our results directly comparable to those of similar studies by Davidson (2001) and Haunz (2007).

An overview of English phonotactic restrictions on initial and final CC and CCC consonant clusters demonstrates that sonority plays a significant role in this language. English branching onsets and codas can be argued to conform to the Sonority Sequencing Principle (the former also to the Minimum Sonority Distance) despite a number of surface violations of sonority well-formedness, represented mainly by initial /s/ + obstruent clusters and final sequences with coronal obstruents. These apparent exceptions to the SSP are frequently assumed to contain a syllable appendix thus they do not constitute violations of the principle in question. Furthermore, English phonotactic patterns provide evidence in favour of the core-periphery structure of the English lexicon. Peripheral consonant clusters, which occur mainly in loanwords, are frequently inconsistent with certain constraints holding in the core vocabulary, such as a ban on labial C_1 and C_2.

On the other hand, the richness of the Polish phonotactic patterns has made some scholars question the validity of the SSP for this language (e.g. Sawicka 1974, 1985, 1995 and Dukiewicz 1995). Others maintain that this principle holds in Polish at a lower level of representation than the surface level (e.g. Rubach and Booij 1990, Bethin 1992 and Szpyra-Kozłowska 1998). Since such theoretical issues are largely irrelevant to our analysis of the experimental data, we adopt no particular stance in this respect. Of crucial importance for our purposes is the surface ill-formedness of numerous Polish clusters with regard to the SSP, which is expected to trigger various repair strategies in the course of their adaptation by native speakers of English.

The traditional approach to sonority is criticised in certain frameworks mainly due to its circularity as well as a doubtful representational status of the phenomenon in question. In Government Phonology, sonority is derived from the internal structure of a segment and corresponds to its relative melodic complexity. Sonority is also viewed as an epiphenomenon in Onset Prominence Phonology, where it is directly related to the position of a segment in the assumed representational hierarchy, with sounds assigned at higher levels being less sonorous than those at lower levels. On the other hand, according to Beats-and-Binding Phonology, in order to account for the phonotactic restrictions governing consonant clusters, it is necessary to take into account the sonority of the segments in a cluster (corresponding to their manner of articulation) as well as their place of articulation and voicing.

A formal analysis of the experimental data in Chapters 4 and 5 will be carried out within the framework of Optimality Theory, a non-derivational model of grammar which claims that grammatical structures attested in the world's languages result from an interaction of universal markedness and faithfulness con raints. In order to nativise a foreign consonant cluster, native speakers of ? iglish have to make it conform to the syllable structure of their language thr ugh the application of various repair strategies. The syllable structure in OT is overned by an interaction of universal markedness constraints, i.e. NUC, C /S, *CODA, *COMPLEX, and relevant faithfulness constraints. In English, all t : syllable well-formedness constraints, with the exception of NUC, are domi- ited by FAITH. This is because English allows onsetless syllables (violation of)NS), syllables with coda consonants (violation of *CODA) as well as branch- ing constituents (violation of *COMPLEX). At the same time, since English on- set and coda clusters satisfy the SSP, the SONORITY constraint must be ranked higher than FAITH. This ranking will provide a basis for the formal account of the experimental results in Chapters 4 and 5.

A survey of similar studies on online loanword adaptation, in particular Davidson (2001), Davidson *et al.* (2004) and Haunz (2007), has revealed some of their limitations. These pertain mainly to a small number of experimental stimuli which represent a limited range of segment combinations in word-initial position only. In this light, it seems necessary to conduct more extensive research in order to verify the validity of the conclusions reached in the studies under discussion. The present monograph attempts to attain this goal.

4 Adaptation of Polish CC consonant clusters by native speakers of English

1 Introduction

In this Chapter we report on an online loanword adaptation experiment in which 30 native speakers of British English reproduced authentic Polish words with initial and final CC consonant clusters which do not occur in English. The major aim of the study is threefold. First, we attempt to uncover the most frequent repair strategies used to nativise ill-formed phonotactic structures as well as to identify the mechanisms governing the adaptation process. Secondly, our aim is to verify the validity of various loan adaptation models discussed in Chapter 2. To this end, we will confront the results of our experiment with the predictions made by the major approaches to loan assimilation. Last but not least, we will offer an adequate formal analysis of the experimental results couched in the framework of Optimality Theory which accounts for the patterns of adaptation as well as the variation attested in the data.

Section 2 deals with the design of the experiments on online adaptation of Polish initial and final CC and CCC clusters by native speakers of English. We start with the presentation of the stimuli employed in the study. Next, we provide information concerning the participants, the experimental procedure as well as the assumptions adopted in the analysis and the categorisation of the results.

Section 3 focuses on the presentation of the results of the experiment. We begin with a general overview of the data in 3.1 Vowel epenthesis emerges as the most frequent repair strategy, followed by a modification of C_1 or C_2 and consonant deletion. In Section 3.2 we examine the factors which exert an influence on the rate of targetlike reproduction of foreign CC sequences, such as the sonority distance between the consonants in a cluster or the relative markedness of feature configurations present in C_1 and/or C_2. The following sections deal with an analysis of clusters repaired by vowel epenthesis (3.3), segment change (3.4) and consonant deletion (3.5) respectively.

Section 4 deals with a formal analysis of the experimental results. First, we examine how the patterns of adaptation revealed in our study relate to the predictions made by the major loan phonology models presented in Chapter 2. It is argued that the relevant data can receive a straightforward explanation in an Optimality Theory analysis similar to Itô and Mester's (1995, 1999, 2001) account of lexical stratification in Japanese. In what follows, we provide a formal OT account of targetlike reproduction (4.2), vowel epenthesis (4.3), segment change (4.4) and consonant deletion (4.5). The conclusions are presented in Section 5.

2 Experimental design

In this section we describe the design of the experiments on the adaptation of Polish CC and CCC consonant clusters by native speakers of English. First, in 2.1 we focus on the materials used in the experiments and next in 2.2 on the participants. Finally, the adopted procedure as well as the assumptions underlying data categorisation are dealt with in 2.3.

2.1 Materials

The stimuli used in Experiment 1 were 103 authentic Polish words containing CC consonant clusters of various types, including:

- 56 items with consonant clusters in word-initial position (48 monosyllabic words and 8 initially-stressed disyllabic words),
- 37 items with consonant clusters in word-final position (all of them monosyllabic),
- 10 distractors (mono- and disyllabic Polish words stressed on the initial syllable with no segmental or phonotactic structures prohibited in English).

The full list of the experimental stimuli can be found in Appendix 1. The sonority-based classification of the structure of the CC sequences examined in the experiment is presented in Tab. 19.

Tab. 19: Sonority-based classification of CC clusters

	initial	final
obstruent + obstruent	27	15
obstruent + sonorant	14	10
sonorant + obstruent	10	8
sonorant + sonorant	5	4
total	56	37

The numbers of clusters in Tab. 19 vary between the groups, in some cases considerably. This is a direct consequence of the lack of proportions in the numbers of Polish CC sequences of different structure permitted in respective word positions, as evidenced in Tab. 20 (Zydorowicz *et al.* 2016).

Tab. 20: Initial and final CC clusters in Polish

	initial	final
obstruent + obstruent	103	32
obstruent + sonorant	88	35
sonorant + obstruent	17	60
sonorant + sonorant	10	18
total	218	145

It may seem that certain clusters, particularly initial obstruent + sonorant and final sonorant + obstruent sequences, are underrepresented in Tab. 19. This stems from the fact that such structures are very frequent in English and there is a considerable overlap between English and Polish with regard to the number of permitted CC sequences of these types. As a result, many such clusters were not included in the set of the experimental materials. Needless to say, the number of stimuli could not be too large given the participants' limited attention span as well as time constraints.

The stimuli used in Experiment 2 were 36 authentic Polish words containing CCC consonant clusters of various types, including:

- 22 items with consonant clusters in word-initial position (15 monosyllabic words and 7 initially-stressed disyllabic words),
- 5 items with consonant clusters in word-final position (all of them monosyllabic),
- 9 distractors (mono- and disyllabic Polish words stressed on the initial syllable with no segmental or phonotactic structures prohibited in English).

The full list of the experimental stimuli can be found in Appendix 4. The classification of the CCC sequences examined in the study according to their sonority is presented in Tab. 21.

Tab. 21: Sonority-based classification of CCC clusters

	initial	final
obstruent + obstruent + obstruent	5	2
obstruent + obstruent + sonorant	8	1
obstruent + sonorant + obstruent	2	0
obstruent + sonorant + sonorant	3	0
sonorant + obstruent + obstruent	1	2
sonorant + obstruent + sonorant	3	0
total	22	5

Again, there is a considerable degree of variation in the numbers of clusters between some groups in Tab. 21. This fact reflects the disproportions in the numbers of Polish CCC sequences of different structure allowed in the initial and final position, as demonstrated in Tab. 22 (Zydorowicz *et al.* 2016).

Tab. 22: Initial and final CCC clusters in Polish

	initial	final
obstruent + obstruent + obstruent	50	6
obstruent + obstruent + sonorant	105	3
obstruent + sonorant + obstruent	13	0
obstruent + sonorant + sonorant	20	0
sonorant + obstruent + obstruent	3	29
sonorant + obstruent + sonorant	16	15
total	207	53

In both experiments the materials included clusters composed of sounds present in the native English inventory as well as sequences containing one or two non-English segments. Such an experimental setup allows for investigating a range of phenomena that cannot be examined if no foreign sounds are included, for instance patterns of segmental adaptation or the influence of the presence/absence of a non-native segment in a consonant cluster on the selection of an adaptation strategy.

The stimuli were recorded by a male native speaker of Polish with no speech impediments and digitised at 44.1 kHz sampling rate. The target words were next presented to two other native speakers of Polish, who were asked to write down the items they had heard. Both subjects reproduced all items accurately, which proves the correctness of the recorded material and its unambiguous pronunciation.

2.2 Participants

The participants in Experiment 1 were 30 native speakers of the southern variety of British English, including 16 women and 14 men, aged between 18 and 30. They were recruited at University College London and St Mary's University College in Twickenham, London. The subjects in Experiment 2 were 15 native speakers of the southern variety of British English, of whom 11 were women and 4 men, aged between 20 and 30, recruited at the University of Reading. Both

118

groups consisted of undergraduate and postgraduate students attending non-linguistic programmes as well as junior members of the teaching staff. The majority of the experimental subjects were monolingual English speakers, nevertheless, all of them had learnt one or two foreign languages at school (usually French, German, Spanish or Italian) and some were fluent in German and/or French. The participants reported no speech or hearing disorders as well as declared no knowledge of Polish and other Slavic languages. Full details concerning the subjects who took part in the studies are included in Appendix 2 (Experiment 1) and Appendix 5 (Experiment 2).

2.3 Procedure and data categorisation

In Experiment 1 the participants were divided into two groups of 15 persons each. They were then informed that they would take part in an experiment involving reproduction of Polish words. Both groups were asked to perform the repetition task similar to that carried out by Haunz (2007), i.e. the participants were requested to repeat the stimuli presented to them auditorily through headphones in a randomised order. Each word was played twice and subsequent items were activated by the experimenter after the response to the preceding stimulus had been completed. The responses were recorded using a Tascam DR-08 digital recorder and digitised at 44.1 kHz sampling rate. The target items used in the experiment were randomly divided into two parts so that Group A adapted half of the words and Group B the other half. The major reason for this division stemmed from the large number of the stimuli in Experiment 1. The main goal of this step was to prevent the occurrence of the fatigue effect, which would have been likely to take place if all the materials had been presented to each participant. Experiment 2 was conducted according to the same procedure, however, given the lower number of the stimuli, no group division was employed.

The recordings were then analysed, both auditorily as well as by means of wide-band spectrograms in Speech Analyzer 3.1 software. The participants' responses were classified into four major categories, namely 'targetlike reproduction', 'vowel epenthesis', 'consonant deletion' and 'segment change'. In addition, in the adaptation of CCC clusters, the category 'vowel epenthesis and consonant deletion' was employed. Where no reliable categorisation could be made, the items were labelled as 'other'.

As regards clusters containing non-English sounds, especially Polish sibilant fricatives and affricates, the responses in which Polish post-alveolars and prepalatals were realised as English palato-alveolars were classified as targetlike, as shown in (78).

(78) Targetlike classification of non-English segments
fricatives: [ʃ] for [ʂ] and [ɕ]; [ʒ] for [ʐ] and [ʑ]
affricates: [tʃ] for [t͡ʂ] and [t͡ɕ]; [dʒ] for [d͡ʐ] and [d͡ʑ]

This assumption was based on the results of several studies (e.g. Lisker 2001, McGuire 2007) showing very poor discrimination rates of a contrast between Polish post-alveolars and pre-palatals by native English listeners, who usually collapse both under the native category of palato-alveolars. In addition, studies on foreign-accented Polish (e.g. Szpyra-Kozłowska & Radomski 2014) demonstrate that the contrast under discussion is one of the most difficult aspects of Polish pronunciation for the majority of foreigners learning this language and one of the most important perceptual properties of foreign-accented Polish.

A comment should also be made concerning the categorisation of /t, d, s, z, n/, which are usually post-dental in Polish and alveolar in English. The reproduction of these segments was considered targetlike when they were realised as coronal consonants, whether post-dental or alveolar.

With regard to epenthesis, the presence of an epenthetic vowel was in most cases clearly visible on the spectrogram, nevertheless, its duration varied considerably. Following Haunz (2007), we assumed that a token should be classified as a case of 'vowel epenthesis' when it contained a vowel-like portion of at least 20 ms or three glottal pulses. The items where, apart from vowel insertion, one of the consonants was modified, e.g. [gʒ] > [gəʃ], were assumed to undergo "changes on the higher prosodic level" (Haunz 2007: 54) and were labelled as cases of 'vowel epenthesis.'

3 Results

In this section we present the results of the experiment on the adaptation of CC consonant clusters by native speakers of English. We begin with a general overview of the data in 3.1. The following sections focus on targetlike reproduction (3.2), vowel epenthesis (3.3), segment change (3.4) and consonant deletion (3.5) respectively.

3.1 General overview of repair strategies

A total of 1395 tokens (93 words x 15 participants) have been obtained in the experiment (excluding the distractors). A general categorisation of the responses is presented in Tab. 23.

Tab. 23: General categorisation of the responses in the experiment

category	number of tokens	percentage of tokens
targetlike production	615	44.09 %
vowel epenthesis	530	37.99 %
segment change	201	14.41 %
consonant deletion	49	3.51 %

The figures in Tab. 23 indicate that the predominant type of response is targetlike production. As regards repair strategies, the most common is vowel epenthesis, followed by segment change. The rate of consonant deletion is negligible. These results are in accordance with a cross-linguistic preference identified by Paradis and LaCharité's (1997), according to which epenthesis is universally favoured over deletion as a strategy of repairing ill-formed structures since it maximally preserves the phonological content of the input. This insight is formalised as the Preservation Principle, stipulating that as much phonological information in the input as possible should be retained in the output unless the cost of preservation is too high (see Section 2.1 in Chapter 2 for a more detailed discussion of Paradis and LaCharité's (1997) loan adaptation model).

The breakdown of the results for initial and final clusters is presented in Fig. 6.

Fig. 6: Initial vs. final CC clusters

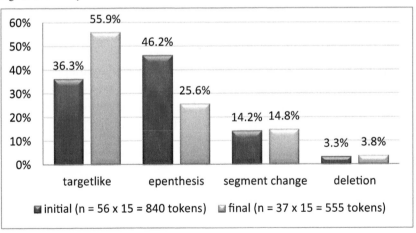

The data in Fig. 6 demonstrate that, on the whole, final clusters are easier to imitate than initial CC sequences, as evidenced by the higher rate of targetlike responses for the former. This means that initial clusters undergo modifications more frequently, especially vowel epenthesis. The rates of segment change and consonant elision are similar for both categories under discussion.

Let us now examine the results for clusters of different segmental structure separately, i.e. obstruent + obstruent, obstruent + sonorant, sonorant + obstruent and sonorant + sonorant sequences respectively. The results for the first group are presented in Fig. 7.

Fig. 7: Obstruent + obstruent clusters

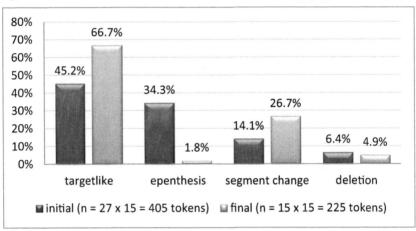

The data in Fig. 7 reveal several interesting patterns. First of all, in the case of obstruent + obstruent clusters, the rate of targetlike responses is considerably higher for the final sequences than for the initial ones. Secondly, in contrast to the initial clusters, which are mostly repaired by vowel epenthesis, the main strategy used to adapt the final sequences is segment change. As regards the latter structures, vowel insertion constitutes only 1.8 % of all responses. The rate of deletion is fairly low for clusters in both positions.

The data for obstruent + sonorant sequences are shown in Fig. 8.

Fig. 8: Obstruent + sonorant clusters

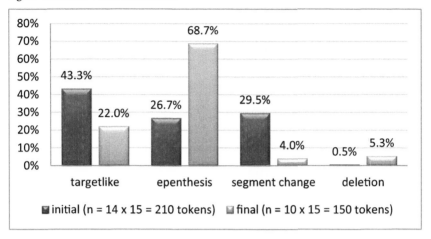

As demonstrated in Fig. 8, initial obstruent + sonorant clusters are easier to reproduce than final ones. The former are mostly repaired by segment change and vowel epenthesis, whereas the latter by vowel epenthesis. Again, the rate of consonant elision is low in both positions, although considerably higher word-finally.

In Fig. 9 we present the results for sonorant + obstruent sequences.

Fig. 9: Sonorant + obstruent clusters

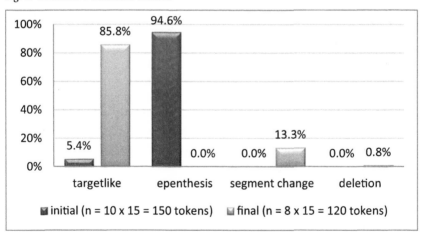

The rate of targetlike responses for initial vs. final sonorant + obstruent sequences is radically different, with the former being faithfully reproduced in only 5.4 % of cases and the latter in 85.8 %. Initial clusters are repaired solely by vowel epenthesis and final sequences by segment change.

The results for the last group of clusters, i.e. sonorant + sonorant, are provided in Fig. 10.

Fig. 10: Sonorant + sonorant clusters

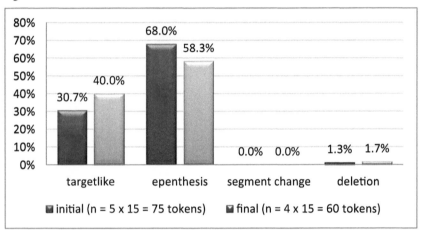

As demonstrated in Fig. 10, initial sonorant + sonorant sequences are more difficult to reproduce faithfully than final clusters of this type. The predominant repair strategy for CC structures in both positions is vowel epenthesis. Deletion occurs marginally and segment change is unattested.

To sum up, an analysis of the data presented in Figs. 6–10 reveals several interesting patterns. First of all, on average, the rate of targetlike responses is higher for final clusters than for initial ones. This may be due to the fact that English allows more CC sequences word-finally than word-initially, mostly due to suffixation (past tense, plurality, third person singular). As demonstrated in Chapter 3, the majority of word-final clusters with /t, d, s, z/ as C_2 arise as a result of adding some inflectional morpheme, e.g. plural <-s> or past tense <-ed>, to the stem. Secondly, in both positions consonant deletion is marginal as opposed to vowel epenthesis, which lends support to Paradis and LaCharité's (1997) Preservation Principle. Finally, the rates of targetlike reproduction for obstruent + sonorant and sonorant + obstruent clusters indicate that sonority-based restrictions on syllable structure might be an important factor influencing the participants' responses. Thus, clusters of rising sonority, i.e. obstruent + sonorant, are easier to imitate word-initially (in onsets) than word-finally (in codas) (43.3 % vs. 22 %). On the other hand, falling sonority sequences, i.e. sonorant + obstruent, are produced targetlike more frequently in word-final (coda) than in word-initial (onset) position (85.8 % vs. 5.4 %). The relationship between the rate of targetlike responses and the clusters' sonority profile is examined in more detail in the following Section.

3.2 Targetlike reproduction

The rates of targetlike reproduction of CC clusters vary considerably, with some sequences easily imitated by the participants, e.g. /#tl/ - 86.7 % and /#tf/ - 86.7 %, and others almost invariably repaired, e.g. /#gb/ - 13.3 % and /#mʂ/ - 6.7 % (percentages refer to the rate of targetlike responses). This is a typical example of differential importation, i.e. a phenomenon whereby certain foreign segments or structures enter the recipient language unadapted, whereas others undergo consistent nativisation (see Chapter 1, Section 3.4.4).[35]

Let us now examine the factors that are relevant for the rate of targetlike responses in our experiment. First of all, we would like to investigate the role of the sonority distance between C_1 and C_2 in order to determine if the sequences conforming to the SSP are easier to imitate than those violating this principle.

Drawing on the generalisations formulated in the previous Chapter, it may be predicted that Polish initial CC clusters which do not conform to the SSP (sonority distance ≤ 0) will be produced targetlike less frequently than those with a sonority rise. However, voiceless sibilant fricative + voiceless plosive sequences, such as /#çp/ and /#ʂp/, may be expected to present little difficulty to the participants as similar structures can be found in English. The results of the experiment seem to confirm these predictions, as demonstrated in Tab. 24.

---

35 One might ask how it is possible for native speakers of English to produce consonant clusters which violate core English phonotactic restrictions. An important argument is that this happens very frequently in fast speech, e.g. *tomorrow* ['tmɒrəʊ] and *potato* ['pteɪtəʊ]. This means that phonotactic constraints are not always satisfied in actual production.

sonority distance (SD)	number of clusters	% targetlike
SD ≥ 1	23	50.4 %
SD ≤ 0	31	21.7 %
/#ɕp/, /#ʂp/	2	100 %

The average rate of targetlike responses for Polish initial CC clusters of rising sonority is considerably higher than for sequences of falling sonority and sonority plateaus (50.4 % vs. 21.7 %). The results of a t-test show that this difference is statistically significant (p < 0.01). As predicted, the participants had no problems with the correct reproduction of /#ɕp/ and /#ʂp/, which violate the SSP, but have a similar segmental makeup to legal or marginal English initial clusters, such as /sp/ and /ʃp/. All these facts indicate that the sonority profile of an initial CC sequence can be regarded as a global predictor of its successful imitation.

The impact of the sonority distance is particularly evident when the rates of targetlike responses are compared for initial obstruent + sonorant and sonorant + obstruent sequences. Thus, the former, well-formed with respect to the SSP, are reproduced correctly in 43.3 % of cases, whereas the latter, violating the principle in question, only in 5.4 % of cases. As far as obstruent + obstruent sequences are concerned, the situation is more complex. Some clusters turn out to be very easy to imitate, e.g. /#pʂ/, /#tf/, /#zv/ or /#tʂ/, whereas others present a considerable difficulty in this respect, e.g. /#ʂtʂ/, /#xʂ/ or /#dʐdʐ/. This is most probably due to the influence of factors other than the sonority distance, such as the segmental structure of a cluster. This issue is discussed in more detail below. Furthermore, it must be noted that the role of the sonority distance as a global predictor of the success rate in cluster reproduction must be viewed as a general tendency rather than as an inviolable principle.

As regards word-final position, it may be predicted that Polish CC sequences not consistent with the SSP (SD ≥ 0) should be produced targetlike less frequently than those with a sonority drop. However, clusters violating the SSP, but similar in terms of segmental structure to English surface exceptions to this principle, i.e. /pʂ#/ and /tʂ#/, may be expected to present little difficulty to native speakers of English. These predictions are corroborated by the experimental data, as evidenced in Tab. 25.

Tab. 25: Targetlike reproduction of Polish final CC clusters

sonority distance (SD)	number of clusters	% targetlike
SD ≤ -1	17	68.2 %
SD ≥ 0	18	39.3 %
/pʂ#/, /tʂ#/	2	100 %

The mean correct response rate for Polish final CC sequences of falling sonority is considerably higher than for those of rising sonority and sonority plateaus (68.2 % vs. 39.3 %). The results of a t-test demonstrate that this difference is statistically significant ($p < 0.01$). As expected, the rate of targetlike responses is very high for /pʂ#/ and /tʂ#/. Given these results, we may argue that, on the whole, the sonority profile of a final CC cluster can be viewed as a global predictor of its faithful reproduction.

The impact of the sonority distance is particularly striking when the rates of targetlike responses are compared for final sonorant + obstruent and obstruent + sonorant sequences. The former, consistent with the SSP, are reproduced faithfully in 85.8 % of cases, whereas the latter, violating this principle, only in 22 % of cases. Again, like in the case of initial clusters, the situation is more complicated with respect to obstruent + obstruent sequences. Thus, some of them are easily imitated, e.g. /ʦk#/, /pʨ#/ or /sf#/, while others almost invariably undergo some modification, e.g. /pʧ#/, /ʂʧ#/ or /fʧ#/. These facts indicate that, although the sonority distance between C_1 and C_2 can be regarded as a global predictor of the success rate in cluster reproduction, it constitutes only one of a number of factors exerting an influence on the patterns of cluster adaptation. This issue is discussed in more detail below.

With regard to sonority, the results of our experiment run counter to similar studies, such as Davidson (2001), Davidson *et al.* (2004) and Haunz (2007), in which the sonority profile is argued to have no influence on the rate of successful reproduction of a cluster. However, as demonstrated in Chapter 3 (Section 8), these studies have several drawbacks, such as a small number of stimuli and a limited range of segmental combinations examined, i.e. only obstruent + obstruent and obstruent + sonorant sequences. Taking all these facts into consideration, it may be argued that the apparent lack of impact of the sonority profile of a cluster on the rate of its successful reproduction in Davidson (2001) and Haunz (2007) is a result of the limited set of experimental stimuli used in both studies.

As has already been mentioned, the sonority distance between C_1 and C_2 is only one of a number of factors that have an impact on the relative ease or difficulty in the faithful rendering of a cluster. Other relevant factors include, for instance, the voicing and place of articulation of C_1 and/or C_2. Our experimental results exhibit a general tendency for clusters where C_1 and/or C_2 contain an unmarked value of a given feature to be reproduced faithfully more frequently. Thus, as regards voicing, given the assumption that voiceless obstruents are unmarked with regard to voiced obstruents (e.g. Lombardi 1991), it might be expected that CC sequences containing the former will be produced targetlike more frequently than those containing the latter, all else being equal. The results of our experiment demonstrate that this is indeed the case. For example, the average rate of successful reproduction of initial obstruent + obstruent clusters for voiceless sequences is 57.6 %, whereas for voiced ones 31.8 % (the difference is statistically significant at p < 0.01). Several examples are presented in (79).

(79) <u>The impact of voicing on the rate of targetlike reproduction</u>

/#tʃ/	86.7 %	/#dv/	33.3 %	/sf#/	86.7 %
/#ftɕ/	40 %	/#vdʑ/	13.3 %	/tf#/	73.3 %

Furthermore, on average, a high rate of targetlike responses can be observed for final obstruent + obstruent sequences, all of which are voiceless (66.7 %).

Another factor which exerts an influence on the rate of targetlike reproduction is the place of articulation of C_1 and/or C_2. Major places of articulation can be arranged into a universal hierarchy reflecting their relative markedness, as demonstrated in (80) (de Lacy 2006: 2).

(80) <u>Major place of articulation markedness hierarchy</u>
dorsal > labial > coronal > glottal
('>' = 'is more marked than')

According to the hierarchy in (80), dorsals are more marked than labials, which are in turn more marked than coronals, etc. The results of our experiment demonstrate a general tendency for clusters containing segments with marked place feature values to be reproduced targetlike less frequently than those with unmarked specifications, all else being equal. This is exemplified in (81).

(81) <u>The impact of place of articulation on the rate of targetlike reproduction</u>

/#db/	40 %	/#gb/	13.3 %
/#zdʑ/	40 %	/#vdʑ/	13.3 %
/#zm/	33.3 %	/#vm/	6.7 %

The data in (81) show that the rate of successful reproduction is higher for clusters with a coronal C_1 than for sequences where this segment is non-coronal.
In general, the more marked feature values a given segment in a cluster has, the less likely it is for this sequence to be realised faithfully. This can be illustrated with a pattern of targetlike responses for initial plosive + plosive clusters in (82).

(82) <u>Targetlike reproduction in initial plosive + plosive clusters</u>
/#pt/	60 %
/#db/	40 %
/#gb/	13.3 %

Since the sequences in (82) have the same sonority distance (SD = 0), this factor cannot account for the differences between them in the rate of targetlike reproduction. They can be explained by reference to the relative markedness of the feature values of C_1 and C_2. Thus, /#pt/ is the easiest because the only marked feature is labiality in C_1. The cluster /#db/ is more difficult due to its increased markedness incurred by the presence of voicing in both C_1 and C_2 as well as labiality in C_2. Finally, /#gb/ is the most difficult, because it has all the marked features of /#db/ plus dorsal C_1.

To sum up, it might be concluded that a number of factors exert impact on the ease or difficulty in the faithful rendering of Polish CC clusters by native speakers of English. These include the sonority distance between C_1 and C_2 as well as the relative markedness of feature values in C_1 and C_2, especially those encoding voicing and the place of articulation. A formal analysis of targetlike reproduction cases will be provided in Section 4.2.

3.3 Vowel epenthesis

Vowel epenthesis is the most frequent repair strategy found in the data as it constitutes 37.99 % of all responses. In the majority of cases, the epenthetic segment, although varying with regard to its duration, is of schwa-like quality. Since a detailed examination of the fine acoustic properties of the vowel under discussion is beyond the scope of the present monograph, it will be consistently represented as /ə/ unless its quality is markedly different from the lax mid central vowel.

As far as initial clusters are concerned, when an ill-formed /#C_1C_2/ sequence undergoes vowel epenthesis, the epenthetic segment may be inserted either before (/#C_1C_2/ → [#VC_1C_2] – prothesis) or inside the cluster (/#C_1C_2/ → [#C_1VC_2] – anaptyxis). The cases of both edge and internal epenthesis are attested in the experimental data, however, the latter occurs in a larger number of sequences than the former. The clusters undergoing anaptyxis are provided in (83).

(83) <u>Internal epenthesis in the adaptation of initial CC clusters</u>
    (a) <u>sonority violation</u>
/#lv/ → [ləv]	100 %	/#gd͡ʑ/ → [gəd͡ʑ]	86.7 %
/#mɲ/ → [mən]	100 %	/#vd͡ʑ/ → [vəd͡ʑ]	86.7 %
/#d͡ʐd͡ʑ/ → [d͡ʐəd͡ʑ]	93.3 %	/#mz/ → [məz]	73.3 %
/#mʂ/ → [məʃ]	93.3 %	/#mn/ → [mən]	66.7 %

/#gb/ → [gəb]	86.7 %	/#dv/ → [dəv]	66.7 %
/#db/ → [dəb]	60 %	/#mr/ → [mər]	40 %
/#dm/ → [dəm]	60 %	/#ml/ → [məl]	33.3 %
/#f͡ɕ/ → [fə͡tʃ]	46.7 %	/#f͡ɕm/ → [t͡ʃəm]	20 %
/#f͡ts/ → [fət]	40 %	/#tʂ/ → [təʃ]	20 %
/#gʐ/ → [gəʒ]	40 %	/#pʂ/ → [pəʃ]	13.3 %
/#pt/ → [pət]	40 %	/#tf/ → [təf]	13.3 %
/#t͡ʂk/ → [t͡ʃək]	40 %	/#t͡sn/ → [t͡sən]	6.7 %

(b) other

/#dl/ → [dəl]	73.3 %	/#vl/ → [vəl]	33.3 %
/#zr/ → [zər]	40 %		

As demonstrated in (83), the vast majority of initial clusters nativised by internal epenthesis violate the SSP or the MSD, or both. Thus, it might be tentatively assumed that in the items listed in (83a) the repair in question is triggered by a sonority violation. It must be noted, however, that the rate of anaptyxis varies considerably among clusters and is usually inversely proportional to the rate of targetlike reproduction. Thus, for example, internal epenthesis is most frequent in sequences where both C_1 and C_2 are voiced consonants and occurs at a considerably lower rate in voiceless clusters, which are more often realised faithfully. Moreover, there are some sequences well-formed with respect to sonority but not occurring in English, yet adapted by internal epenthesis (83b). We assume that in these cases vowel epenthesis is triggered by an increased markedness of the feature values present in C_1 and/or C_2.

The clusters where prothesis rather than anaptyxis takes place are presented in (84).

(84) Edge epenthesis in the adaptation of initial CC clusters

    (a) /r/ + obstruent

/#rt/ → [ərt]	100 %	/#rv/ → [ərv]	93.3%
/#rd/ → [ərd]	93.3 %		

    (b) /w/ + obstruent

/#wg/ → [ʊwg]	100 %	/#wz/ → [ʊwz]	100 %
/#wb/ → [ʊwb]	100 %	/#wk/ → [ʊwk]	93.3 %

    (c) /z/ + consonant

/#zd/ → [əzd]	53.3 %	/#d͡ʑb/ → [əzb]	20 %
/#zd͡ʑ/ → [əzd͡ʒ]	46.7 %	/#d͡ʑv/ → [əzv]	20 %
/#zb/ → [əzb]	40 %	/#zw/ → [əzw]	20 %
/#zm/ → [əzm]	33.3 %	/#zv/ → [əzv]	13.3 %

    (d) other

/#ln/ → [əln]	100 %	/#vm/ → [əvm]	86.7 %

The overwhelming majority of initial clusters in (84) violate the SSP or the MSD, or both, the only exception being /#zw/. The sequences in (84) can be divided into several categories in terms of their segmental structure. First of all, edge epenthesis takes place in sequences of /r/ or /w/ followed by an obstruent (84a & 84b). The rate of vowel insertion is very high in both cases, but the quality of the epenthetic segment is different. Thus, in /r/-initial clusters it is the lax mid central vowel /ə/, whereas in /w/-initial sequences it is the lax high back rounded vowel /ʊ/. Furthermore, prothesis takes place in clusters with /z/ or /d͡z/ as C_1 (84c). However, the rate of the repair in question is considerably lower than in (84a) or (84b). Finally, there are two sequences which do not belong to any of the three groups (84d).

As far as final CC sequences are concerned, the epenthetic vowel may be inserted either after (/C_1C_2#/ → [C_1C_2V#] – paragoge) or inside the cluster (/C_1C_2#/ → /C_1VC_2#/ – anaptyxis). The former option is almost invariably selected by the participants, as evidenced in (85).

(85) Vowel epenthesis in the adaptation of final CC clusters

   (a) /C_1C_2#/ → [C_1C_2V#]

/kw#/ → [kwə]	100 %		/çɲ#/ → [ʃnə]	93.3 %
/dm#/ → [dmə]	93.3 %		/rɲ#/ → [rnə]	86.7 %
/sw#/ → [swə]	93.3 %		/pɲ#/ → [pnə]	73.3 %
/çm#/ → [ʃmə]	66.7 %		/tw#/ → [twə]	40 %
/çl#/ → [ʃlə]	66.7 %		/fr#/ → [frə]	20 %
/rm#/ → [rmə]	53.3 %		/ʂp#/ → [ʃpə]	20 %
/tr#/ → [trə]	40 %		/sf#/ → [sfə]	6.7 %

   b) /C_1C_2#/ → /C_1VC_2#/

   /mn#/ → [mən]   93.3 %

The vast majority of clusters undergoing paragoge, except for /rɲ#/, /rm#/ and /ʂp#/, are sequences of flat or rising sonority, thus they violate the SSP. It should be pointed out that, as in the case of initial sequences, the rate of insertion varies considerably and is usually inversely proportional to the rate of targetlike reproduction. The only cluster adapted via internal epenthesis is /mn#/.

To sum up, vowel epenthesis in both initial and final clusters seems to be triggered by violations of the SSP and/or the MSD. However, a number of patterns observed in the experimental data require further explanation, including

a) epenthesis site (internal vs. edge) in the adaptation of initial and final clusters,
b) different quality of an epenthetic vowel in /wC/ clusters.

These issues will be addressed in Section 4.3, where a formal analysis of the epenthesis data within an OT framework will be provided.

3.4 Segment change

Segment change constitutes 14.41 % of all responses and is the second most frequent repair strategy found in the experimental data. It targets mostly affricates, which are realised as plosives or fricatives. Other changes, such as devoicing or altering the place of articulation, are also attested but relatively infrequent. We start with a discussion of the nativisation of affricates in 3.4.1 and then move on to other modifications in 3.4.2.

3.4.1 Affricates

There are 28 clusters containing an affricate in the experimental stimuli, including 8 with the voiceless dental affricate /t͡s/, 7 with the voiceless post-alveolar affricate /t͡ʃ/, 7 with the voiceless pre-palatal affricate /t͡ɕ/, 2 with the voiced dental affricate /d͡z/, 1 with the voiced post-alveolar affricate /d͡ʒ/ and 3 with the voiced pre-palatal affricate /d͡ʑ/. Let us now discuss the patterns of adaptation of each segment in turn.

The voiceless dental affricate /t͡s/ occurs in 8 CC structures, including 4 initial and 4 final sequences, as evidenced in Tab. 26.

Tab. 26: Clusters with the voiceless dental affricate /t͡s/

CLUSTER	TARGETLIKE	EPENTHESIS	DELETION	SEGMENT CHANGE
/t͡s#/	13.3 %	0 %	0 %	86.7 % [ft]
/#t͡sw/	26.7 %	0 %	0 %	73.3 % [tw]
/lt͡s#/	40 %	0 %	0 %	60 % [lt]
/#ft͡s/	20 %	40 % [fət]	0 %	40 % [ft]
/nt͡s#/	80 %	0 %	0 %	20 % [nt]
/#t͡sn/	33.3 %	6.7 % [t͡sən]	0 %	60 % [sn]
/#t͡sf/	86.7 %	0 %	0 %	13.3 % [sf]
/t͡sk#/	100 %	0 %	0 %	0 %

The data in Tab. 26 demonstrate that the segment in question is predominantly substituted with the coronal plosive [t] in 4 CC sequences, namely /t͡s#/, /#t͡sw/, /lt͡s#/ and /#ft͡s/. It should be added that /#ft͡s/ is nativised either as [ft] or [fət], i.e. sometimes it undergoes double repair: /ə/ epenthesis to break up an ill-formed structure and the segmental modification of /t͡s/ → [t]. Interestingly, [t] is selected as the correspondent of the affricate, although [s] would result in an equally well-formed output. The same preference for [t], despite the availability of alternatives, such as [s] or [ts], can be observed in the adaptation of the remaining three clusters. Thus, /#t͡sw/ may be repaired as [tw] or [sw] since both constitute legal English structures, yet the former is clearly preferred. The same applies to final clusters /ft͡s#/ and /lt͡s#/. Their logically possible licit English renderings are [fts] / [lts], [ft] / [lt] and [fs] / [ls]. As regards /ft͡s#/, [ft] is selected in almost 90 % of cases. The other sequence, i.e. /lt͡s#/, displays more variability, with 60 % of [lt] and 40 % of [lt͡s] realisations, nevertheless, /t͡s/ → [t] replacement is still predominant. An exception to this regularity is /nt͡s#/, where target-like reproduction constitutes 80 % of responses and [t] only 20 %. The above results therefore indicate that the voiceless dental affricate /t͡s/ tends to be nativised as [t], even though [s] (or sometimes [ts] in final position) gives rise to equally well-formed structures in terms of English phonotactics.

The remaining three clusters, i.e. /#t͡sn/, /#t͡sf/ and /t͡sk#/, exhibit different patterns of segmental adaptation of /t͡s/. In /#t͡sn/ the affricate is substituted with the coronal fricative [s] in 60 % of cases, which produces a legal English sequence [sn]. As a matter of fact, this is the only repair that results in a well-formed output, as /t͡s/ → [t] would yield [tn], a cluster violating the MSD. As far as /#t͡sf/ is concerned, the only repair resulting in a legal English output is substituting the affricate with the fricative [s] (/#t͡sf/ → [sf]). Adapting the affricate as [t] produces an illicit cluster [tf]. However, in the vast majority of cases /t͡s/ is reproduced targetlike in spite of the fact that the outcome is not consistent with English phonotactics. Apparently, the pressure to preserve the phonological content is stronger here than sonority restrictions. As for the final /t͡sk#/ cluster, the adaptation which best satisfies English phonotactic constraints is [sk], nonetheless, it is unattested. Instead, the predominant response is [tsk], a marginal sequence in English occurring mostly in foreign place names, e.g. *Irkutsk, Yakutsk* and *Okhotsk*. The mapping /t͡s/ → [t], resulting in an ill-formed sequence [tk], is avoided.

On the whole, the data demonstrate that the voiceless dental affricate /t͡s/ tends to be substituted with [t], except when this gives rise to an illicit cluster, such as [#tf], [tk#] or [#tn]. In some cases, targetlike reproduction of the affricate is preferred, although substitution with a fricative would yield a better formed structure in terms of English phonotactics.

The voiceless post-alveolar affricate /t͡ʃ/ is present in 7 clusters, including 3 in initial position and 4 in final position. In Tab. 27 we present the patterns of segmental adaptation of /t͡ʃ/ in these sequences.

Tab. 27: *Clusters with the voiceless post-alveolar affricate /t͡ʂ/*

CLUSTER	TARGETLIKE	EPENTHESIS	DELETION	SEGMENT CHANGE
/#t͡ʂk/	60 %	40 % [t͡ʂək]	0 %	0 %
/#ʂt͡ʂ/	0 %	0 %	0 %	100 % [ʃt]
/#t͡ʂw/	0 %	0 %	0 %	100 % [tw]
/pt͡ʂ#/	0 %	0 %	0 %	100 % [pt]
/t͡ʂp#/	86.7 %	0 %	0 %	13.3 % [ʃp]
/ʂt͡ʂ#/	6.7 %	0 %	0 %	93.3 % [ʃt]
/rt͡ʂ#/	80 %	0 %	0 %	20 % [rt]

The figures in Tab. 27 indicate that the segment under discussion is nativised as the coronal plosive [t] in 4 CC structures, namely /#t͡ʂw/, /#ʂt͡ʂ/, /pt͡ʂ#/ and /ʂt͡ʂ#/. In all cases, the /t͡ʂ/ → [t] adaptation constitutes the best repair strategy in terms of English phonotactics. This is because it results in well-formed sequences [tw], [pt] and [ʃt] for /#t͡ʂw/, /pt͡ʂ#/ and /ʂt͡ʂ#/ respectively, and a marginal cluster [ʃt] for /#ʂt͡ʂ/. It should be noted that the substitution with the fricative [ʃ] produces outputs which are either ill-formed, e.g. /#ʂt͡ʂ/ → *[ʃʃ], /ʂt͡ʂ#/ → *[ʃʃ] and /pt͡ʂ#/ → *[pʃ], or, as in /#t͡ʂw/ → [ʃw], peripheral. Given these results, it may be argued that the voiceless post-alveolar affricate /t͡ʂ/ is nativised as [t], because other alternatives yield illicit outputs.

In the remaining three clusters, /t͡ʂ/ is mostly produced targetlike, i.e. as a voiceless palato-alveolar affricate [t͡ʃ]. As regards /#t͡ʂk/ and /t͡ʂp#/, the /t͡ʂ/ → [t] mapping is unattested, presumably because it results in ill-formed outputs of two plosives, i.e. *[tk] and *[tp]. Again, as in the case of /t͡ʂ/, the faithful reproduction of the affricate is preferred over the substitution with the fricative [ʃ]. The difference between /t͡ɕ/ and /t͡ʂ/ is that the adaptation to [s] gives rise to well-formed clusters for the former, whereas for the latter both targetlike reproduction as well as replacement with a fricative produce illicit structures. The affricate in /rt͡ʂ#/ is rendered targetlike in 80 % of cases, although neither *[rt͡ʃ#] nor *[rt#] is an attested sequence in English. Still, a more faithful alternative is selected.

To sum up, the above results indicate that the voiceless post-alveolar affricate /t͡ʂ/ tends to be adapted as [t], except when this gives rise to an illicit sequence, e.g. of two plosives. If this is the case, then the faithful reproduction of the affricate is preferred over the substitution with a fricative, even if the latter repair produces a better formed output.

The voiceless pre-palatal affricate /t͡ɕ/ occurs in 7 clusters, including 3 initial and 4 final sequences. The figures concerning /t͡ɕ/ nativisation are presented in Tab. 28.

Tab. 28: Clusters with the voiceless pre-palatal affricate /t͡ɕ/

CLUSTER	TARGETLIKE	EPENTHESIS	DELETION	SEGMENT CHANGE
/#ft͡ɕ/	40 %	46.7 % [fət͡ɕ]	0 %	13.3 % [ft]
/#ɕt͡ɕ/	60 %	0 %	0 %	40 % [st͡ʃ]
/#t͡ɕm/	80 %	20 % [t͡ɕəm]	0 %	0 %
/pt͡ɕ#/	100 %	0 %	0 %	0 %
/ɕt͡ɕ#/	40 %	0 %	0 %	60 % [ʃt]
/ft͡ɕ#/	100 %	0 %	0 %	0 %
/jt͡ɕ#/	100 %	0 %	0 %	0 %

As demonstrated in Tab. 28, the segment in question is predominantly reproduced targetlike. The only clusters with some variation between [t͡ʃ] and [t] are /ɕt͡ɕ#/ and /#ft͡ɕ/, nevertheless, the faithful reproduction of the affricate is still more frequent than the substitution with the voiceless coronal stop. The targetlike realisation of /t͡ɕ/ is attested both in those sequences where the /t͡ɕ/ → [t] mapping yields an illicit output, e.g. /#t͡ɕm/ → *[tm], as well as in clusters where this modification results in well-formed or at least marginal structures, e.g. /ɕt͡ɕ#/ → [ʃt], /ft͡ɕ#/ → [ft] or /pt͡ɕ#/ → [pt]. This pattern seems somewhat surprising given that in very similar clusters the dental /t͡s/ and the post-alveolar /t͡ʂ/ are mostly substituted with [t], as evidenced in Tab. 29.

Tab. 29: Divergent adaptation of /t͡s/ and /t͡ʂ/ vs. /t͡ɕ/

adapted as [t]	adapted as [t͡ʃ]
/#ft͡s/	/#ft͡ɕ/
/#ʂt͡ʂ/	/#ɕt͡ɕ/
/ʂt͡ʂ#/	/ɕt͡ɕ#/
/ft͡s#/	/ft͡ɕ#/
/pt͡ʂ#/	/pt͡ɕ#/

This naturally raises the question concerning the reasons behind the divergent adaptation of /t͡s/ and /t͡ʂ/ vs. /t͡ɕ/.

To sum up, an examination of the patterns of adaptation of Polish voiceless affricates by native speakers of English reveals the following general tendencies:

1. The voiceless dental and post-alveolar affricates tend to be nativised as [t], except when this gives rise to an ill-formed sequence. The adaptation to the coronal stop is selected despite the availability of alternative repairs, e.g. the substitution with a fricative, which yield phonotactically well-formed outputs.
2. The pre-palatal affricate is realised as [t͡ʃ] in all contexts, even though the adaptation to a plosive or a fricative produces better formed English CC sequences.

The data concerning the nativisation of Polish voiced affricates are provided in Tab. 30.

Tab. 30: Clusters with voiced affricates

CLUSTER	TARGETLIKE	EPENTHESIS	DELETION	SEGMENT CHANGE
/#d͡zb/	13.3 %	20 % [əzb]	0 %	66.7 % [zb]
/#d͡zv/	6.7 %	20 % [əzv]	0 %	73.3 % [zv]
/#d͡zd͡ʐ/	0 %	93.3 % [d͡ʒəd͡ʒ]	6.7 % [d͡ʒ]	0 %
/#gd͡ʐ/	13.3 %	86.7 % [gəd͡ʒ]	0 %	0 %
/#vd͡ʐ/	13.3 %	86.7 % [vəd͡ʒ]	0 %	0 %
/#zd͡ʐ/	40 %	46.7 % [əzd͡ʒ]	0 %	13.3 % [st͡ʃ]

As demonstrated in Tab. 30, the only voiced affricate undergoing segmental modification is the dental /d͡z/, realised mostly as [z] in /#d͡zb/ and /#d͡zv/. It should be noted that both the substitution with a plosive as well as with a fricative create sequences violating sonority restrictions, i.e. [db] / [zb] and [dv] / [zv], yet the latter option is consistently selected by the participants. The clusters containing the post-alveolar /d͡ʐ/ or pre-palatal /d͡ʑ/ are predominantly repaired by vowel epenthesis, with no segmental changes affecting the affricates.

Taking into consideration the results concerning the adaptation of affricates, our main goal will be to account for the divergent realisations of the dental and the post-alveolar vs. the pre-palatal affricates. Furthermore, we need to explain the preference for /d͡z/ → [z] rather than /d͡z/ → [d] adaptation as well as target-like reproduction of /d͡ʐ/ and /d͡ʑ/. These issues will be dealt with in Section 4.4.

3.4.2 Other changes

Other segmental changes included mainly consonant devoicing and a segment modification in the place of articulation, however, their incidence was low or very low. The clusters repaired through devoicing are presented in (86).

(86) Consonant devoicing in CC clusters

/#zm/ → [sm]	33.3 %	/#zdʑ/ → [sʧ]	13.3 %
/#zw/ → [sw]	33.3 %	/#zv/ → [sf]	13.3 %
/#zr/ → [sr]	20 %	/#vm/ → [fm]	6.7 %
/#vl/ → [fl]	20 %	/#dl/ → [tl]	6.7 %

The data in (86) indicate that devoicing usually results in well-formed English clusters. The only exceptions are /#zr/ → [sr], /#vm/ → [fm] and /#dl/ → [tl].

The clusters in which the place of articulation of C_1 or C_2 is modified are listed in (87).

(87) Place of articulation modification in CC clusters

/#ɕɲ/ → [ʃn]	53.3 %	/#tl/ → [kl]	6.7 %
/ʂp#/ → [sp]	20 %	/tf#/ → [ts]	6.7 %
/pɲ#/ → [pn]	13.3 %	/wʂ#/ → [ws]	6.7 %

As demonstrated in (87), the place of articulation modification occurs extremely rarely. The only segment which undergoes this repair in a larger number of cases is the pre-palatal nasal /ɲ/, realised consistently as the coronal nasal [n], which is not surprising as /ɲ/ is not found in English.

The clusters in which other segmental changes occur are provided in (88).

(88) Other segmental modifications in CC clusters

| /tw#/ → [tf] | 20 % | /#xf/ → [kf] | 6.7 % |
| /xf#/ → [fk] | 20 % | /fr#/ → [lf] | 6.7 % |

The modifications in the CC sequences in (88) include devoicing + change in the place of articulation (/tw#/ → [tf]), change in the manner of articulation + metathesis (/xf#/ → [fk], /fr#/ → [lf]) and change in the manner of articulation (/#xf/ → [kf]).

On the whole, our main goal will be to account for a general avoidance of devoicing and place modification as repair strategies in the adaptation of Polish CC clusters by native speakers of English. This will be discussed in Section 4.4.

3.5 Consonant deletion

Consonant elision is generally dispreferred in the overwhelming majority of clusters. Thus, no instances of this repair are found in 50 out of 56 initial CC sequences. The rates of deletion in the remaining 6 clusters are presented in (89), with segments undergoing the process under discussion in parentheses (in the case of /#d͡ʐd͡ʐ/, it is impossible to determine whether C_1 or C_2 is deleted).

(89) Consonant deletion in initial CC clusters

/#(x)ş/ → [ʃ]	86.7 %	/#(t)ş/ → [ʃ]	6.7 %
/#(x)f/ → [f]	73.3 %	/#m(r)/ → [m]	6.7 %
/#(d͡ʐ)(d͡ʐ)/ → [d͡ʒ]	6.7 %	/#t(l)/ → [t]	6.7 %

As demonstrated in (89), the rate of consonant deletion is usually very low, i.e. it amounts to 6.7 %. The only exceptions are clusters of voiceless fricatives, i.e. /#xf/ and /#xş/, where it constitutes 73.3 % and 86.7 % of responses respectively and is the most frequent repair strategy. In the cases under discussion, the segment that is invariably removed is the voiceless velar fricative /x/. This might be due to the fact that this consonant is not part of the native English inventory. Interestingly, no instances of the repair under discussion are found in the adaptation of the voiced fricative + fricative sequence /#zv/, which is produced targetlike in the majority of cases (73.3 %).

Consonant deletion is slightly more frequent in final clusters. However, although it is attested in almost one fourth of all such sequences (9 out of 37), its incidence is usually marginal, as shown in (90).

(90) Consonant deletion in final CC clusters

/(x)f#/ → [f]	46.7 %	/(r)f#/ → [f]	6.7 %
/t(w)#/ → [t]	26.7 %	/r(m)#/ → [r]	6.7 %
/(t)f#/ → [f]	20 %	/s(f)#/ → [s]	6.7 %
/t(r)#/ → [t]	13.3 %	/p(ɲ)#/ → [p]	6.7 %
/f(r)#/ → [f]	6.7 %		

The rate of consonant elision is the highest in the /xf#/ cluster. Again, the segment undergoing the process in question is /x/. In other CC sequences, deletion occurs marginally, with the exception of /tw#/ and /tf#/, where it constitutes 26.7 % and 20 % of responses respectively.

In what follows our main goal will be to account for a general avoidance of consonant deletion as a repair strategy in the nativisation of Polish CC clusters by native speakers of English as well as to explain why elision targets mostly the voiceless velar fricative /x/. We will deal with these issues in Section 4.5.

4 Analysis and discussion

This Section is devoted to a formal analysis of the experimental data presented in Section 3. We start with a discussion of how the patterns revealed in our study relate to the predictions made by the major loan phonology models discussed in Chapter 2. The following Sections focus on accounts of targetlike reproduction (4.2), vowel epenthesis (4.3), segment change (4.4) and consonant deletion (4.5) in the adaptation of Polish CC consonant clusters by native speakers of English within the model of OT.

4.1 Experimental results vs. predictions of different loan adaptation approaches

Let us now consider which approach to loanword adaptation best accounts for the patterns found in the experimental data.

As regards the phonological approximation view, one of the most popular loan nativisation models within that approach is the Theory of Constraints and Repair Strategies Loanword Model (TCRS LM) (Paradis and LaCharité 1997), which claims that loanword adaptation is governed by a set of universal inviolable principles (see Chapter 2, Section 2.1). The most important of these is the Preservation Principle, stipulating that as much phonological information in the input as possible should be retained in the output. The Preservation Principle is limited by the Threshold Principle stating that a particular segment will be saved unless its rescue requires more than two steps of repair. If this is the case, that is, if the preservation of a segment is too costly, then it is predicted to undergo elision. As a result, epenthesis is universally favoured over deletion as a strategy of repairing ill-formed structures since it maximally preserves the phonological content of the input. In the case of phonotactic adaptations, this means that illegal combinations of well-formed segments should undergo epenthesis, whereas clusters with at least one foreign sound should be repaired by deletion. This is because a repair through vowel epenthesis in the latter case would entail 1) insertion of a nucleus between the consonants, 2) supplying the nucleus with the segmental content via vowel or glide spreading and 3) adaptation of the illicit segment. Such a solution involves three steps of repair thus it is too costly in terms of the Threshold Principle.

On the one hand, the results of our experiment indeed show the preference for vowel epenthesis, especially in initial clusters, and avoidance of deletion, which is in line with the Preservation Principle. On the other hand, some results for the CC structures containing non-English segments run counter to the predictions made by the TCRS LM. Thus, clusters with /x/, a non-English segment, are indeed adapted through consonant elision. However, other foreign sounds, such as /ɲ/ or /ʦ/ are consistently preserved and sequences containing them are predominantly repaired by vowel epenthesis or segment change rather than elision. It seems therefore that the major flaw of the model under discussion is a rigid threshold of two steps of repair, which clearly cannot be maintained in the light of the experimental evidence presented in this Chapter.

The phonetic approximation view, as advocated by Peperkamp and Dupoux (2002, 2003), Peperkamp (2005), Peperkamp *et al.* (2008) and Boersma and Hamann (2009) (see Chapter 2, Section 3.2) challenges the idea that L2 words are faithfully perceived and mapped onto L1 underlying forms which are subsequently computed by the native phonological grammar. Instead, it proposes that loanword adaptation takes place in perception. The input to speech perception consists of a continuous acoustic signal, mapped by the phonetic decoder onto the phonetically closest native structures in the process called perceptual assimilation. Phonetic closeness is defined as similarity in terms of either acoustic distance (Kuhl 2000) or articulatory gestures (Best and Strange 1992). Perceptual assimilation takes place before production grammar applies. This means that the output of perception is already well-formed in the recipient language.

Under this view, illicit phonotactic structures should be invariably altered so as to fit the target language phonological system and cases of native-like reproduction should be extremely rare. As the results of our experiment show, this is not the case as the percentage of targetlike responses is relatively high. Our data are inconsistent with the claim that perception is overwhelmingly unfaithful. This in turn means that the modifications affecting loanwords cannot take place solely in perception, but they have to be computed by the production grammar.

The perceptual similarity view (e.g. Yip 2002, Kang 2003), based on the concept of the P-Map proposed by Steriade (2001/2008) (see Chapter 2, Section 4.2), also emphasises the role of perception in loanword adaptation. It rests on the assumption that speakers possess knowledge of perceptual similarity between certain pairs of structures in particular contexts. The major difference with regard to the phonetic approximation view is that this knowledge is encoded in the form of output-output faithfulness constraints exerting pressure towards perceptually minimal repairs. This means that in loanword adaptation, borrowers aim to maximise the perceptual similarity between source items and the output of adaptation in that they employ strategies resulting in the least perceptible deviations from the source as possible.

The major problem with this approach is that in many cases it does not predict which adaptation strategy produces the output most perceptually similar to the source form. For example, initial clusters such as /#zm/ or /#vl/ can be repaired by either devoicing of C_1 or vowel epenthesis. In order to claim that [sm], [əzm] or [zəm] is the best perceptual match for /zm/, it is necessary to obtain experimental data on the relative perceptual similarity of these forms to /zm/. Thus, whether the approach in question correctly predicts the adaptation patterns of Polish consonant clusters by native speakers of English remains an open question as it needs to be verified by independent experimental studies, e.g. eliciting perceptual similarity judgements. Therefore, we leave this matter for future research.

In the present monograph, we will argue that our data can receive an adequate description and explanation in an Optimality Theory analysis similar to Itô and Mester's (1995, 1999, 2001) account of lexical stratification in Japanese (see Chapter 2, Section 2.2). Under this view, there is no need for a separate loan phonology component. This is because the vast majority of modifications occurring in borrowings result from the application of the native hierarchy of phonological constraints. Importation as well as different degrees of nativisation attested in loanwords can be accounted for by reranking of FAITH with respect to an invariant hierarchy of markedness constraints. In what follows we will demonstrate that the repair strategies employed in the majority of the experimental data can be explained as a direct reflection of the native English phonological grammar. Any data that seem to be inconsistent with the core native phonology will be shown to result from the FAITH promotion or demotion with respect to a constant ranking of well-formedness constraints.

Under this view, faithfulness constraints are floating constraints (e.g. Anttila 1998, Boersma 1998), i.e. their position in the ranking is variable. Such a view is consistent with the fundamental assumption of the Extended Richness of the Base principle (see Davidson et al. 2004: 340 for details) which states that "[t]he final state of the grammar is in general a partial ranking containing floating faithfulness constraints." This means that the phonological grammar of a given language is understood not as a fixed ranking of markedness and faithfulness constraints, but rather as a partial ranking, where the latter may occupy different positions. This has an important consequence for the nativisation of loanwords. As argued by Davidson et al. (2004: 341), "[i]nputs that are not drawn from the native lexicon will in general yield variable outputs; with Faithfulness elevated from the base grammar, outputs of non-native inputs will in general violate the surface generalisations of the language." In other words, cases of partial adaptation or non-adaptation of foreign items occur due to the promotion of FAITH with respect to the base ranking, i.e. the one producing core native outputs. Gradual elevation of FAITH results in the deactivation of subsequent markedness constraints, which, in turn, produces increasingly faithful outputs violating the surface generalisations of the language.

However, there is another possibility not discussed by Davidson et al. (2004), namely demotion of FAITH with respect to the base ranking. In such a case, the output also violates the surface patterns of a language, this time not because of its increased faithfulness to the source item but rather because of a decrease in markedness with regard to what is required by the core phonology expressed by the base ranking. In other words, the output of adaptation satisfies more markedness constraints than native outputs. When such a situation arises, we are dealing with a case of the emergence of the unmarked in loanword nativisation (see Chapter 1, Section 3.4.5), where borrowed items are made to conform to stricter structural restrictions than the native vocabulary.

The effects of floating FAITH in English are summarised in (91) (M_n stands for a markedness constraint).

(91) <u>Floating FAITH in English</u>

base ranking	$M_1 >> M_2 >> FAITH >> M_3$	native English (core)
FAITH promotion	$M_1 >> FAITH >> M_2 >> M_3$	partial nativisation
	$FAITH >> M_1 >> M_2 >> M_3$	importation
FAITH demotion	$M_1 >> M_2 >> M_3 >> FAITH$	emergence of the unmarked

The base ranking defines core English phonology and produces outputs consistent with English surface generalisations. The gradual promotion of FAITH yields partially adapted or unadapted outputs violating these generalisations. It can be argued that the peripheral consonant clusters discussed in Chapter 3 (Section 2) have entered English via this mechanism. On the other hand, demotion of FAITH results in cases of the emergence of the unmarked, i.e. outputs which satisfy more markedness constraints than the native vocabulary.

In what follows we will demonstrate how floating FAITH accounts for the patterns of nativisation of Polish CC clusters attested in the experimental results presented in Section 3. It will be argued that the majority of adaptations are produced by the base English ranking, i.e. they are consistent with English surface phonotactic patterns. However, we will also investigate cases of importation (Section 4.2) as well as the emergence of the unmarked (Section 4.3.1), which arise due to FAITH promotion and FAITH demotion respectively. Some examples of partial adaptation will be examined in Chapter 5 (Section 3.2).

4.2 Targetlike reproduction

Let us start with an analysis of targetlike reproduction cases, which clearly violate native English surface phonotactic patterns. Our account is based on the assumption that the English lexicon is organised into the core-periphery structure, where the core stratum includes native vocabulary, with all phonological wellformedness requirements satisfied, whereas items located in the peripheral strata, such as unassimilated loanwords, obey only a subset of the core constraints.

Although, as demonstrated in Section 3.2, clusters conforming to the SSP are easier to imitate than those inconsistent with the principle in question, there are still cases of the faithful reproduction of CC sequences disobeying SONORITY, e.g. /#pt/ (60 %), /#db/ (40 %) and /#mʐ/ (26.7 %). Such items might be interpreted as belonging to the peripheral stratum of the lexicon, where SONORITY is deactivated. This is achieved through reranking of FAITH with respect to markedness constraints, as shown in (92).

(92) Core vs. periphery constraint rankings
Core stratum (native vocabulary)
SONORITY >> FAITH (MAX-IO, DEP-IO) >> ONS, *CODA, *COMPLEX
Peripheral stratum (unassimilated loanwords)
FAITH (MAX-IO, DEP-IO) >> SONORITY >> ONS, *CODA, *COMPLEX

FAITH promotion at the peripheral stratum means that faithfulness to the input takes precedence over well-formedness in terms of sonority and the universal syllable structure. As a result, foreign items enter the target language unadapted.

Tableau 7 demonstrates an example of the targetlike reproduction of a Polish CC cluster.

Tableau 7: Targetlike reproduction of /#pt/ in ptak /ptak/ 'a bird'

/ptak/	MAX-IO	DEP-IO	SONORITY	ONS	*CODA	*COMPLEX
☞ ptak			*		*	*
pə.tak		*!			*	
pak	*!				*	
tak	*!				*	

In Tableau 7 the candidates incurring some violation of faithfulness, whether MAX-IO or DEP-IO, are ruled out. In consequence, the fully faithful form emerges as optimal despite its ill-formedness with respect to SONORITY, *CODA and *COMPLEX.

To sum up, cases of targetlike reproduction can be regarded as belonging to the peripheral stratum of the English lexicon, where certain structural constraints, such as SONORITY, are deactivated due to FAITH promotion.

4.3 Vowel epenthesis

Since none of the CC clusters used in the experiment constitute well-formed English initial or final sequences, native speakers of English have to modify them in order to make them conform to the phonotactic patterns of their language.

They can achieve this goal by means of a number of repair strategies, including vowel epenthesis, consonant deletion as well as segment change, yet the experimental results demonstrate that the first of them is most frequently employed. This is a typical example of the so-called too-many-solutions-problem, i.e. a situation in which a foreign input may be repaired through several modifications, each of which yields a well-formed output, but adapters clearly prefer one nativisation strategy (see Chapter 1, Section 3.4.1). In terms of Optimality Theory, the strong preference for vowel insertion as opposed to other repairs indicates that the faithfulness constraint prohibiting epenthesis, i.e. DEP-IO, is low-ranked with respect to those disallowing elision, i.e. MAX-IO, or segment change, i.e. IDENT-IO (McCarthy and Prince 1995). Thus, our experimental results provide direct insight into the ranking of constraints for which there is little or no evidence in the native phonology.

In this Section, we provide a formal OT analysis of vowel epenthesis as a repair strategy in the adaptation of Polish CC consonant clusters by native speakers of English. Initial and final clusters are examined in Sections 4.3.1 and 4.3.2. respectively.

4.3.1 Initial clusters

As regards vowel epenthesis in initial clusters, there are several logically possible syllabifications with an epenthetic segment (in parentheses), as evidenced in (93).

(93) Logically possible syllabifications of /C_1C_2VC/ with an epenthetic vowel
    a) /#C_1C_2VC#/ → [(V)C_1C_2.VC]
    b) /#C_1C_2VC#/ → [(V)C_1.C_2VC]
    c) /#C_1C_2VC#/ → [C_1(V)C_2.VC]
    d) /#C_1C_2VC#/ → [C_1(V).C_2VC]

The first logical possibility is to insert a vowel before a CC sequence and either syllabify both C_1 and C_2 as the coda of the initial syllable (93a) or only C_1 as the coda of the initial syllable and C_2 as the onset of the following syllable (93b). The other logical possibility is to insert an epenthetic vowel between C_1 and C_2. In such a case, C_2 may be syllabified as the coda of the initial syllable (93c) or as the onset of the following syllable (93d).

The syllabifications in (93) differ with respect to their relative well-formedness. Tableau 8 contains their evaluation in terms of universal syllable structure markedness constraints.

Tableau 8: Evaluation of possible syllabifications of /#C$_1$C$_2$VC#/ with vowel epenthesis

/#C$_1$C$_2$VC#/	*COMPLEX	ONS	*CODA
(V)C$_1$C$_2$.VC	*	**	***
(V)C$_1$.C$_2$VC		*	**
C$_1$(V)C$_2$.VC		*	**
☞ C$_1$(V).C$_2$VC			*

As demonstrated in Tableau 8, the optimal syllabification of /#C$_1$C$_2$VC#/ with an epenthetic vowel is [C$_1$(V).C$_2$VC] as it incurs only a single violation of *CODA. The remaining candidates are harmonically bounded by the winner, i.e. they cannot win under any ranking of the relevant constraints.[36] In this light, it should be expected that the Polish initial CC sequences nativised via vowel epenthesis will be predominantly adapted through internal rather than edge epenthesis and will be syllabified as [C$_1$(V).C$_2$VC], unless other factors come into play.

The results of our experiment are in accordance with this prediction, with the majority of clusters undergoing anaptyxis, as shown in Section 3.3 Tableau 9 demonstrates the pattern in question.

Tableau 9: Anaptyxis in /#dv/ in dwa /dva/ 'two'

/dva/	SONORITY	MAX-IO	DEP-IO	ONS	*CODA	*COMPLEX
dva	*!					*
☞ də.va			*			
dəv.a			*	*!	*	
əd.va			*	*!	*	
ədv.a	*!		*	**!	**	*
da		*!				
va		*!				

The fully faithful candidate as well as [ədv.a] are immediately ruled out due to a SONORITY violation, while forms with a deleted C$_1$ or C$_2$ are eliminated by MAX-IO. Since all the remaining candidates contain an epenthetic vowel, they

---

36 See e.g. Samek-Lodovici and Prince (1999) for a discussion of harmonic bounding relations.

fail to satisfy DEP-IO. The item [də.va] is selected as optimal because it is best-formed in terms of the syllable structure constraints.

However, certain initial clusters undergo prothesis rather than anaptyxis. These include sequences with /r/, /w/ or /z/ as C_1. In these cases, the /#C_1C_2VC#/ → [(V)C_1.C_2VC] adaptation is usually selected rather than /#C_1C_2VC#/ → [C_1(V).C_2VC], even though it is suboptimal with regard to ONS and *CODA. Clearly, some other factor(s) must take priority over these syllable well-formedness constraints.

Let us discuss the /r/- and /w/-initial sequences first, where the segments in question are syllabified into the coda of the initial syllable, as evidenced in (94).

(94) /r/ and /w/ syllabified into the coda

| /rdɛst/ | → | [ər.dɛst] | *[rə.dɛst] |
| /wza/ | → | [ʊw.za] | *[wʊ.za] |

This is surprising for two reasons. First of all, these outputs violate the surface generalisations of English according to which neither /r/ nor /w/ can occur in the coda position. Secondly, the forms in question are treated in a different way than the vast majority of initial CC clusters, where C_1 is syllabified into the onset of the initial syllable, not the coda, in accordance with the pattern demonstrated in Tableau 8.

In what follows, we will argue that the cases under discussion represent instances of the emergence of the unmarked, i.e. forms which satisfy more markedness constraints than the native vocabulary. This will be formally expressed through FAITH demotion with respect to certain markedness constraints.

Our crucial claim is that the main reason behind the divergent behaviour of the /r/- and /w/- initial sequences is that universally /r/ and /w/ make better codas than onsets. According to the Sonority Dispersion Principle (SDP) (Clements 1990), while the sonority rise from the onset to the nucleus should be maximised, the sonority drop from the nucleus to the coda should be minimised. This means that obstruents make the best singleton onsets in a CV syllable as they are maximally distant from vowels in terms of sonority. On the other hand, sonorants constitute better codas than obstruents because the sonority drop between vowels and sonorants is lower than between vowels and obstruents.

In optimality-theoretic terms, this can be formally expressed by means of Peak and Margin Constraint Hierarchies (e.g. Prince and Smolensky 1993/2004, Baertsch 2002, 2012) prohibiting segments of a particular sonority value from occupying a given syllable position. In the present monograph, we adopt Baertsch's (2002, 2012) split margin approach to the syllable, which employs three constraint hierarchies, namely the Peak Hierarchy, the M_1 Hierarchy and the M_2

Hierarchy. The first ranking expresses a preference for segments of high sonority in the syllable nucleus, while the remaining ones govern different positions within the onset and the coda. Both margin hierarchies directly relevant to our discussion are provided in (95) (Baertsch 2012: 9, 21).

(95) Syllable margin hierarchies
M_1 Hierarchy (singleton onset, C_1 in onset cluster, C_2 in coda cluster)
$*A_1 \gg *I_1 \gg *U_1 \gg *R_1 \gg *L_1 \gg *N_1 \gg *T_1$
M_2 Hierarchy (singleton coda, C_1 in coda cluster, C_2 in onset cluster)
$*T_2 \gg *N_2 \gg *L_2 \gg *R_2 \gg *U_2 \gg *I_2 \gg *A_2$

The capital letters in the rankings in (95) stand for the following groups of sounds: T = obstruent, N = nasal, L = lateral, R = rhotic, U = high back vowel or glide, I = high front vowel or glide, A = non-high vowel. The M_1 Hierarchy favours segments of low sonority in singleton onsets as well as in C_1 position in onset clusters and in C_2 position in coda sequences. On the other hand, the M_2 Hierarchy expresses a preference for segments of high sonority in singleton codas as well as in C_1 position in coda clusters and C_2 position in branching onsets. The rankings under discussion are universal and the types of segments allowed in particular positions within the onset or the coda in a given language depend crucially on the relative ranking of FAITH.

In the core English vocabulary any consonant, including a glide, may appear in the onset, so FAITH dominates all the constraints in the M_1 Hierarchy, except for $*A_1$. As regards the coda, since obstruents are found in this position in English, FAITH must dominate $*T_2$ and, by transitivity, the remaining M_2 Hierarchy constraints.[37] The relevant rankings are presented in (96) (Baertsch 2012: 9, 21).

(96) Ranking of FAITH in English in M_1 and M_2 Hierarchy
M_1 Hierarchy
$*A_1 \gg$ FAITH $\gg *I_1 \gg *U_1 \gg *R_1 \gg *L_1 \gg *N_1 \gg *T_1$
M_2 Hierarchy
FAITH $\gg *T_2 \gg *N_2 \gg *L_2 \gg *R_2 \gg *U_2 \gg *I_2 \gg *A_2$

The situation is different with regard to some loanwords. The results of our experiment indicate that during loan adaptation native speakers of English prefer to syllabify /r/ and /w/ into the syllable coda rather than the onset. This can be formally expressed as the demotion of FAITH below $*R_1$ in the M_1 Hierarchy, as evidenced in (97).

---

37 As observed by Baertsch (2012: 21), vowels do not occur in the coda position due to the interaction with the Peak Hierarchy constraints.

(97) FAITH demotion in M_1 Hierarchy in English

$*A_1 >> *I_1 >> *U_1 >> *R_1 >> FAITH >> *L_1 >> *N_1 >> *T_1$

If FAITH is demoted below $*R_1$, then only laterals, nasals and obstruents will be able to surface in the syllable onset. Segments of higher sonority will be syllabified either into the nucleus or the coda, depending on the interaction with other constraints.

Tableau 10 demonstrates the effect of FAITH demotion.

Tableau 10: Prothesis in /#rd/ in rdɛst /rdɛst/ 'a knotweed'

/rdɛst/	SONORITY	$*R_1$	MAX-IO	DEP-IO	ONS	*CODA	*COMPLEX
rdɛst	*!	*				**	*
rə.dɛst		*!		*		**	*
rəd.ɛst		*!		*	*	***	*
☞ ər.dɛst				*	*	***	*
ərd.ɛst				*	**!	****	**
dɛst		*!				**	*

The fully faithful form is ruled out due to a SONORITY violation, whereas the items with /r/ in the onset are eliminated by $*R_1$. The choice between [ər.dɛst] and [ərd.ɛst] is determined by the syllable structure constraints, with the former candidate emerging as optimal.

The evaluation of /w/-initial clusters proceeds in a similar fashion, with the forms containing /w/ in the onset eliminated by $*U_1$. However, in these cases there is an additional phenomenon to explain, namely the quality of the epenthetic segment, realised as the lax high back rounded vowel /ʊ/ rather than as /ə/. Our claim is that the pattern under discussion may be accounted for on the assumption that the epenthetic segment is an underspecified featureless vowel (e.g. Oostendorp 1995). The vowel in question becomes schwa by default in the vast majority of cases but when it is adjacent to /w/, it receives backness and rounding from this segment through assimilation. According to this proposal, the epenthetic schwa is different from the lexical schwa in English. As pointed out by Hall (2011), there are several studies which provide evidence for such a claim, e.g. Davidson and Stone (2003) demonstrate that there are significant differences in the position of the tongue between the lexical schwa and the epenthetic schwa pronounced by native speakers of English to repair ill-formed initial consonant clusters. Further support is provided by the divergent behaviour of schwa + /w/ sequences in core English phonology and in loan adaptation. Thus, the lexical schwa in English does not assimilate to /w/ in terms of backness and rounding, hence /əw/ sequences surface as such in e.g. *away, aware* or *awake*. On the other hand, assimilation takes place in the same context in loan nativisation, as demonstrated above. This indicates that the epenthetic schwa is different from the lexical schwa in English.

Finally, prothesis rather than anaptyxis occurs in the clusters with /z/ as C_1, such as /#zd/ or /#zb/. However, it must be noted that the sequences in question are frequently reproduced in a targetlike manner and the rate of initial epenthesis is relatively low. The most likely explanation for the ease of imitation is a structural similarity of /zC/ clusters to legal English /sC/ sequences, such as /sp, st, sk/. Nonetheless, some participants modify them by inserting a vowel before C_1. This is in accordance with a cross-linguistic tendency observed by a number of scholars (e.g. Broselow 1992, Gouskova 2001, Yildiz 2005) for falling sonority onset sequences to be repaired by initial rather than internal epenthesis. Various explanations for this phenomenon have been put forward, for instance analysing /sC/ clusters as complex segments (Broselow 1992, Yildiz 2005) or attributing the pattern in question to the role of the Syllable Contact Law (Gouskova 2001). The results of our experiment seem to be consistent with the former approach. The latter makes predictions which are inconsistent with our data, i.e. that the default epenthesis site is before the cluster and anaptyxis takes place only in rising sonority onsets to avoid a violation of the SCL that would arise as a result of prothesis. However, our data demonstrate that internal epenthesis takes place in clusters with a sonority fall (e.g. /#lv/, /#mʂ/, /#mʐ/), rise (e.g. /#dv/, /#dm/, /#mr/) as well as in plateaus (e.g. /#db/, /#mn/, /#gb/) thus the role of the SCL is limited. Instead, in the majority of cases the outputs of adaptation conform to the universal basic syllable well-formedness constraints, i.e. ONS, *CODA and *COMPLEX.

4.3.2 Final clusters

As regards vowel insertion in final clusters, there are several logically possible syllabifications with an epenthetic vowel, as demonstrated in (98).

(98) Logically possible syllabifications of /#CVC₁C₂#/ with an epenthetic vowel
  a) /#CVC₁C₂#/ → [CV.C₁C₂(V)]
  b) /#CVC₁C₂#/ → [CVC₁.C₂(V)]
  c) /#CVC₁C₂#/ → [CVC₁.(V)C₂]
  d) /#CVC₁C₂#/ → [CV.C₁(V)C₂]

The first theoretical possibility is to insert a vowel after the C_1C_2 sequence, in which case C_1C_2 are both syllabified into the onset of the final syllable (98a) or they are split between the coda of the initial syllable and the onset of the final syllable (98b). The other logical option is to insert a vowel between C_1 and C_2, with C_1 syllabified either into the coda of the initial syllable (98c) or the onset of the final syllable (98d).

The outputs in (98) differ with regard to their relative well-formedness. In Tableau 11, we provide their evaluation in terms of universal basic syllable structure constraints.

Tableau 11: Evaluation of possible syllabifications of /#C_1C_2VC#/ with vowel epenthesis

/#CVC_1C_2#/	*COMPLEX	ONS	*CODA
☞ $CV.C_1C_2(V)$	*		
☞ $CVC_1.C_2(V)$			*
$CVC_1.(V)C_2$		*	**
☞ $CV.C_1(V)C_2$			*

As evidenced in Tableau 11, the optimal syllabifications of /#CVC_1C_2#/ with an epenthetic vowel include [$CV.C_1C_2(V)$], [$CVC_1.C_2(V)$] and [$CV.C_1(V)C_2$] as they incur only a single violation of some markedness constraint each. Given this, we should expect variation in the vowel epenthesis site unless other constraints come into play (e.g. [$CV.C_1C_2(V)$] is possible only if the sequence C_1C_2 constitutes a well-formed onset).

However, the results of our experiment show that final clusters are almost invariably adapted via paragoge rather than anaptyxis. Thus, although [$CV.C_1C_2(V)$], [$CVC_1.C_2(V)$] and [$CV.C_1(V)C_2$] are equally well-formed in terms of syllable structure, only the first two outputs are attested in the data (with the exception of the /mn#/ cluster). Clearly, some other constraint must influence the outcome of adaptation of final sequences. Our claim is that the relevant constraint is CONTIGUITY (McCarthy and Prince 1995, Gouskova 2001).

(99) CONTIGUITY constraint
CONTIGUITY: Elements adjacent in the input must be adjacent in the output.

CONTIGUITY militates against both deletion as well as breaking up sequences of segments with an epenthetic vowel. Due to an active role of CONTIGUITY, edge rather than internal epenthesis is preferred in the adaptation of coda clusters. This is demonstrated in Tableau 12.

Tableau 12: Paragoge in /dm#/ in kadm /kadm/ 'cadmium'[38]

/kadm/	SONORITY	MAX-IO	DEP-IO	ONS	*CODA	*COMPLEX	CONT
kadm	*!				**	*	
☞ kad.mə			*		*		
ka.dmə	*!		*			*	
ka.dəm			*		*		*!
kad.əm			*	*	**!		*
kad		*!			*		*
kam		*!			*		*

The selection between candidates with paragoge and anaptyxis, i.e. [kad.mə] and [ka.dəm], crucially depends on CONTIGUITY, which favours the former output. CONTIGUITY must be ranked below syllable well-formedness constraints in order to prevent the occurrence of edge epenthesis in initial clusters, as shown in Tableau 13.

Tableau 13: Inactivity of CONTIGUITY in /#dv/ in dwa /dva/ 'two'

/dva/	SONORITY	MAX-IO	DEP-IO	ONS	*CODA	*COMPLEX	CONT
dva	*!					*	
☞ də.va			*				*
dəv.a			*	*!	*		*
əd.va			*	*!	*		
ədv.a	*!		*	**!	**	*	
da		*!					*
va		*!					*

---

38 Final clusters with a nasal or lateral as C_2 could in principle be adapted through making the sonorant syllabic, however, this option is not attested in the experimental results. On the one hand, it may reflect a general trend in British English whereby syllabic consonants are increasingly replaced with sequences of schwa plus a non-syllabic consonant (e.g. Cruttenden 2014: 85). Another possible explanation is a kind of the emergence of the unmarked effect, i.e. FAITH demotion below the constraint against consonantal nuclei (*P/C, Prince and Smolensky 1993/2004) forces all the outputs of adaptation to satisfy the latter.

151

Tableau 13 demonstrates that CONTIGUITY does not affect the outcome of initial clusters adaptation when it is ranked below ONS, *CODA and *COMPLEX.

To sum up, the vast majority of vowel epenthesis cases result from a straightforward application of the native English ranking of phonological constraints. However, in some cases, the outputs of adaptation conform to stricter structural requirements than the native vocabulary, as in /rC/, /wC/ and /zC/ clusters. The nativisation of these sequences can be regarded as an instance of the emergence of the unmarked phenomenon, formally expressed through FAITH demotion with respect to relevant markedness constraints.

4.4 Segment change

In this Section we provide a formal OT analysis of segment change in the adaptation of Polish CC clusters by native speakers of English. We start with an examination of the modifications affecting affricates (4.4.1) and next we deal with other segmental changes, such as devoicing and altering the place of articulation (4.4.2).

4.4.1 Affricates

As regards the patterns of adaptation of Polish voiceless affricates by native speakers of English, the central problem concerns the reasons behind the divergent adaptation of /ts/ and /tʂ/ vs. /tɕ/. As demonstrated in Section 3.4.1, the dental and post-alveolar affricates tend to be nativised as [t], except when this gives rise to an ill-formed sequence. The adaptation to the coronal stop is selected despite the availability of alternative repairs, e.g. the substitution with a fricative. On the other hand, the pre-palatal affricate is realised as [tʃ] in all contexts, even though the adaptation to a plosive or a fricative produces better formed English CC sequences.

Before we provide an analysis of segmental modification of affricates, it is necessary to explain why clusters with an affricate are not repaired by vowel epenthesis. After all, they are evaluated by the same hierarchy of constraints as sequences composed of other segments. In the Optimality Theory framework, the answer is straightforward, namely the clusters in question do not undergo vowel epenthesis because there is some faithfulness constraint ranked below DEP-IO whose violation results in a well-formed output.

The most common segmental modification affecting /ts/ is a change to the coronal plosive [t], e.g. /#tsw/ → [tw]. Whenever this would produce an ill-formed output, the coronal fricative [s] is selected instead of [t], e.g. /#tsn/ → [sn] (*[tn]).

Given the assumption that affricates are strident stops (e.g. Jakobson *et al.* 1952, Rubach 1994), differing from plosives only in that they are [+strident], the following faithfulness constraints belonging to IDENT-IO family (McCarthy and Prince 1995) are violated in order to ensure the satisfaction of higher ranked markedness constraints in the nativisation of /t͡s/:

(100) IDENT-IO constraints violated in the nativisation of /t͡s/
IDENT-IO[strid]: Correspondent segments in input and output have identical values for [strident].
IDENT-IO[cont]: Correspondent segments in input and output have identical values for [continuant].
IDENT-IO[cont] >> IDENT-IO[strid]

IDENT-IO[cont] must be ranked above IDENT-IO[strid] since the value of [continuant] is altered only if the modification of [strident] fails to produce a well-formed output. In addition, three markedness constraints are necessary to account for the lack of dental, post-alveolar as well as pre-palatal affricates in English. These are informally defined in (101).

(101) Markedness constraints against dental, post-alveolar and pre-palatal affricates
*[t͡s]: No dental affricates.
*[t͡ʂ]: No post-alveolar affricates.
*[t͡ɕ]: No pre-palatal affricates.

Tableau 14 accounts for the realisation of /t͡s/ as [t] in the cluster /#t͡sw/.[39]

Tableau 14: /t͡s/ → [t] adaptation in /#t͡sw/ in cto /t͡swɔ/ 'a tariff'

/t͡swɔ/	*[t͡s]	SONORITY	MAX-IO	DEP-IO	IDENT-IO [cont]	IDENT-IO [strid]
t͡swɔ	*!					
☞ twɔ						*
swɔ					*!	
t͡sə.wɔ	*!			*		
tə.wɔ				*!		*
wɔ			*!			

---

39 Syllable structure constraints and CONTIGUITY have been omitted from the tableaux in this Section, as they play no active role in the selection of optimal outputs in the case of clusters with affricates.

All candidates with [t͡s] are ruled out by the high-ranked *[t͡s]. The forms with an epenthetic vowel or a deleted consonant are eliminated by DEP-IO and MAX-IO respectively. The choice between [twɔ] and [swɔ] is determined by IDENT-IO[cont], which favours the former candidate.[40]

Tableau 15 accounts for the realisation of /t͡s/ as [s] in the cluster /#t͡sn/.

Tableau 15: /t͡s/ → [s] adaptation in /#t͡sn/ in cnota */t͡snɔta/ 'a virtue'*

/t͡snɔta/	*[t͡s]	SONORITY	MAX-IO	DEP-IO	IDENT-IO [cont]	IDENT-IO [strid]
t͡snɔ.ta	*!	*				
tnɔ.ta		*!				*
☞ snɔ.ta					*	
t͡sə.nɔ.ta	*!			*		
tə.nɔ.ta				*!		*
sə.nɔ.ta				*!	*	
tɔ.ta			*!			*

In Tableau 15 evaluation proceeds in a similar fashion as in Tableau 14. However, the affricate in /#t͡sn/ is realised as the coronal fricative [s] rather than plosive [t] because the latter output incurs a violation of SONORITY due to an insufficient sonority distance between C_1 and C_2 (*[tn]).

A question arises why /t͡ʂ/ and /t͡ɕ/ are treated differently in that the former is usually substituted with [t], whereas the latter with [t͡ʃ], e.g. /pt͡ʂ#/ → [pt] vs. /pt͡ɕ#/ → [pt͡ʃ]. Our claim is that the divergent adaptation of /t͡ʂ/ vs. /t͡ɕ/ is crucially related to certain place features of Polish and English affricates. In Tab. 31 we provide the relevant place feature values of the segments in question (based on Szpyra 1995 and Hall 1997).

40 The selection of [t] may be facilitated by the fact that it is the most unmarked consonant, realised through default, as demonstrated by studies on underspecification and markedness (e.g. Kiparsky 1985, Avery and Rice 1989, Paradis and Prunet 1991). It should also be noted that the voiceless coronal stop is the second most frequent consonant in English (Cruttenden 2014: 235).

Tab. 31: Place feature values of Polish and English affricates

POLISH	post-alveolars	pre-palatals
[anterior]	-	-
[distributed]	-	+

ENGLISH	palato-alveolars
[anterior]	-
[distributed]	+

As demonstrated in Tab. 31, English palato-alveolar affricates are identical to Polish pre-palatals with respect to the values of [anterior] and [distributed]. On the other hand, they differ from Polish post-alveolars with regard to the value of [distributed]. The actual outputs of adaptation indicate that the feature [distributed] is of key importance in the selection of optimal candidates in that its modification is generally avoided, as illustrated in (102).

(102) Avoidance of [distributed] modification
/ʧ/ → [t]   [-dist] → [-dist]   */ʨ/ → [t]   [+dist] → [-dist]
*/ʧ/ → [ʧ]   [-dist] → [+dist]   /ʨ/ → [ʧ]   [+dist] → [+dist]

The adaptations involving a change in the value of [distributed], i.e. /ʧ/ → [ʧ] and /ʨ/ → [t], are dispreferred. Instead, the substitutions which preserve the value of this feature, i.e. /ʧ/ → [t] and /ʨ/ → [ʧ], are selected, the effect being the divergent adaptation of /ʧ/ vs. /ʨ/. It should also be noted that altering the value of [anterior] is allowed, as in /ʧ/ → [t] ([-ant] → [+ant]). The constraints against modifications of [distributed] and [anterior] are presented in (103).

(103) IDENT-IO constraints
IDENT-IO[dist]: Correspondent segments in input and output have identical values of [distributed].
IDENT-IO[ant]: Correspondent segments in input and output have identical values of [anterior].
IDENT-IO[cont], IDENT-IO[dist] >> IDENT-IO[strid], IDENT-IO[ant]

In order to derive the correct results, IDENT-IO[dist] must be ranked higher than IDENT-IO[strid], otherwise the /ʧ/ → [ʧ] adaptation, which preserves stridency, would be favoured over the /ʧ/ → [t] substitution, where IDENT-IO[strid] is violated. On the other hand, IDENT-IO[ant] must be low in the hierarchy as the actual outputs fail to satisfy this constraint.

The effect of IDENT-IO(dist) in the adaptation of clusters with /ʦ̺/ is illustrated in Tableau 16.

Tableau 16: /ʦ̺/ → [t] adaptation in /pʦ̺#/ in depcz /dɛpʦ̺/ 'to trample, imp.'

/dɛpʦ̺/	SON	MAX-IO	DEP-IO	IDENT-IO [cont]	IDENT-IO [dist]	IDENT-IO [strid]	IDENT-IO [ant]
depʧ					*!		
☞ dept						*	*
depʃ				*!			
de.pəʧ			*!				
de.pət			*!			*	*
de.pəʃ			*!	*			
dep		*!					
deʧ		*!					
det		*!				*	*

The candidates with an epenthetic vowel or a deleted consonant are ruled out by DEP-IO and MAX-IO respectively, whereas [depʃ] is eliminated by IDENT-IO[cont]. The choice between [depʧ] and [dept] is crucially determined by IDENT-IO[dist], which favours the latter output.

The active role of IDENT-IO[dist] in the nativisation of sequences with /ʨ/ is demonstrated in Tableau 17.

Tableau 17: /ʨ/ → [ʧ] adaptation in /pʨ#/ in kopć /kɔpʨ/ 'to smoke, imp.'

/kɔpʨ/	SON	MAX-IO	DEP-IO	IDENT-IO [cont]	IDENT-IO [dist]	IDENT-IO [strid]	IDENT-IO [ant]
☞ kɔpʧ							
kɔpt					*!	*	*
kɔpʃ				*!			
kɔ.pəʧ			*!				
kɔ.pət			*!			*	*
kɔ.pəʃ			*!	*			
kɔp		*!					
kɔʧ		*!					
kɔt		*!				*	*

The evaluation in Tableau 17 proceeds in a similar fashion as in Tableau 16. Again, IDENT-IO[dist] plays a key role in the selection of the optimal output choosing [kɒptʃ] over [kɒpt].

Adaptation of voiced affricates can be accounted for in the same way as nativisation of voiceless affricates. Thus, dental [d͡z] is realised as [z] rather than [d], because the latter adaptation would result in ill-formed outputs violating SONORITY. Clusters /#d͡zb/ and /#d͡zv/ are therefore nativised as [zb] and [zv] respectively. Even though these items are inconsistent with SONORITY too, they are still better than [db] and [dv], most probably due to their structural similarity to legal English /sC/ sequences. The pre-palatal /d͡ʑ/ is realised as [d͡ʒ], because the /d͡ʑ/ → [d] adaptation entails a modification in the value of [distributed] therefore a cluster like /gd͡ʑ/ is nativised as /gəd͡ʒ/ rather than /gəd/. The only voiced affricate treated differently from its voiceless counterpart is the post-alveolar /d͡ʐ/, which is adapted as [d͡ʒ] rather than [d]. However, since there is only one cluster with /d͡ʐ/ in the experimental data, it is difficult to draw a definite conclusion concerning the nativisation of this segment.

To sum up, there is compelling evidence that the divergent adaptation of Polish dental and post-alveolar vs. pre-palatal affricates in CC clusters is mainly an effect of IDENT-IO[dist], a constraint militating against the modification in the value of the feature [distributed]. The features which native speakers of English most frequently alter in affricates in order to ensure the conformity of loanwords with these segments to the native phonology are [strident] and [anterior], followed by [continuant].

4.4.2 Other changes

Other segmental modifications include mainly consonant devoicing and a change in the segment's place of articulation, however, their rate is low or very low. As a result, our main goal is to account for a general avoidance of these repair strategies in the adaptation of Polish CC clusters by native speakers of English.

The scarcity of consonant devoicing can be accounted for by the high-ranked IDENT-IO[voice], i.e. a constraint prohibiting differences in the value of the feature [voice] between input and output segments (McCarthy and Prince 1995). The constraint is formally defined in (104).

(104) IDENT-IO[voice] constraint
IDENT-IO[voice]: Correspondent segments in input and output have identical values for [voice].

If IDENT-IO[voice] is ranked above DEP-IO, then vowel epenthesis is preferred to voicing change, all else being equal.

This can be illustrated with the adaptation of the initial sequence /vl/. Before we present a tableau with the evaluation of output candidates, it is necessary to introduce a new constraint which accounts for the peripheral status of /vl/ in English established in Chapter 3. Since the cluster is question satisfies SONORITY, its peripherality in English can be attributed to a high degree of markedness of its members. Thus, C_1 is marked due to a non-coronal place of articulation, the presence of voicing as well as the presence of [+continuant]. In addition, the fact that /v/ is followed by another consonant rather than a vowel increases the markedness of the sequence (Davidson *et al.* 2004: 353). All these observations can be formally expressed as a local conjunction constraint provided in (105).

(105) *N-COR & *VOI$_{SON}$ & *F & *CC constraint
*N-COR & *VOI$_{SON}$ & *F & *CC: No non-coronal voiced fricative before any consonant in the same syllable.

The active role of constraint (105) is demonstrated in Tableau 18.

Tableau 18: Vowel epenthesis in /#vl/ in wlot */vlɔt/ 'an inlet'*

/vlɒt/	*N-COR & *VOI$_{SON}$ & *F & *CC	SONORITY	MAX-IO	IDENT-IO [voice]	DEP-IO
vlɒt	*!				
flɒt				*!	
☞ və.lɒt					*
vɒt			*!		
lɒt			*!		

The fully faithful candidate is eliminated by *N-COR & *VOI$_{SON}$ & *F & *CC. Given the dominance of IDENT-IO[voice] over DEP-IO, the candidate with an epenthetic vowel is preferred to the one with devoiced C_1.

However, some participants nativise the cluster under discussion (as well as some other sequences) through devoicing of C_1 rather than vowel insertion. In optimality-theoretic terms this means that they assume a different ranking of IDENT-IO[voice] and DEP-IO, with the latter dominating the former. This is illustrated in Tableau 19.

Tableau 19: Consonant devoicing in /#vl/ in wlot /vlɔt/ 'an inlet'

/vlɔt/	*N-COR & *VOI$_{SON}$ & *F & *CC	SONORITY	MAX-IO	DEP-IO	IDENT-IO [voice]
vlɔt	*!				
☞ flɔt					*
və.lɔt				*!	
vɔt			*!		
lɔt			*!		

Tableaux 18 and 19 illustrate how the variation in the nativisation strategies employed by the experimental subjects can be accounted for in an analysis couched in the framework of Optimality Theory. Under this view, the phenomenon under discussion directly reflects the differences in the rankings of faithfulness constraints assumed by particular participants.

Changes in the major place of articulation, e.g. substituting a labial segment with a coronal or a dorsal one, are extremely rare. They may be formally expressed as a high-ranked constraint prohibiting input-output disparities with regard to the major articulator.

(106) IDENT-IO[PLACE] constraint
IDENT-IO[PLACE]: Correspondent segments in input and output have identical major articulator.

However, certain place modifications do occur in the experimental data but they are restricted to altering the values of the dependent features of a particular PLACE class node, mostly CORONAL. We assume that the CORONAL node dominates the features [strident] (e.g. Pulleyblank 1989, Lahiri and Evers 1991, Shaw 1991), [anterior] and [distributed] (e.g. Sagey 1986, McCarthy 1988, Clements and Hume 1995). We have already seen examples of modifications of the first two features in the nativisation of affricates, e.g. /t͡s/ → [t] ([+strident] → [-strident]) and /t͡ʂ/ → [t] ([-anterior] → [+anterior]).

A change affecting the value of [distributed] can be illustrated with the adaptation of the pre-palatal nasal /ɲ/, mostly adapted as the alveolar nasal [n]. The constraint against the pre-palatal nasal is informally formulated in (107).

(107) Markedness constraint against the pre-palatal nasal
*[ɲ]: No pre-palatal nasal.

An example of the /ɲ/ → [n] substitution is provided in Tableau 20.

Tableau 20: /ɲ/ → [n] adaptation in /#ɕɲ/ in śnieg /ɕɲɛk/ 'snow'

/ɕɲek/	*[ɲ]	SONORITY	MAX-IO	DEP-IO	IDENT-IO [dist]	IDENT-IO [ant]
ʃɲek	*!					
☞ ʃnek					*	*
ʃə.nek				*!	*	*
ʃek			*!			

The faithful output is ruled out by the high-ranked *[ɲ]. The forms with an epenthetic vowel or a deleted consonant incur fatal violations of DEP-IO and MAX-IO respectively. The winning candidate is [ʃnek] in spite of its violation of IDENT-IO[dist] and IDENT-IO[ant].

To sum up, the scarcity of major place modifications and consonant devoicing is a reflection of a high ranking of faithfulness constraints militating against these repair strategies.

4.5 Consonant deletion

As demonstrated in Section 3.5, consonant deletion is the least frequent repair strategy found in the data. It is generally dispreferred, with the exception of the /#xʂ/, /#xf/ and /xf#/ clusters, where it targets the voiceless velar fricative /x/. The avoidance of elision is a direct reflection of the MAX-IO >> DEP-IO hierarchy. Under this ranking, vowel epenthesis is always preferred to consonant deletion as a repair strategy. As a result, the hierarchy of phonological constraints established in previous Sections fails to account for the /x/ deletion cases, as evidenced in Tableau 21.

Tableau 21: Failure to account for /x/ deletion in /#xf/ in chwast /xfast/ 'a weed'

/xfast/	*[x]	SONORITY	MAX-IO	DEP-IO	IDENT-IO [cont]
xfaːst	*!	*			
kfaːst		*!			*
xə.faːst	*!			*	
☜ kə.faːst				*	*
☞ faːst			*!		
kaːst			*!		*

In Tableau 21 the candidates with [x] are ruled out by the high-ranked *[x], a constraint prohibiting velar fricatives. The item [kfɑːst] is ill-formed with regard to SONORITY. The actual output is eliminated by MAX-IO and, as a result, the candidate with an epenthetic vowel, i.e. [kə.fɑːst], emerges as optimal.

In order for the actual surface form, i.e. [fɑːst], to be selected, it would be necessary to rerank DEP-IO or IDENT-IO[cont] above MAX-IO. However, such a ranking would yield incorrect results for clusters repaired by vowel epenthesis or segment modification. Thus, we are faced with a ranking paradox.

We would like to claim that in order to account for /x/ deletion it might be necessary to take perceptual factors into account. One possibility is that /x/ in the /#xʂ/, /#xf/ and /xf#/ clusters is deleted in perception, thus it is not part of the input to the production grammar. It can be argued that when /x/ occurs in the context of another voiceless fricative, it is perceptually non-salient and, in consequence, more likely to be deleted in perception. As demonstrated by Radomski and Sydorenko (2016), the results of a similar study on online adaptation of Ukrainian consonant clusters by native speakers of English show that /x/ undergoes elision much more frequently when the other consonant in a cluster is voiceless than when it is voiced (108).

(108)   The rate of /x/ deletion in Ukrainian clusters
    (a) /#ʧx/ → [ʧ]   64 %   (b) /#xv/ → [v]   20 %
       /#sx/ → [s]   64 %   /#xr/ → [r]   8 %
       /#ʃx/ → [ʃ]   60 %

The data in (108) indicate that the rate of /x/ deletion depends on whether the other segment in a sequence is voiced or voiceless. If /x/ is adjacent to a voiceless consonant, it is more likely to be deleted, possibly due to its perceptual non-salience in this context (although this may also be related to the position of /x/ in the cluster). Obviously, this is merely a tentative proposal, which needs to be verified by perception research.

Another possible explanation why [fɑːst] rather than [kə.fɑːst] emerges as the actual output of nativisation of /xfast/ is that the former is perceptually more similar to the input than the latter. If this were the case, then it would be necessary to postulate some output-output faithfulness constraint, which would eliminate [kə.fɑːst] as an excessive departure from the input in terms of perceptual similarity. Again, in order to confirm the validity of such a proposal, it is necessary to carry out an independent study eliciting perceptual similarity judgements.

In conclusion, it has been demonstrated that the /x/ deletion cases are inconsistent with the ranking of the production grammar constraints which yields correct results for items with vowel epenthesis or segment change. In this light, it seems that perceptual factors must be invoked in order to account for /x/ elision. We have suggested two alternative explanations. According to the first one, /x/ is prone to deletion in perception due to its perceptual non-salience when it is adjacent to another voiceless consonant. Alternatively, the outputs in which /x/ is deleted might be judged by the borrowers as perceptually more similar to the input than the ones with an epenthetic vowel. The validity of both proposals needs to be verified by further research.

5 Conclusions

This Chapter has reported on an online loanword adaptation experiment in which 30 native speakers of Standard Southern British English were asked to reproduce authentic Polish words with initial and final CC consonant clusters unattested in English. The major goals of the study have been to identify the most frequent repair strategies the participants applied in order to adapt illicit consonant sequences, to discover the mechanisms governing the nativisation processes, to verify the validity of various loan adaptation models as well as to provide a formal OT analysis of the adaptation patterns and variation in the data.

A general overview of the data has demonstrated that the most frequent repair strategy is vowel epenthesis, followed by a modification of C_1 or C_2, with consonant deletion occurring marginally. With regard to targetlike reproduction, it has been argued that a number of factors have an impact on the rate of accurate imitation of a cluster. First, sequences violating the Sonority Sequencing Principle are reproduced targetlike less frequently than those which conform to this generalisation. The difference has been found to be statistically significant for both initial and final clusters. These results run counter to the conclusions reached by Davidson (2001) and Haunz (2007), who claim that the sonority distance between consonants has no significant influence on the rate of successful reproduction of a cluster. We have argued that the differences in the attested results stem from the fact that the studies in question, contrary to the present research, examine a small set of experimental stimuli representing a limited range of segment combinations. Another factor which determines the relative ease or difficulty of faithful cluster reproduction is the markedness of feature values inherent in C_1 and/or C_2. A general tendency can be observed whereby the more marked feature values a given consonant in a sequence has, e.g. [+voice] for obstruents, the less likely it is for this cluster to be realised targetlike.

An examination of vowel epenthesis cases has demonstrated that in initial clusters a vowel is usually inserted between C_1 and C_2, with the exception of the sequences with /r/, /w/ or /z/ as C_1, where edge epenthesis is preferred.

Additionally, in /w/-initial clusters, the quality of the epenthetic vowel is different than in the remaining cases in that it is the lax high back rounded vowel /ʊ/ rather than /ə/. In final sequences, the predominant epenthesis site is after the illicit cluster.

Segment change affects mainly affricates. The voiceless dental and postalveolar affricates tend to be nativised as [t], except when this gives rise to an ill-formed sequence. The adaptation to the coronal stop is selected despite the availability of alternative repairs, e.g. the substitution with a fricative, which yield phonotactically well-formed outputs. On the other hand, the pre-palatal affricate is realised as [tʃ] in all contexts, even though the adaptation to a plosive or a fricative produces better formed English CC sequences. Voiced affricates exhibit similar behaviour as their voiceless counterparts. Other repair strategies involving segmental modifications, such as consonant devoicing or change in the place of articulation are generally avoided. Consonant deletion occurs marginally, with the exception of clusters with /x/, where this segment is frequently removed.

A juxtaposition of the experimental results with the predictions made by the major approaches to loan adaptation has revealed several problematic issues inherent in the theories under discussion. As regards the TCRS LM, our data are generally in accordance with the Preservation Principle, which expresses the dispreference for deletion as a means of resolving phonotactic conflicts. However, the results for clusters with non-English segments run counter to the predictions made by this model. This indicates that the rigid threshold of two steps of repair imposed by the TCRS LM cannot be maintained in the light of the experimental evidence.

Our data are also inconsistent with the basic claim of the phonetic approximation view that perception is overwhelmingly unfaithful. A relatively high percentage of targetlike responses demonstrates that this is not the case. As a result, modifications affecting loanwords must be predominantly computed by the production grammar.

The central problem with the perceptual similarity approach is that in many cases it does not predict which repair strategy yields an output most perceptually similar to the input. To this end, it requires carrying out independent experimental studies eliciting perceptual similarity judgements. Therefore, the validity of this proposal in accounting for our data must be verified by further research on perception.

Our experimental results can receive a straightforward explanation in an Optimality Theory analysis similar to Itô and Mester's (1995, 1999, 2001) account of lexical stratification in Japanese, in which no separate loanword phonology component is necessary. Given the assumption of the Extended Richness of the Base principle that the phonological grammar of a language is not a fixed ranking of constraints, but rather a partial ranking with floating faithfulness constraints, it can be argued that the vast majority of modifications taking place in borrowings are an effect of the hierarchy of native constraints. Outputs which violate the surface generalisations of a language are produced by reranking of relevant faithfulness constraints with regard to markedness constraints, either FAITH promotion or demotion. Given these assumptions, the instances of targetlike reproduction can be interpreted as belonging to a peripheral stratum of the English lexicon, where certain structural constraints, such as SONORITY, are deactivated due to FAITH promotion.

The majority of vowel epenthesis cases are consistent with the core ranking of phonological constraints in English. However, in some instances, the outputs of adaptation conform to stricter structural requirements than the native vocabulary, as in /rC/ and /wC/ clusters, where /r/ and /w/ are syllabified into the coda rather than the onset in accordance with a universal tendency for sonorants to make better codas than onsets. The nativisation of these sequences can be regarded as an example of the so-called emergence of the unmarked phenomenon, resulting from FAITH demotion.

The divergent adaptation of Polish post-alveolar vs. pre-palatal affricates in CC sequences has been argued to result from IDENT-IO[dist], a constraint prohibiting modification in the value of the feature [distributed]. The features which native speakers of English most frequently alter in affricates in order to ensure the conformity of loanwords with these segments to native phonology are [strident] and [anterior], followed by [continuant]. These facts can be formally expressed as the ranking IDENT-IO[cont], IDENT-IO[dist] >> IDENT-IO[strid], IDENT-IO[ant]. The scarcity of major place modifications and consonant devoicing is a reflection of a high ranking of the faithfulness constraints militating against these repair strategies. Variation in the nativisation strategies employed by the participants has been demonstrated to take place due to the differences in the ranking of faithfulness constraints assumed by particular subjects.

The cases of /x/ deletion are inconsistent with the ranking of production grammar constraints established for items with vowel epenthesis or segment change. Therefore, perceptual factors must be invoked in order to account for /x/ elision. A potential explanation is that /x/ is prone to deletion in perception due to its perceptual non-salience when it is adjacent to another voiceless consonant. Alternatively, outputs in which /x/ is deleted might be judged by the borrowers as perceptually more similar to the input than the ones with an epenthetic vowel.

The validity of both proposals needs to be verified by independent perception studies.

In the next Chapter we will confront our findings against another set of experimental data in order to verify the validity of our analysis. Our goal will be to examine the patterns of adaptation of Polish CCC consonant clusters by native speakers of southern British English.

5 Adaptation of Polish CCC consonant clusters. Established versus online loans

1 Introduction

In Chapter 4 it has been demonstrated that the substantial majority of modifications taking place in online adaptation of Polish CC consonant clusters by native speakers of British English can be viewed as resulting from the English ranking of universal phonological constraints with floating FAITH. The goal of this Chapter is to confront these findings against another set of experimental data. To this end, we will examine the patterns of adaptation of Polish initial and final CCC sequences by native speakers of Standard Southern British English. Another objective is to compare the experimental results with the nativisation strategies applied to consonant clusters in established loanwords. This will allow us to draw theoretical conclusions regarding the stratification of borrowings in English.

Section 2 is devoted to the presentation of the results of the experiment. We start with a general overview of the data in 2.1. Vowel epenthesis is demonstrated to be the most frequent repair strategy, followed by consonant deletion and segment change. The next sections deal with targetlike reproduction cases (2.2) as well as clusters repaired by vowel epenthesis (2.3) and other modifications (2.4) respectively.

Section 3 focuses on a formal analysis of the experimental results. We examine the patterns of adaptation revealed in the study on CCC clusters by means of the same constraint rankings that were used for the CC sequences in Chapter 4. In what follows, we provide an OT account of targetlike reproduction (3.1), vowel epenthesis (3.2) and other repair strategies (3.3).

Section 4 deals with a comparison of the nativisation strategies applied to word-initial and word-final consonant clusters in online adaptations and established loanwords. First, a selection of representative examples of the latter type of borrowings is presented. Next, we investigate the major differences between the two groups of loans as well as provide their interpretation in terms of the core-periphery distinction.

Finally, in Section 5 we present the conclusions as well as the implications that the experimental results have for a general theory of loanword adaptation. It is argued that there is no need for a separate loanword phonology component given the assumption of the Extended Richness of the Base principle (Davidson *et al.* 2004) that the phonology of a language consists of a partial ranking with floating faithfulness constraints. The role of perceptual modifications in loan-word nativisation is claimed to be relatively limited.

2 Results

In this Section we present the experimental data on the adaptation of CCC consonant clusters by native speakers of English. First, a general overview of the data is provided in 2.1. The following sections focus on targetlike reproduction (2.2), vowel epenthesis (2.3) and other modifications (2.4) respectively.

2.1 General overview of repair strategies

A total of 405 tokens (27 words x 15 participants) have been obtained in the experiment (excluding the distractors). A general categorisation of the responses is presented in Tab. 32.

Tab. 32: General categorisation of the responses in the experiment

category	number of tokens	percentage of tokens
targetlike production	87	21.5 %
vowel epenthesis	204	50.4 %
consonant deletion	54	13.3 %
segment change	43	10.6 %
vowel epenthesis & consonant deletion	17	4.2 %

The figures in Tab. 32 indicate that the predominant repair strategy is vowel epenthesis, followed by consonant deletion and segment change. In a small number of cases, vowel insertion and consonant elision co-occur. Targetlike reproduction cases constitute around one fifth of all the responses.

The breakdown of the results for the initial and final clusters is presented in Fig. 11.

Fig. 11: Initial vs. final CCC clusters

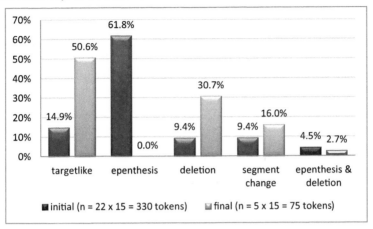

As shown in Fig. 11, the rate of targetlike reproduction is considerably higher for final CCC sequences. On the other hand, initial clusters are relatively difficult to imitate faithfully, with the majority of them being repaired through vowel epenthesis. This modification is unattested in final clusters, where the predominant repair strategies are consonant deletion and segment change.

Let us now compare the results for CC and CCC sequences. The rates of targetlike responses for initial and final clusters are presented in Fig. 12.

Fig. 12: Targetlike reproduction

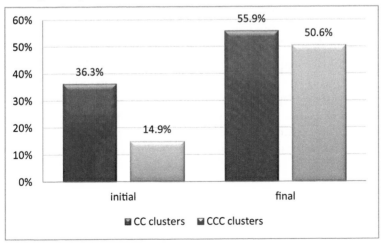

On the whole, CC sequences are easier to reproduce faithfully than CCC ones, especially in word-initial position. This may be due to the fact that English permits a very limited set of initial CCC clusters, as demonstrated in Chapter 3 (Section 2). As regards word-final position, both CC and CCC sequences are rendered target-like more frequently than initial clusters, which reflects the fact that a wider range of segment combinations is allowed in English word-finally than word-initially, as shown in Chapter 3 (Section 2).

A comparison of the rates of vowel epenthesis for CC and CCC clusters in both positions is provided in Fig. 13.

Fig. 13: Vowel epenthesis

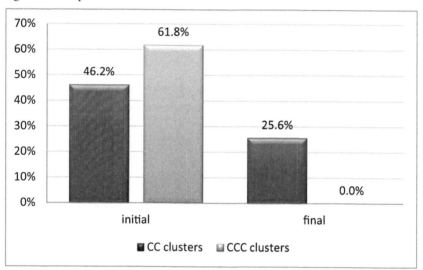

Vowel epenthesis constitutes the most frequent strategy used by the participants in order to nativise both CC and CCC sequences. However, its incidence is considerably higher in the adaptation of initial clusters. As has already been mentioned, final consonant sequences are generally easier to reproduce faithfully than initial ones, which may contribute to the low rate of vowel epenthesis.

The figures concerning segment change in the clusters under discussion are compared in Fig. 14.

Fig. 14: Segment change

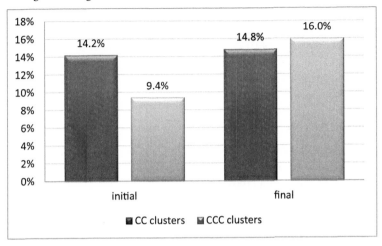

As demonstrated in Fig. 14, there are no significant differences in the rates of segment change for initial vs. final consonant clusters. This strategy is the second most frequent repair for CC sequences and third for CCC structures, after vowel epenthesis and consonant deletion.

The incidence of consonant elision for CC and CCC clusters in both positions is presented in Fig. 15.

Fig. 15: Consonant deletion

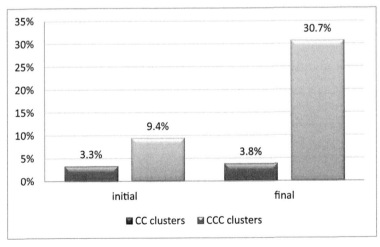

At first glance, it seems that consonant deletion is considerably more frequent for CCC sequences, especially in final position. However, the high percentage of the repair in question is mainly due to two clusters, i.e. /xtr#/ and /stf#/, in which elision is the predominant strategy. Given a limited number of stimuli with final CCC clusters (n = 5), the responses for these two sequences heavily influence the overall results for the relevant category. In this light, consonant elision remains a generally dispreferred nativisation strategy.

2.2 Targetlike reproduction

In the vast majority of cases, the rate of targetlike responses is relatively low, with the exception of the final clusters /psk/ and /nṣt/ as well as certain initial sequences, as evidenced in (109).

(109) Targetlike reproduction in CCC clusters

initial		final	
/#stf/	60 %	/psk#/	100 %
/#tkn/	40 %	/nṣt#/	100 %
/#skn/	33.3 %	/stf#/	46.7 %
/#smr/	33.3 %		

The data in (109) indicate that initial clusters which are most easily imitated include mainly /sCC/ structures (the only exception being /#tkn/). This is not surprising given the fact that only /s/ can occur in C_1 position in initial sequences of three consonants in English. As regards the final clusters with the highest rate of accurate reproduction, their preservation might be due to their structural similarity to legal English sequences, e.g. /nṣt/ vs. /nst/ as in *against* and /psk/ vs. /pst/ as in *lapsed*. A formal analysis of targetlike reproduction cases is provided in Section 3.1.

2.3 Vowel epenthesis

Vowel epenthesis constitutes the most frequent repair strategy in the experimental data. It is the predominant response in 17 out of 22 initial sequences, with its incidence varying to a greater or lesser extent. In the adaptation of final clusters, vowel insertion is unattested. However, since only 5 such items were used in the study, this may result from a limited number of the experimental stimuli. The clusters with high rates of vowel epenthesis are presented in (110).

(110) Vowel epenthesis in CCC clusters
  a) C₁VC₂C₃

/#mgl/ → [məgl]   100.0 %   /#vzg/ → [vəzg]   73.3 %
/#mʧ͡ʧ/ → [məsʧ]   93.3 %   /#vzl/ → [vəzl]   66.7 %
/#mgn/ → [məgn]   93.3 %   /#pʂʈʂ/ → [pəsʧ]   53.3 %
/#gʐm/ → [gəʐm]   86.7 %   /#tkn/ → [təkn]   53.3 %
/#mdw/ → [mədw]   80.0 %   /#tkf/ → [təkf]   46.7 %
/#bzd/ → [bəzd]   73.3 %

  b) C₁C₂VC₃

/#skn/ → [skən]   66.7 %   /#zgn/ → [zgən]   66.7 %
/#zmɲ/ → [zmən]   66.7 %   /#smr/ → [smər]   60.0 %

  c) C₁VC₂C₃ / C₁C₂VC₃

/#brn/ → [bərn] (60.0 %) / [brən] (33.3 %)   93.3 %
/#drg/ → [dərg] (53.3 %) / [drəg] (40.0 %)   93.3 %

As demonstrated in (110), the majority of CCC sequences are adapted with an epenthetic vowel between C_1 and C_2C_3. A different epenthesis site is selected only in /sCC/ and /zCC/ clusters, where the vowel is inserted between C_1C_2 and C_3. In two cases, there is variation between $C_1VC_2C_3$ and $C_1C_2VC_3$ adaptations.

Given the data above, our main goal is to account for a general preference for $C_1VC_2C_3$ nativisation. Furthermore, it is necessary to explain the divergent behaviour of /sCC/ and /zCC/ clusters as well as variation in the epenthesis site in some clusters. A formal analysis of these patterns is provided in Section 3.2.

2.4 Other modifications

Other repair strategies, such as consonant deletion and segment change, were relatively infrequent and limited to a small number of experimental stimuli. The clusters with the highest rate of consonant elision are presented in (111).

(111) Consonant deletion in CCC clusters
  initial
/#pxl/   93.3 % ([pl] – 66.7 %, [pr] – 26.6 %)
/#tkf/   26.7 % [kf]
/#vbr/   26.7 % [br]
/#krf/   26.7 % ([kf] – 20 %, [kr] – 6.7 %)
/#sxl/   20 % ([sl] – 13.3 %, [fl] 6.7 %)
  final
/xtr#/   86.7 % ([θt] – 33.3 %, [ft] – 26.7 %, [xt] – 26.7 %)
/stf#/   53.3 % [st]

The data in (111) demonstrate that consonant deletion is most frequent in the /#pxl/ and /xtr#/ clusters, where it constitutes over 85 % of the responses. In the former sequence, the sound undergoing elision is /x/, whereas in the latter it is the final segment, i.e. /r/. The final consonant is also removed in /stf#/ in 53.3 % of cases. In the remaining clusters, the rate of the modification in question is relatively low.

The clusters with the highest rate of segment change are provided in (112).

(112) <u>Segment change in CCC clusters</u>
initial
/#sxl/   73.3 % [sfl]
/#pʂ͡ʈʂ/   33.3 % ([psʧ] – 20 %, [pʃt] – 13.3 %)
/#vbr/   26.6 % ([fbr] – 13.3 %, [fpr] – 13.3 %)
/#zgɲ/   26.6 % ([skn] – 13.3 %, [zgn] – 13.3 %)
/#zmɲ/   26.6 % ([smn] – 13.3 %, [zmj] – 13.3 %)
final
/jst͡s#/   80 % [jst]

As demonstrated in (112), segment change is the most frequent repair strategy in the /jst͡s#/ and /#sxl/ clusters. In the former sequence, the dental affricate /t͡s/ is realised as the coronal plosive [t], whereas in the latter the voiceless velar fricative /x/ is adapted as the labio-dental fricative [f]. In the remaining clusters, the repair under discussion is relatively infrequent. A formal account of both consonant deletion and segment change is provided in Section 3.3.

3 Analysis and discussion

This Section is devoted to a formal analysis of the experimental data on the adaptation of CCC clusters. We start with a brief account of targetlike reproduction in 3.1. The following Sections focus on vowel epenthesis (3.2) and other modifications (3.3) respectively. Finally, in 3.4 we conclude with a general discussion of the implications that our results carry for a theory of loanword adaptation.

3.1 Targetlike reproduction

The cases of targetlike reproduction of CCC clusters can be accounted for in the same manner as faithful imitation of CC sequences. The items in question might be interpreted as belonging to the peripheral stratum of the lexicon, where SONORITY is deactivated. This is achieved through promotion of FAITH with respect to markedness constraints. For convenience, we repeat the relevant rankings in (113).

(113) Core vs. periphery constraint rankings
Core stratum (native vocabulary)
SONORITY >> FAITH (MAX-IO, DEP-IO) >> ONS, *CODA, *COMPLEX
Peripheral stratum (unassimilated loanwords)
FAITH (MAX-IO, DEP-IO) >> SONORITY >> ONS, *CODA, *COMPLEX

At the peripheral stratum, faithfulness to the input takes precedence over well-formedness in terms of sonority and the basic syllable structure. In consequence, foreign items enter the target language unadapted.

Tableau 22 demonstrates the targetlike reproduction of a Polish CCC cluster.

Tableau 22: Targetlike reproduction of /#vzl/ in wzlot /vzlɔt/ *'ascent'*

/vzlɔt/	MAX-IO	DEP-IO	SONORITY	ONS	*CODA	*COMPLEX
☞ vzlɔt			*		*	*
vəz.lɔt		*!			**	
vlɔt	*!				*	*
vzɔt	*!		*		*	*

The forms incurring some violation of faithfulness, whether MAX-IO or DEP-IO, are eliminated. As a result, the fully faithful candidate is selected as optimal in spite of its ill-formedness with respect to SONORITY, *CODA and *COMPLEX.

In conclusion, the cases of targetlike reproduction can be regarded as belonging to a peripheral stratum of the English lexicon, where certain well-formedness restrictions, such as SONORITY, are deactivated due to FAITH promotion.

3.2 Vowel epenthesis

With regard to vowel epenthesis in initial CCC clusters, there are several logically possible syllabifications with an epenthetic segment (in parentheses), as demonstrated in (114).

(114) Logically possible syllabifications of /$C_1C_2C_3$VC/ with an epenthetic vowel
a) /#$C_1C_2C_3$VC#/ → [(V)$C_1C_2.C_3$VC]
b) /#$C_1C_2C_3$VC#/ → [(V)$C_1.C_2C_3$VC]
c) /#$C_1C_2C_3$VC#/ → [C_1(V)C_2C_3.VC]
d) /#$C_1C_2C_3$VC#/ → [C_1(V).C_2C_3VC]
e) /#$C_1C_2C_3$VC#/ → [C_1(V)$C_2.C_3$VC]
f) /#$C_1C_2C_3$VC#/ → [C_1C_2(V)C_3.VC]
g) /#$C_1C_2C_3$VC#/ → [C_1C_2(V).C_3VC]

175

The first possibility is to insert a vowel before a CCC sequence and either syllabify C_1C_2 as the coda of the initial syllable and C_3 as the onset of the following syllable (114a) or C_1 as the coda of the first syllable and C_2C_3 as the onset of the following syllable (114b). It should be noted that such syllabifications can be selected only if C_1C_2 constitutes a well-formed coda and C_2C_3 a well-formed onset. Another option is to insert an epenthetic vowel between C_1 and C_2C_3. In such a case C_2C_3 may be syllabified as the coda of the initial syllable (114c) (only if it constitutes a well-formed coda), as the onset of the following syllable (114d) (only if it constitutes a well-formed onset) or it may be split between the coda of the initial syllable and the onset of the following syllable (114e). Finally, if C_1C_2 is a permissible onset, an epenthetic vowel may be inserted between C_1C_2 and C_3. If this is the case, C_3 may be syllabified as the coda of the initial syllable (114f) or as the onset of the following syllable (114g).

Tableau 23 presents an evaluation of all logically possible adaptations of a CCC consonant cluster with an epenthetic vowel carried out in terms of the universal syllable well-formedness constraints.

Tableau 23: Evaluation of logically possible syllabifications of /$C_1C_2C_3VC$/ with vowel epenthesis

/$C_1C_2C_3VC$/	*COMPLEX	ONS	*CODA
(V)C_1C_2.C_3VC	*	*	***
(V)C_1.C_2C_3VC	*	*	**
C_1(V)C_2C_3.VC	*	*	***
☞ C_1(V).C_2C_3VC	*		*
☞ C_1(V)C_2.C_3VC			**
C_1C_2(V)C_3.VC	*	*	**
☞ C_1C_2(V).C_3VC	*		*

As demonstrated in Tableau 23, the optimal syllabifications of /$C_1C_2C_3VC$/ are [C_1(V).C_2C_3VC], [C_1(V)C_2.C_3VC] and [C_1C_2(V).C_3VC] as they incur only two violations each. Given this, we should expect native speakers of English to adapt CCC consonant clusters in /$C_1C_2C_3VC$/ words as [C_1(V).C_2C_3VC], [C_1(V) C_2.C_3VC] and/or [C_1C_2(V).C_3VC], depending on whether or not C_1C_2 and C_2C_3 constitute well-formed onsets. If C_1C_2 is not permitted, then the adaptation with an epenthetic vowel inserted after C_1 should be selected as optimal, i.e. either [C_1(V).C_2C_3VC] or [C_1(V)C_2.C_3VC], depending on the well-formedness of C_2C_3 as an onset sequence. On the other hand, if C_1C_2 is allowed, then we should expect some variation between the adaptations with an epenthetic vowel inserted after C_1 and after C_2, unless other factors intervene.

First of all, let us examine the sequences in which C_1C_2 is prohibited as an onset and thus the $[C_1C_2(V).C_3VC]$ adaptation is ruled out by higher-ranked sonority constraints. These clusters should be predominantly adapted with an epenthetic vowel inserted between C_1 and C_2C_3. The syllabification of the C_2C_3 sequence will be determined by other factors. Thus, if C_2C_3 constitutes a well-formed onset, it may either be syllabified as $[C_1(V).C_2C_3VC]$ or as $[C_1(V)C_2.C_3VC]$, unless other constraints come into play. On the other hand, if C_2C_3 is not a permissible onset, only the $[C_1VC_2.C_3VC]$ syllabification is possible.

Out of 17 clusters in which vowel epenthesis is the predominant repair strategy, C_1C_2 is an ill-formed English onset in 13 cases, as evidenced in (115).

(115) Vowel epenthesis in CCC clusters where C_1C_2 is an ill-formed English onset

/#mgl/	→ [məgl]	100.0 %	/#vzl/	→ [vəzl]	66.7 %
/#mʧ̑ɕ/	→ [məsʧ̑]	93.3 %	/#zmɲ/	→ [zmən]	66.7 %
/#mgɲ/	→ [məgn]	93.3 %	/#zgɲ/	→ [zgən]	66.7 %
/#gʐm/	→ [gəʒm]	86.7 %	/#pʂʧ̑ʂ/	→ [pəsʧ̑]	53.3 %
/#mdw/	→ [mədw]	80.0 %	/#tkn/	→ [təkn]	53.3 %
/#bzd/	→ [bəzd]	73.3 %	/#tkʃ/	→ [təkʃ]	46.7 %
/#vzg/	→ [vəzg]	73.3 %			

The data in (115) demonstrate that the vast majority of CCC clusters in which C_1C_2 is not a well-formed onset sequence are adapted with an epenthetic vowel inserted between C_1 and C_2C_3. The syllabification of C_2C_3 is determined by whether or not this sequence constitutes a well-formed onset. Thus, if this is the case, as in /#mgl/ and /#mdw/, C_2C_3 is syllabified as the onset of the second syllable, as shown in Tableau 24. The constraint ranking in this tableau is identical to the one accounting for vowel epenthesis in CC clusters. However, for CCC sequences it is necessary to take into account an additional constraint, namely SCL, in order to obtain the desired outcome. This constraint is formulated in (116) (Gouskova 2001).

(8) SCL constraint
SCL: Sonority must not rise across a syllable boundary.

Tableau 24 demonstrates vowel epenthesis in /#mgl/ in *mglisty* /mglistɨ/ 'foggy.'

Tableau 24: Vowel epenthesis in /#mgl/ in mglisty /mglistɨ/ 'foggy'

/mglistɨ/	SONORITY	MAX-IO	DEP-IO	*COMPLEX	*CODA	ONS	SCL
mgli.stɪ	*!			**			
mgi.stɪ	*!	*		**			
gli.stɪ		*!		**			
əm.gli.stɪ			*	**	*!	*	
əmg.li.stɪ			*	**	*!*	*	*
mgə.li.stɪ	*!		*	**	*		
məg.li.stɪ			*	*	*		*!
☞ mə.gli.stɪ			*	**			

The choice between [mə.gli.stɪ] and [məg.li.stɪ] is determined by the SCL constraint in favour of the former candidate. Both forms fail to satisfy DEP-IO and incur two violations of the syllable markedness constraints, but [mə.gli.stɪ] is preferred to [məg.li.stɪ] because it involves a steep sonority fall between the final segment of the initial syllable and the initial segment of the second syllable.

On the other hand, if C_2C_3 cannot be syllabified as an onset sequence due to a SONORITY violation, C_2 surfaces in the coda of the initial syllable and C_3 in the onset of the second syllable. This is the case with the remaining clusters in (115), except for /z/-initial clusters, i.e. /#zmɲ/ and /#zgɲ/.

In Tableau 25 an evaluation of the input /mgɲɛɲɛ/ is demonstrated as an example of an adaptation of a CCC sequence where C_2C_3 is split between the heterosyllabic coda and onset in order to avoid a SONORITY violation.

Tableau 25: Vowel epenthesis in /#mgɲ/ in mgnienie /mgɲɛɲɛ/ 'a blink'

/mgɲɛɲɛ/	SONORITY	MAX-IO	DEP-IO	*COMPLEX	*CODA	ONS	SCL
mgne.ne	*!			*			
mge.ne	*!	*		*			
gne.ne	*!	*		*			
əm.gne.ne	*!		*	*	*	*	
əmg.ne.ne			*	*	*!*	*	*
mgə.ne.ne	*!		*	*			
☞ məg.ne.ne			*		*		*
mə.gne.ne	*!		*	*			

All candidate forms in Tableau 25, except for [əmg.ne.ne] and [məg.ne.ne] fail to satisfy SONORITY as neither [mg] nor [gn] is a permitted onset sequence. The latter emerges as the optimal realisation of the input because it is better formed in terms of syllable structure.

The only clusters in (115) which do not conform to the pattern of the $[C_1(V) C_2 C_3]$ adaptation are /z/-initial sequences, i.e. /#zmɲ/ and /#zgɲ/. In these cases, an epenthetic vowel is inserted between $C_1 C_2$ and C_3 in spite of the fact that $C_1 C_2$ is not an attested onset sequence in English. A question naturally arises as to why the $[C_1 C_2(V)C_3]$ adaptation is preferred to $[C_1(V)C_2 C_3]$. The most likely explanation is that native speakers of English treat /z/-initial clusters in an analogous way to /s/-initial clusters, such as /#sm/ or /#sk/. In other words, if /#sC/ sequences do not violate SONORITY due to /s/ being a syllable appendix, or for some other reason, by analogy, neither do /#zC/ clusters.

An evaluation of the input /#zgɲ/ is presented in Tableau 26.

Tableau 26: Vowel epenthesis in /#zgɲ/ in zgnić /zgɲiʧ/ 'to rot'

/zgɲiʧ/	SONORITY	MAX-IO	DEP-IO	*COMPLEX	*CODA	ONS	SCL
zgɲiʧ	*!			*	*		
zgiʧ		*!		*	*		
gɲiʧ	*!	*		*	*		
əz.gɲiʧ	*!		*	*	**	*	
əzg.ɲiʧ			*	*	**!*	*	*
☞ zgə.ɲiʧ			*	*	*		
zə.gɲiʧ	*!		*	*	*		
zəg.ɲiʧ			*		**		*!

As demonstrated in Tableau 26, if [zg] is not ruled out by SONORITY as an onset sequence, then the selection between [zgə.ɲiʧ] and [zəg.ɲiʧ] depends crucially on the SCL constraint. Since the former candidate satisfies this requirement, as opposed to the latter, it is chosen as the optimal form.

It should be noted that there is an exception in the experimental data to the pattern of adaptation predicted in Tableau 23. This is the initial cluster /#vbr/ in *wbrew* [vbref] 'against'. The responses for this sequence are presented in (117).

(117) The responses for /#vbr/ in *wbrew* [vbref] 'against'

targetlike	20.0 %	deletion	26.7 % [br]
epenthesis	26.7 % [vəbr]	segment change	26.7 % [fbr] / [fpr]

The figures in (117) indicate that there is no clearly established repair strategy for the sequence /#vbr/, with vowel epenthesis, consonant deletion and segment change occurring with the same frequency. Since /vb/ cannot be syllabified as an onset cluster, an epenthetic vowel is inserted between C_1 and C_2C_3, in accordance with the pattern established in Tableau 23. The most puzzling phenomenon in the case of /vbr/ adaptation is an increased rate of C_1 deletion. In similar clusters in (115), this repair is virtually unattested, with the exception of the sequence /#tkf/, where /t/ is omitted in 26.7 % of responses. In voiced clusters, consisting of both two and three elements, consonant elision does not occur. A possible explanation for a higher incidence of /v/ deletion in /#vbr/ is the perceptual similarity between the Polish word *wbrew* [vbref] and English *breath* [breθ]. In other words, some participants might have interpreted the stimulus [vbref] as not different in any significant way from English *breath*. This interpretation becomes even more likely in light of the fact that in those responses where deletion took place the final consonant was [θ] rather than [f]. Other participants either managed to reproduce /#vbr/ faithfully or devoiced C_1 or C_2. The variation under discussion may also be attributed to the differences in the ranking of faithfulness constraints assumed by the participants (see Chapter 4, Section 3.4.2 for a discussion of a similar case).

Let us now examine the adaptation of CCC clusters in which the C_1C_2 sequence constitutes a permissible English onset. In these cases, both the $[C_1C_2(V).C_3]$ and $[C_1(V).C_2C_3]$ / $[C_1(V)C_2.C_3]$ nativisations are equally well-formed in terms of the universal syllable structure constraints. As a result, some variation between these adaptations should be expected, unless other factors come into play. Out of 17 clusters with vowel epenthesis as the predominant repair strategy, C_1C_2 is a permitted English onset in 4 cases, as shown in (118).

(118) CCC clusters in which C_1C_2 is a well-formed English onset

/#brn/	→	[bərn] (60.0 %) / [brən] (33.3 %)	93.3 %
/#drg/	→	[dərg] (53.3 %) / [drəg] (40.0 %)	93.3 %
/#skn/	→	[skən]	66.7 %
/#smr/	→	[smər]	60.0 %

The data in (118) demonstrate that variation in the epenthesis site is found in the case of /#brn/ and /#drg/, but not in the case of /#skn/ and /#smr/. It should also be noted that in the nativisation of the former clusters, /r/ is preserved despite the fact that the outputs violate a core phonological constraint prohibiting this segment in coda position in British English. These cases may be interpreted as instances of partial nativisation where due to FAITH promotion, the constraint against the rhotic in the coda is deactivated. In other words, faithfulness to the input in this respect takes precedence over the satisfaction of the relevant structural constraint. Nevertheless, the outputs are not fully faithful to the source forms as they contain epenthetic vowels which break up illicit sequences of consonants. Thus, although FAITH is elevated over the constraint against the rhotic in the coda, it is still dominated by SONORITY. The effect is the partial adaptation of /#brn/ and /#drg/ clusters.

The variation in the nativisation of these sequences is predicted in Tableau 23. In accordance with this prediction, both the $[C_1C_2(V).C_3]$ and $[C_1(V)C_2.C_3]$ adaptations are attested ($[C_1(V).C_2C_3]$ is ruled out by SONORITY). This is illustrated in Tableau 27.

Tableau 27: Vowel epenthesis in /#drg/ in drgać /drgaʨ/ 'to twitch'

/drgaʨ/	SONORITY	MAX-IO	DEP-IO	*COMPLEX	*CODA	ONS	SCL
drgaʨ	*!			*	*		
draʨ		*!		*	*		
rgaʨ	*!		*	*	*		
əd.rgaʧ	*!		*	*	**	*	*
ədr.gaʧ	*!		*	*	***	*	
☞ drə.gaʧ			*	*	*		
də.rgaʧ	*!		*	*	*		
☞ dər.gaʧ			*		**		

In Tableau 27 two optimal candidates are selected, i.e. [drə.gaʧ] and [dər.gaʧ], each incurring three violation marks, one for DEP-IO and two for syllable structure constraints. Since both forms satisfy the SCL, this constraint cannot choose between them and, as a result, both adaptations are attested.

The situation is different with the /#skn/ and /#smr/ clusters, where no variation in the epenthesis site is found. In these forms, an epenthetic vowel is inserted only between C_1C_2 and C_3. Tableau 23 predicts that $[C_1(V).C_2C_3]$ and $[C_1(V) C_2.C_3]$ are equally well-formed with respect to the universal syllable structure constraints, yet these adaptations are not found in the case of /#skn/ and /#smr/. As demonstrated in Tableau 28, this is because they violate other constraints.

Tableau 28: Vowel epenthesis in /#skn/ in sknera /sknɛra/ '*a miser*'

/sknɛra/	SONORITY	MAX-IO	DEP-IO	*COMPLEX	*CODA	ONS	SCL
sknɛ.ra	*!			*			
skɛ.ra		*!		*			
snɛ.ra		*!		*			
əs.knɛ.ra	*!		*	*	*	*	
əsk.nɛ.ra			*	*	*!*	*	*
☞ skə.nɛ.ra			*	*			
skən.ɛ.ra			*	*	*!	*	*
sə.knɛ.ra	*!		*	*			
sək.nɛ.ra			*		*		*!

The $[C_1(V).C_2C_3]$ adaptation, i.e. [sə.knɛ.ra], is eliminated by the top-ranked SONORITY because [kn] cannot be syllabified as an onset sequence. On the other hand, the $[C_1(V)C_2.C_3]$ parse, i.e. [sək.nɛ.ra] is suboptimal due to an SCL violation. As a result, the $[C_1C_2(V).C_3]$ candidate, i.e. [skə.nɛ.ra], is selected as the optimal form.

To sum up, we have demonstrated that the majority of vowel epenthesis cases result from an application of the core English ranking of phonological constraints. In general, the patterns of vowel insertion in the adaptation of both CC and CCC clusters can be predicted on the basis of the constraint hierarchy that holds in core English phonology.

3.3 Other modifications

As demonstrated in Section 2.4, other repair strategies, such as consonant deletion and segment change, are relatively infrequent and limited to a small number of CCC sequences.

As far as the former modification is concerned, the only clusters with a high rate of segment loss include /#pxl/, /xtr#/ and /stf#/. The general avoidance of elision is a direct reflection of the MAX-IO >> DEP-IO hierarchy. Under this ranking, vowel epenthesis is always preferred to consonant deletion as a repair strategy. As a result, the hierarchy of phonological constraints which produces the correct results for the majority of the CCC data fails to account for the segment loss cases in the same way as it fails to do so for /x/ elision in CC clusters.

Given the situation above, we would like to argue that in order to account for deletion in some CCC sequences it might be necessary to take perceptual factors into consideration. In the case of /x/ elision in /#pxl/, a possible explanation is that the participants interpret the [px] sequence as strongly aspirated [p] due to the voicelessness of [x] and, as a result, realise a sequence of three consonants as two segments, i.e. [pl]. It should be noted that when /x/ is found in a different context, e.g. in /#sxl/ or /xtr#/, it is preserved and adapted in the majority of cases rather than deleted. This suggests that certain phonological environments facilitate /x/ misperception, or render this segment perceptually non-salient. This is in line with the results of online adaptation of Ukrainian CC clusters by native speakers of English reported by Radomski and Sydorenko (2016), where /x/ is found to undergo elision much more frequently when the other consonant in a cluster is voiceless than when it is voiced. Obviously, further experimental research is necessary to verify the validity of this proposal.

As regards consonant deletion in /xtr#/ and /stf#/, it is invariably the final segment that is removed. The consonants under discussion might be especially prone to elision for two reasons, namely due to their being voiceless (in Polish /r/ is completely devoiced word-finally after a voiceless consonant) and cluster-peripheral at the same time.

The clusters with the highest rate of segment change include /jst͡s#/ and /#sxl/. In the former, the dental affricate /t͡s/ is realised as the coronal plosive [t] in accordance with the pattern observed in the adaptation of affricates in CC sequences. What seems puzzling is rendering /#sxl/ mostly as [sfl], a cluster unattested in English, given the availability of a legal, though rare, English sequence [skl] with C_2 having the same place of articulation as Polish [x]. A possible explanation is that the former output is perceptually more similar to the input than the latter. If this were the case, then it would be necessary to postulate some output-output faithfulness constraint, which would eliminate [skl] as an excessive departure from the input in terms of perceptual similarity. Again, in order to confirm the validity of such a proposal, it is necessary to carry out an independent study eliciting perceptual similarity judgements.

4 Adaptation of consonant clusters in established vs. online loans

This Section is devoted to a comparison of the nativisation patterns observed in our experimental data with those attested in established loanwords in English.[41] In particular, our aim is to find out whether there is convergence between the

---

41 Examples of the latter have been taken from Wells (2008) and Merriam-Webster.com online dictionary.

repair strategies used in both types of borrowings in the adaptation of non-native consonant clusters as well as to draw theoretical conclusions concerning the stratification of loanwords in English. It should be noted that the observations made in this Section are preliminary in character as a detailed analysis of established loans is beyond the scope of the present monograph.

As regards online adaptations, it has been shown that the predominant nativisation strategies are those which preserve the source phonological material, i.e. targetlike reproduction, vowel epenthesis and segment change. As demonstrated in Chapters 4 and 5, they account for 96.49 % and 82.5 % of all responses for CC and CCC clusters respectively (in CCC sequences, vowel epenthesis co-occurs with consonant elision in further 4.2 % of cases). Consonant deletion occurs marginally, which indicates that the removal of phonological content is strongly avoided.

However, an examination of the nativisation of consonant clusters in established loanwords reveals that segment loss is by no means infrequent, especially in initial CC sequences, as evidenced in (119).

(119) Consonant deletion in established loanwords in English

initial CC

/bd/ → [d]	*bdellium*
/dn/ → [n]	*Dnepropetrovsk, Dniester, Dneper* (optionally [dn])
/ɦr/ → [r]	*hryvna*
/kn/ → [n]	*Knorr, knackwurst*
/ks/ → [z]	*Xerox, Xerxes*
/mn/ → [n]	*mnemonic, Mnemosyne*
/pf/ → [f]	*pfennig, Pfeiffer, Pfizer*
/pn/ → [n]	*pneumonia, pneumatic*
/ps/ → [s]	*psalm, pseudonym, psychic, psychology*
/pt/ → [t]	*pterodactyl, pterosaur*

The data in (119) show that initial CC consonant clusters in numerous loans from various languages have been adapted to the native English phonology through consonant deletion rather than some repair strategy which preserves the phonological content. The segment which is invariably removed is C_1, most probably because of its marginal position in the syllable or the impossibility of incorporating it into the onset of the initial syllable due to sonority restrictions.

On the other hand, vowel epenthesis occurs less frequently than consonant elision and seems to be restricted to the adaptation of initial nasal + obstruent clusters and final obstruent + /ʁ/ sequences in loans from French. Several representative examples are presented in (120).

184

(120) Vowel epenthesis in established loanwords in English[42]

initial CC

/mb/ → [əmb]   *Mbabane, Mbeki, mbaqanga*
/mp/ → [əmp]   *Mpumalanga*
/nd/ → [ənd]   *Ndola, Ndebele*
/ŋk/ → [əŋk]   *Nkomo*

final CC

/vʁ/ → [vrə][42]   *Havre, joie de vivre, oeuvre, savoir-vivre, chef d'oeuvre, Sevres*
/tʁ/ → [trə]   *raison d'être, Montmartre*
/dʁ/ → [drə]   *double entendre*
/pʁ/ → [prə]   *Ypres*

initial CCC

/kʃt/ → [gəʃt]   *Gstaad*
/ŋkr/ → [əŋkr]   *Nkrumah*
/vlt/ → [vəlt]   *Vltava*

final CCC

/ŋgr/ → [ŋgrə]   *bhangra*

An epenthetic vowel is inserted before initial nasal + obstruent sequences and after final obstruent + /ʁ/ sequences. The former pattern is in accordance with a cross-linguistic tendency for initial falling sonority clusters to be repaired by prothesis rather than anaptyxis (e.g. Gouskova 2001). The latter can be viewed as spelling-based adaptations. Instances of other consonant sequences nativised through vowel epenthesis are rare.

In some cases, there is variation between vowel insertion, consonant deletion and/or targetlike reproduction, as demonstrated in (121).

(121) Variation in established loanwords in English

initial CC

/gd/ → [gəd] / [d]   *Gdańsk*
/gn/ → [gən] / [n]   *gneiss*
/kn/ → [kn] / [kən]   *Knesset*
/pn/ → [pn] / [pən] / [n]   *Phnom Penh*
/pt/ → [pt] / [pət] / [t]   *Ptah*

initial CCC

/kʁw/ → [krw] / [kw] / [kr]   *croissant, Croix*

The variation observed in items in (121) indicates that no single fixed repair strategy has been established for them yet.

---

42 Note an exception: *au poivre* [əʊ 'pwɑːv].

Furthermore, some loanwords have been adapted by means of segment change. These include mainly borrowings from German with initial /ʃC/ or /ʃCʁ/ clusters, exemplified in (122).

(122) Segment change in established loanwords in English
    initial CC

/ʃk/ → [sk]	*Skoda* (optionally [ʃk])
/ʃt/ → [st]	*Steiner, stoss* (optionally [ʃt]), *Stuka, Stein, Stalag*
/ʃv/ → [ʃw]	*Schwann, Schwartz, Schwartzenegger, Schwartzschild, Schwarzkopf, Schwarzwald, Schweitzer* (optionally [ʃv] in *Schwartz, Schwarzkopf, Schwarzwald* and *Schweitzer*)
/sr/ → [ʃr]	*Sri Lanka* (optionally [sr])
/sv/ → [sw]	*Swedenborg*
/tsv/ → [zw]	*Zwingli, zwieback*

    final CC

/xt/ → [kt]	*Maastricht* (optionally [xt])

    initial CCC

/ʃpʁ/ → [spr]	*Springer, spritzer*
/ʃtʁ/ → [str]	*Strauss, strudel, Strasburg*

In the majority of cases the segment modified in initial /ʃC/ and /ʃCʁ/ sequences is /ʃ/, which is realised as [s] (additionally, the quality of the rhotic changes in the nativisation of the latter structures, i.e. [ʁ] is substituted with [r]). This modification results in the formation of legal English /sC/ and /sCr/ clusters and may be due to various factors such as phonological or/and phonetic similarity between [ʃ] and [s] or the influence of orthography. Nonetheless, it should be noted that in some loanwords [ʃ] is tolerated as C_1 giving rise to peripheral clusters such as those examined in Chapter 3 (Section 2). Furthermore, the adaptation of /ʃv/ and /sv/ as [ʃw] and [sw] respectively can be viewed as based on the English grapheme-to-phoneme correspondence rule according to which <w> is pronounced as [w].

Finally, certain foreign consonant sequences have been borrowed into English without alteration. We have seen some instances of importation of initial CC clusters in Chapter 3 (Section 2). Below we provide representative cases of non-adaptation of final CCC sequences.

(123) Importation in established loanwords in English
    final CCC

/fsk/	*Dnepropetrovsk, Brest-Litovsk, Petropavlovsk, Sverdlovsk*
/lsk/	*Arkhangelsk*
/msk/	*Omsk, Tomsk*
/nsk/	*Minsk*
/psk/	*Vitebsk*

The examples in (123) are Russian place names with the final /Csk/ clusters. The sequences in question are borrowed without modification, which indicates that they present no difficulty to the native speakers of English. This is corroborated by the high percentage of targetlike responses for the /psk/ cluster in our online adaptation experiment.

A comparison of the nativisation strategies observed in online adaptations and established loanwords reveals several differences. First of all, consonant deletion is considerably more frequent in the latter type of borrowings. On the other hand, in online loans the source phonological material is preserved in the overwhelming majority of cases, with consonant elision being very rare, except for a handful of clusters, such as those containing the voiceless velar fricative /x/. Secondly, vowel epenthesis is not the most frequent repair strategy in established loans in contrast to online adaptations. In the former, the proportion between vowel insertion, consonant deletion and segment change is significantly more balanced than in the latter, where vowel epenthesis is clearly predominant. Finally, targetlike reproduction, or importation, of foreign phonotactic structures is more common in online adaptations than in established borrowings.

The lack of a clearly predominant repair strategy in some established loanwords can be attributed to the fact that a larger number of factors are potentially involved in determining their final phonological shape than in the case of online loans. For example, some established borrowings are evidently influenced by the spelling (e.g. /sv/ → [sw] in *Swedenborg*), which plays no role in online adaptations elicited in a repetition task in which no written input is available to the adapters. Furthermore, as pointed out by Szpyra-Kozłowska (2015) (after Bartmińska and Bartmiński 1997), the influence of orthography is particularly powerful in the case of proper names as it facilitates their faithful reproduction and, consequently, the preservation of their identity. Additionally, temporal factors may further complicate the nativisation patterns found in established loans. In general, it can be assumed that the longer a particular foreign item functions in the target language, the more likely it is to undergo various modifications to conform to the native patterns. Variation observed in established loans also stems from the fact that different adapters have different knowledge of foreign languages, as demonstrated by the following quotes from Wells (2008: xxix),

(124) <u>Knowledge of foreign languages in the adaptation of established loans</u>

"Names from foreign languages can either be pronounced in a way that imitates the foreign language or be integrated into the English sound system. Although this applies mainly to personal and geographical names, to some extent it applies to ordinary words too."

"(…) those speakers of English who have some knowledge of the foreign language may well pronounce such words or names in a way that imitates the phonetics of the foreign language, or occupies some half-way stage between the foreign-language pronunciation and the anglicization."

"Educated speakers of BrE usually know some French. So do Canadians. They will therefore try to pronounce French names in a French way."

Thus, proficiency in a foreign language facilitates faithful reproduction of non-native structures.

On the whole, established borrowings are more closely integrated into the core phonological system of English than online ones as evidenced by a lower rate of importation for the former. Given the assumption that online adaptations represent an initial stage of loan nativisation, it might be argued that at this stage the maximally faithful rendering of a foreign item takes precedence over ensuring its conformity to the surface generalisations of the recipient language. In optimality-theoretic terms, it means that initially faithfulness constraints dominate markedness constraints. This explains a relatively high percentage of targetlike reproduction cases in online adaptations in comparison with established loanwords. Over time, as foreign items become established borrowings, they usually exhibit an increasing degree of nativisation until they fully conform to the core phonology of the target language and are no longer recognised by native speakers as words of foreign origin. To put it differently, at the initial stage of adaptation a loanword belongs to the peripheral stratum of native phonology, where certain markedness constraints are deactivated due to the promotion of faithfulness constraints. The process whereby a borrowing becomes established can be interpreted as a gradual movement from the periphery to the core, where markedness takes priority over faithfulness. During this kind of transition, different surface forms of a loanword may coexist, including an unadapted version which violates core phonological generalisations and thus lies in the periphery as well as a fully nativised version which conforms to all core constraints. Cases of partial nativisation are also possible. Some examples of established loanwords with consonant clusters can be interpreted as undergoing the process in question, as evidenced by variation between importation and complete nativisation of an offending sequence (125).

(125) Established loanwords in the process of periphery to core transition
initial CC

/kn/ → [kn] / [kən]	*Knesset*
/pn/ → [pn] / [pən] / [n]	*Phnom Penh*
/pt/ → [pt] / [pət] / [t]	*Ptah*
/sr/ → [sr] / [ʃr]	*Sri Lanka*
/ʃp/ → [ʃp] / [sp]	*spiel*
/ʃt/ → [ʃt] / [st]	*stoss*
/ʃk/ → [ʃk] / [sk]	*Skoda*

final CC

/xt/ → [xt] / [kt]	*Maastricht*

initial CCC

/kʁw/ → [krw] / [kw] / [kr]	*croissant, Croix*

The coexistence of foreign and nativised consonant clusters in the items in (125) indicates that the process of the periphery to core transition is underway in their case. This approach predicts that over time the forms conforming to the core phonology will prevail over the ones with importation.[43]

However, not all established loanwords exhibit variation between targetlike reproduction and full nativisation. Apart from the cases in (125), two more groups of borrowings can be distinguished. On the one hand, there are words of foreign origin in which consonant clusters are invariably repaired in some way and importation is not attested. Representative examples are provided in (126).

(126) Established loanwords with no consonant cluster importation
a)	voiced plosive + voiced plosive (e.g. *bdellium, Gdańsk*)	(sonority plateau)
b)	nasal + plosive (e.g. *Mbabane, Ndola, Nkomo*)	(sonority reversal)
c)	nasal + nasal (e.g. *mnemonic, Mnemosyne*)	(sonority plateau)
d)	voiceless plosive + voiceless fricative (e.g. *psalm, pfennig*)	(small sonority rise)

---

43 The opposite may also happen in some cases, i.e. a nativised form may be replaced with a foreign one. For example, Scottish *loch* used to be pronounced mostly as [lɒk], with the [x] → [k] substitution. According to Wells (2008), the version with the velar fricative [x], i.e. [lɒx], is more common now. This change is probably due to an increasing popularity of Scottish English and the word *loch* in particular.

As evidenced in (126), importation is not found in the case of initial consonant sequences which violate SONORITY, i.e. the SSP (126a, b, c) or the MSD (126d). These cases might be interpreted in two ways. According to the first interpretation (Hypothesis A), the lack of importation indicates that their movement from the periphery to the core has been completed. On the other hand, it can be argued that they never belonged to the periphery and were fully nativised, i.e. included into the core, at the moment of their introduction into the target language (Hypothesis B). Let us now examine how the results of our experiments shed light on these issues.

There were two initial clusters of voiced plosives in the experimental stimuli, namely /db/ and /gb/. The rates of their accurate reproduction were 40 % and 13.3 % respectively, which indicates that the former sequence turned out to present relatively less difficulty than the latter. Thus, the results for /gb/ provide support for Hypothesis B as this sequence undergoes some repair in the vast majority of cases as opposed to /db/, where the proportion of importation to substitution is more balanced. It seems therefore that whether Hypothesis A or B is more likely depends on the relative markedness of C_1 and/or C_2's place of articulation (see Chapter 4, Section 3.2 for a discussion of markedness as a factor which exerts influence on the ease of faithful reproduction of a cluster). In general, clusters composed of segments with marked place feature values, e.g. dorsals, are more difficult to reproduce faithfully and thus more likely to undergo repair in nativisation than those with unmarked specifications, e.g. coronals, all else being equal.

As regards the initial nasal + plosive clusters, no such sequences were employed in the experiment as they are not found in Polish. However, there were some other sonorant + obstruent clusters, such as nasal + fricative (e.g. /mʂ/) or glide + plosive (e.g. /wb/), which constitute sonority reversals. The average rate of targetlike reproduction for these sequences was very low (5.4 %). This suggests that Hypothesis B is more likely than Hypothesis A in cases similar to (126b), i.e. sonority reversals hardly ever enter the periphery and are immediately adapted to satisfy core requirements.

With regard to the initial nasal + nasal clusters, the experimental data do not offer a clear answer which hypothesis is more plausible. While the sequence /mn/ is reproduced faithfully in 33.3 % of cases, the cluster /mɲ/ is always adapted, most probably because the palatal nasal /ɲ/ is not part of the English consonant inventory.

Finally, the responses for the voiceless plosive + voiceless fricative sequences provide support for Hypothesis A as they are easily imitated by the participants (/tʂ/ – 73.3 %, /tf/ – 86.7 %, /pʂ/ – 86.7 %). In this light, the forms in (126d) might be regarded as the final result of the periphery to core transition.

Another group of loanwords in which variation is not attested includes items with importation of foreign phonotactic patterns without nativisation. Selected examples are presented in (127).

(127) Established loanwords with no consonant cluster nativisation
   a) voiced fricative + approximant (e.g. [vl] in *Vladimir*, [vr] in *Wrocław*, [vw] in *voila*, [zl] in *złoty*)
   b) voiceless coronal fricative + consonant (e.g. [sf] in *sphere*, [sr] in *Srebrenica*, [sv] in *Svalbard*, [ʃv]/[ʃw] in *Schwartz*, [ʃl] in *schlep*, [ʃt] in *schtick*, [ʃm] in *schmaltz*, [ʃn] in *schnapps*)

As demonstrated in (127), no repair strategy takes place in borrowings with initial sequences of voiced fricative + approximant and voiceless coronal fricative + consonant. The former are all well-formed with respect to SONORITY, whereas among the latter only some sequences satisfy this constraint.

A possible interpretation of these cases is that they represent an initial stage of the periphery to core transition. On the one hand, the results of our experiment indicate that this might be the case with voiced fricative + approximant clusters, in which the variation between importation and nativisation has been found (the rates of targetlike reproduction: /zr/ – 40 %, /vl/ – 46.7 %, /zw/ – 46.7 %). On the other hand, since the majority of the items in question are proper names (e.g. *Vlad*, *Vladimir*, *Vladivostok*, *Wrocław*), the pressure to undergo nativisation may be counterbalanced by the influence of spelling which facilitates faithful reproduction.

As regards the voiceless coronal fricative + consonant clusters, they were almost invariably reproduced accurately, e.g. /ʂp/ – 100 %, /ɕp/ – 100 %, /ɕl/ – 100 % and /ɕɲ/ – 46.7 % (the rate of targetlike responses for /ɕɲ/ is considerably lower due to the presence of the palatal nasal). The experimental data thus confirm that sequences of this structure present little or no difficulty to native speakers of English and are readily admitted into the periphery. Some of them may undergo nativisation and become part of the core, e.g. /ʃt/ in *stoss* might be realised either as [ʃt] or [st]. Others, especially proper names, are more likely to remain in the periphery and retain their foreignness, e.g. [ʃm] in *Schmidt*.

To sum up, we have argued that there may be three main adaptation scenarios which account for the nativisation patterns found in established loans. According to the first one, at the initial stage of adaptation borrowings enter the periphery of native phonology, where some markedness constraints do not hold due to the promotion of faithfulness constraints. The process whereby a loanword becomes established has been interpreted as a gradual transition from the periphery to the core, where markedness is given priority over faithfulness. This is evidenced by loanwords in the case of which alternative forms with importation and nativisation coexist. In the second scenario, borrowings do not enter the periphery but are immediately adapted to satisfy core requirements. This is especially frequent in foreign items containing structures which gravely violate core constraints, e.g. sonority reversals in the onset. Finally, some borrowings may enter the periphery and remain there for an indefinite period of time. These include mainly forms with less severe violations of core requirements as well as proper names.

5 Theoretical implications and conclusions

This Chapter has reported on an online loanword adaptation experiment in which 15 native speakers of Standard Southern British English reproduced authentic Polish words with initial and final CCC consonant clusters not found in English. Our major goal has been to provide an adequate formal analysis of the experimental data as well as to confront it against the results examined in Chapter 4. Moreover, we have provided a comparison of the nativisation strategies applied in online versus established loans and analysed the major differences between them in terms of the core-periphery distinction.

A general overview of the results in Section 2.1 has demonstrated that the most frequent repair strategy is vowel epenthesis, followed by consonant deletion and segment change. The rate of targetlike reproduction is relatively low, with the exception of the final /psk/ and /nʂt/ clusters as well as the initial /sCC/ sequences. As regards vowel epenthesis, the majority of CCC sequences are adapted with an epenthetic vowel between C_1 and C_2C_3. A different epenthesis site is selected only in the /sCC/ and /zCC/ clusters, where the vowel is inserted between C_1C_2 and C_3. In two cases there is variation between $[C_1(V)C_2C_3]$ and $[C_1C_2(V)C_3]$ adaptations. Other repair strategies, such as consonant deletion and segment change, are relatively infrequent and limited to a small number of experimental stimuli.

In an OT analysis of the experimental data in Section 3 the targetlike reproduction cases have been interpreted as belonging to a peripheral stratum of the English lexicon, where certain structural constraints, such as SONORITY, are deactivated due to FAITH promotion. The application of the core English ranking of phonological constraints has allowed us to account for the majority of the vowel epenthesis cases. We have concluded that the patterns of vowel insertion in the adaptation of both CC and CCC clusters can be predicted on the basis of the constraint hierarchy that holds in the core English phonology. Finally, the instances of consonant deletion have turned out to be inconsistent with the ranking of production grammar constraints established for the items where vowel epenthesis takes place. A possible explanation is that perceptual factors must be invoked in order to account for these forms. However, independent perception research is necessary in order to verify the validity of this proposal.

As demonstrated in Chapters 4 and 5, the results of our experiments on online adaptation of Polish CC and CCC consonant clusters by native speakers of English lend support to the phonological approximation view to loan nativisation, according to which the process in question is mainly computed by the production grammar, with a relatively limited role of perception. Given the assumption that the phonology of English is not a fixed hierarchy of markedness and faithfulness constraints, but rather a partial ranking, where the latter are floating constraints, there is no need for a separate loanword phonology component.

The vast majority of modifications that foreign items undergo are consistent with the core English ranking of phonological constraints. However, there are some cases of non-conformity to the surface generalisations of English. These include the following:

1) instances of targetlike reproduction, or importation, where the source structures are not altered in spite of their ill-formedness with respect to the native phonological constraint ranking,

2) cases of partial adaptation, i.e. outputs which satisfy only a subset of core markedness constraints, as in the nativisation of the /#brn/ and /#drg/ clusters as [bərn] and [dərg] respectively, where SONORITY is satisfied but the constraint against the rhotics in the coda is violated,

3) the emergence of the unmarked cases, where foreign items conform to stricter structural requirements than those imposed by core phonology, as in the adaptation of /r/- and /w/-initial CC sequences, where /r/ and /w/ are syllabified into the syllable coda in accordance with the universal preference for sonorant coda segments.

The first two phenomena, i.e. targetlike reproduction and partial adaptation, result from FAITH promotion with respect to the base ranking which yields core native outputs. In the case of partial adaptation, although FAITH is elevated from its base position, it is still dominated by some markedness constraint(s). In consequence, the outputs comply with certain markedness requirements violating others at the same time. For instance, in the adaptation of the /#brn/ and /#drg/ clusters as [bərn] and [dərg], the constraint prohibiting the rhotic in the coda is deactivated, but the outputs still satisfy SONORITY. Targetlike reproduction is achieved through giving priority to FAITH over all markedness constraints. As argued by Davidson *et al.* (2004), FAITH promotion requires allocating greater cognitive resources to the processing of non-native inputs. The experimental task employed in our studies, i.e. repetition of foreign items, facilitates accurate reproduction as it "makes available ample cognitive resources" (p. 343). In this light, a relatively high percentage of targetlike responses in our results may be partly due to the adopted experimental design.

On the other hand, the emergence of the unmarked cases result from FAITH demotion with respect to the base ranking. In consequence, the outputs of adaptation satisfy more markedness constraints than native items. The cases under discussion may be argued to reflect default settings of Universal Grammar.

In addition, there is a handful of adaptations which are consistent with the surface generalisations of English, but fail to be produced by the core constraint ranking. These include consonant deletion cases, especially of the voiceless velar fricative /x/. In order to account for such forms, it might be necessary to take perceptual factors into consideration. On the one hand, consonant deletion may result from a segment non-perception or poor perception due to its low perceptual salience in certain contexts. On the other hand, clusters adapted by consonant deletion might be judged as perceptually more similar to the input than other potential outputs. This would be encoded in the form of output-output faithfulness constraints eliminating certain adaptations as excessive departures from the input. It has been pointed out that in order to confirm the validity of such proposals, it is necessary to carry out independent perception studies e.g. focusing on eliciting perceptual similarity judgements.

On the whole, the results of both experiments demonstrate that loanword phonology is mainly native phonology understood in accordance with the crucial assumption of the Extended Richness of the Base principle (Davidson et al. 2004) as a partial ranking with floating faithfulness constraints. Thus, our data provide evidence in favour of the phonological approximation view to loan nativisation. The role of perception is relatively limited, however, it may be responsible for some adaptations, especially when segments of low perceptual salience are found in the input.

A comparison of the nativisation strategies used in the adaptation of initial and final consonant clusters in online vs. established loans has revealed a number of differences between these two types of borrowings, such as a higher rate of consonant deletion as well as a lower rate of vowel epenthesis and targetlike reproduction in the latter category of items. Three main groups of established loanwords have been distinguished, namely those with variation between importation and full nativisation of a non-native cluster, those in which consonant sequences are invariably repaired in some way and those with importation of foreign phonotactic patterns without nativisation. Three major adaptation scenarios have been proposed for established loans. The first possibility is that initially foreign items enter the periphery of native phonology, where some markedness constraints are deactivated through the promotion of faithfulness constraints. The process in which a borrowing becomes established can be understood as a movement from the periphery to the core, where markedness takes precedence over faithfulness. The second option is that loanwords undergo full nativisation at the time of their introduction into the target language. Finally, foreign words may enter the periphery and remain there for an indefinite period of time.

Conclusion

Given a variety of theoretical models of loan adaptation proposed in phonological literature in recent years (see Chapter 2), it is necessary to test their validity against experimental data in order to verify their predictions and theoretical relevance. The study of online adaptations presented in this thesis provides significant insight into the mechanisms governing the nativisation processes as well as constitutes an invaluable source of information concerning the synchronic phonology of the borrowing language. The choice of Polish and English as the source language and the target language respectively allows us to observe a wider range of repair strategies than vowel epenthesis and consonant deletion, which are examined in the majority of studies on phonotactic loan adaptation. Since both languages allow many consonant clusters, there is also a possibility of modifying the quality of one or both segments in a sequence.

The present thesis has intended to attain three major objectives. First, we have attempted to uncover the most frequent repair strategies used to anglicise Polish consonant clusters as well as to identify the mechanisms behind the adaptation process. Another aim has been to verify the validity of various loan integration models by means of experimental data. But first and foremost, our goal has been to provide an adequate formal account of the collected material for which we have selected an Optimality Theory framework.

In order to achieve these aims, it has been necessary to place the experimental results in a broader theoretical perspective. This objective has been accomplished in the first three Chapters of the present dissertation. Chapter 1 has provided the necessary background to the issue of phonological loanword adaptation in general and in English in particular. We have focused on a number of relevant issues, such as the definition and classification of loans as well as the key factors conditioning loanword integration along with some problematic patterns emerging in this process and a history of foreign influence in English. Our discussion has demonstrated that phonological loan adaptation is shaped by a number of variables, including the nature of input representation, the role of orthography and the degree of the borrowing community bilingualism. Research on loanwords is further complicated by the occurrence of certain puzzling patterns in phonological nativisation which are difficult to account for in terms of native processes or constraints, including the too-many-solutions problem, divergent repair, unnecessary repair, differential importation and retreat to the unmarked.

The goal of Chapter 2 has been to examine the major contemporary approaches to loan nativisation whose validity has been subject to verification by the experimental data in Chapter 4 and 5. The models in question can be divided into three major groups depending on the degree of importance they attach to the role of phonetics vs. phonology in this process. Analyses which belong to the phonological approximation view, e.g. the Theory of Constraints and Repair Strategies Loanword Model (Paradis and LaCharité 1997) and Itô and Mester's (1995, 1999, 2001) Optimality Theory account, are based on the assumption that loanword adaptation is computed by the phonological component of grammar. On the other hand, phonetic approaches, e.g. a psycholinguistic three-level model (Peperkamp 2005, Peperkamp *et al.* 2008) and Boersma and Hamann's (2009) bidirectional model of L1 speech processing, claim that loan assimilation takes place in perception. Finally, according to mixed frameworks, e.g. Silverman's (1992) two-tier model and the perceptual similarity approach (Kang 2003), both the perception grammar and the production grammar play an active role in processing sound changes which affect borrowings.

Chapter 3 has focused on relevant aspects of English and Polish phonotactics and syllable structure as well as previous research on online loan nativisation. A comparison of the initial and final CC and CCC consonant clusters in English and Polish has revealed profound differences concerning both the number of permitted sequences as well as their segmental structure. Furthermore, it has been demonstrated that universal sonority-based laws, such as the Sonority Sequencing Principle, the Minimum Sonority Distance and the Sonority Dispersion Principle, play a significant role in English phonotactic restrictions. Previous research on online loanword adaptation, e.g. Davidson (2001), Davidson *et al.* (2004) and Haunz (2007), has a number of limitations, including a small number of experimental stimuli which represent a limited range of segment combinations in word-initial position only. This Chapter has also introduced the framework of Optimality Theory, within which the experimental results are formally analysed in Chapters 4 and 5.

A general overview of the data collected in the experiments on online adaptation of Polish initial and final CC and CCC consonant clusters by native speakers of English has demonstrated that the most frequent repair strategy is vowel epenthesis, followed by a modification of C_1 or C_2, with consonant elision occurring marginally. In addition, a relatively high percentage of targetlike reproduction cases have been observed. A number of factors exert an influence on the rate of accurate imitation of a cluster, including the sonority distance between the segments in a sequence as well as the relative markedness of feature values inherent in them.

These results have been analysed within the framework of Optimality Theory in Chapters 4 and 5. Our crucial claim has been that there is no need for a separate loanword phonology component since the vast majority of modifications that foreign items undergo can be accounted for with the native English ranking of phonological constraints. This is possible given the assumption of the Extended Richness of the Base principle (Davidson *et al.* 2004) that the phonological grammar of a particular language is a partial ranking with floating faithfulness constraints. Although the majority of borrowings are consistent with the core ranking, i.e. the one which yields native outputs, certain groups of items violate surface generalisations of English. These include 1) targetlike reproduction cases, where the source structures are not altered by the borrowers in spite of their ill-formedness, 2) instances of partial adaptation and 3) the emergence of the unmarked cases, where foreign items conform to stricter structural requirements than those imposed by the native phonology.

All these phenomena have been explained in an optimality-theoretic framework by the mechanism of FAITH reranking, similar to the one put forward by Itô and Mester (1995, 1999, 2001) for lexical stratification in Japanese as well as for different degrees of nativisation found in borrowings into German. Thus, targetlike reproduction and partial adaptation reflect different degrees of FAITH promotion, while the emergence of the unmarked of FAITH demotion with respect to an invariant hierarchy of structural well-formedness constraints. On the whole, our thesis lends support to the claim that loanword phonology is mainly native phonology in action supplemented with the mechanism of FAITH promotion or demotion. The role of perception in loanword nativisation seems to be relatively limited. Thus, our research provides evidence in favour of the phonological approximation view to loan adaptation.

A comparison of the nativisation strategies used in online vs. established loans has provided further arguments for the stratification of borrowings in English. The latter group of loanwords can be divided into three categories, depending on the presence or absence of importation vs. substitution, i.e. into those with variation between importation and complete adaptation of a foreign consonant cluster, those with full nativisation without the possibility of importation and those with importation of foreign structures without nativisation. Three main adaptation scenarios have been distinguished for established loanwords. First, a foreign item may enter the periphery of native phonology (as evidenced by importation of non-native structures) and become established over time by moving towards the core. Secondly, a loanword may be fully nativised at the time of its introduction into the recipient language. Thirdly, a borrowing may enter the periphery and remain there permanently.

Last but not least, it should be pointed out that the data collected in online adaptation experiments are usually heavily influenced by the adopted experimental design. Thus, it is likely that a modification in the number of participants or the types of clusters employed in the study would alter the obtained results to a greater or lesser degree. In this light, it seems necessary to verify the conclusions drawn in the present thesis with further research on online nativisation.

Appendix 1 CC clusters – experimental stimuli

INITIAL CLUSTERS			
CLUSTER	TARGET WORD	TRANSCRIPTION	GLOSS
OBSTRUENT + OBSTRUENT			
1.	/pt/	ptak	/ptak/	'a bird'
2.	/gb/	gbur	/gbur/	'a boor'
3.	/db/	dbać	/dbaʨ/	'to care'
4.	/gd͡ʑ/	gdzie	/gd͡ʑɛ/	'where'
5.	/t͡ʂk/	czka	/t͡ʂka/	'to hiccup, 3ʳᵈ p. sgl.'
6.	/d͡ʑb/	dzban	/d͡ʑban/	'a jug'
7.	/t͡sf/	cwał	/t͡sfaw/	'gallop'
8.	/d͡ʐd͡ʐ/	dżdżysty	/d͡ʐd͡ʐɨstɨ/	'rainy'
9.	/tʂ/	trzy	/tʂɨ/	'three'
10.	/tf/	twarz	/tfaʂ/	'a face'
11.	/pʂ/	przód	/pʂut/	'front'
12.	/dv/	dwa	/dva/	'two'
13.	/gʐ/	grzyb	/gʐɨp/	'a mushroom'
14.	/d͡zv/	dzwon	/d͡zvɔn/	'a bell'
15.	/ʂp/	szpak	/ʂpak/	'a starling'
16.	/ɕp/	śpi	/ɕpi/	'to sleep, 3ʳᵈ p. sgl.'
17.	/zb/	zbir	/zbir/	'a thug'
18.	/zd/	zdun	/zdun/	'a stove fitter'
19.	/ft͡ɕ/	wcisk	/ft͡ɕisk/	'a snap-in'
20.	/ft͡s/	wcale	/ft͡salɛ/	'at all'
21.	/ʂt͡ʂ/	szczaw	/ʂt͡ʂaf/	'sorrel'
22.	/ɕt͡ɕ/	ściana	/ɕt͡ɕana/	'a wall'
23.	/vd͡ʑ/	wdziać	/vd͡ʑaʨ/	'to put on'
24.	/zd͡ʑ/	zdziałać	/zd͡ʑawaʨ/	'to achieve'
25.	/zv/	zwarty	/zvartɨ/	'compact'
26.	/xf/	chwast	/xfast/	'a weed'
27.	/xʂ/	chrzest	/xʂɛst/	'a baptism'

		INITIAL CLUSTERS		
	CLUSTER	**TARGET WORD**	**TRANSCRIPTION**	**GLOSS**
		OBSTRUENT + SONORANT		
1.	/vm/	*wmów*	/vmuf/	'to talk into, imp.'
2.	/dl/	*dla*	/dla/	'for'
3.	/dm/	*dmuch*	/dmux/	'a blow'
4.	/zr/	*zryw*	/zrɨf/	'a dash'
5.	/zm/	*zmowa*	/zmɔva/	'a plot'
6.	/vl/	*wlot*	/vlɔt/	'an inlet'
7.	/zw/	*zło*	/zwɔ/	'evil'
8.	/t͡ɕm/	*ćma*	/t͡ɕma/	'a moth'
9.	/t͡sn/	*cnota*	/t͡snɔta/	'a virtue'
10.	/t͡ʂw/	*człon*	/t͡ʂwɔn/	'a segment'
11.	/t͡sw/	*cło*	/t͡swɔ/	'a tariff'
12.	/ɕɲ/	*śnieg*	/ɕɲɛk/	'snow'
13.	/tl/	*tlen*	/tlɛn/	'oxygen'
14.	/ɕl/	*ślad*	/ɕlat/	'a trace'

		SONORANT + OBSTRUENT		
1.	/rt/	*rtęć*	/rtɛ̃t͡ɕ/	'mercury'
2.	/lv/	*lwy*	/lvɨ/	'a lion' pl.
3.	/wg/	*łgać*	/wgat͡ɕ/	'to lie'
4.	/wb/	*łby*	/wbɨ/	'a head' pl.
5.	/wz/	*łza*	/wza/	'a tear'
6.	/mʂ/	*msza*	/mʂa/	'a mass'
7.	/rd/	*rdest*	/rdɛst/	'a knotweed'
8.	/rv/	*rwać*	/rvat͡ɕ/	'to tear'
9.	/wk/	*łkać*	/wkat͡ɕ/	'to sob'
10.	/mʐ/	*mżyć*	/mʐɨt͡ɕ/	'to drizzle'

		SONORANT + SONORANT		
1.	/ml/	*mlecz*	/mlɛt͡ʂ/	'a sow thistle'
2.	/mr/	*mrok*	/mrɔk/	'gloom'

INITIAL CLUSTERS			
CLUSTER	TARGET WORD	TRANSCRIPTION	GLOSS
3. /mn/	*mnogi*	/mnɔgi/	'numerous'
4. /ln/	*lnu*	/lnu/	'linen, Gen. sgl.'
5. /mɲ/	*mnich*	/mɲix/	'a monk'

FINAL CLUSTERS			
CLUSTER	TARGET WORD	TRANSCRIPTION	GLOSS
OBSTRUENT + OBSTRUENT			
1. /pt͡ʂ/	*depcz*	/dɛpt͡ʂ/	'to trample, imp.'
2. /pt͡ɕ/	*kopć*	/kɔpt͡ɕ/	'to smoke, imp.'
3. /t͡sk/	*Kock*	/kɔt͡sk/	'a town name'
4. /t͡ʂp/	*liczb*	/lit͡ʂp/	'a number, Gen. pl.'
5. /tʂ/	*patrz*	/patʂ/	'to look, imp.'
6. /pʂ/	*pieprz*	/pjɛpʂ/	'pepper'
7. /tf/	*płetw*	/pwɛtf/	'a fin, Gen. pl.'
8. /ft͡s/	*szewc*	/ʂɛft͡s/	'a shoemaker'
9. /ʂt͡ʂ/	*bluszcz*	/bluʂt͡ʂ/	'ivy'
10. /ɕt͡ɕ/	*gość*	/gɔɕt͡ɕ/	'a guest'
11. /ʂp/	*służb*	/swuʂp/	'a service, Gen. pl.'
12. /ft͡ɕ/	*sprawdź*	/spraft͡ɕ/	'to check, imp.'
13. /ɕp/	*gróźb*	/gruɕp/	'a threat, Gen. pl.'
14. /sf/	*nazw*	/nasf/	'a name, Gen. pl.'
15. /xf/	*żuchw*	/ʐuxf/	'a mandible, Gen. pl.'

OBSTRUENT + SONORANT			
1. /kw/	*piekł*	/pjɛkw/	'to bake, 3rd p. sgl. past'
2. /dm/	*kadm*	/kadm/	'cadmium'
3. /sw/	*prysł*	/prisw/	'to vanish, 3rd p. sgl. past'
4. /ɕɲ/	*baśń*	/baɕɲ/	'a fairy tale'
5. /pɲ/	*wapń*	/vapɲ/	'calcium'
6. /ɕm/	*taśm*	/taɕm/	' a tape, Gen. pl.'

FINAL CLUSTERS			
CLUSTER	TARGET WORD	TRANSCRIPTION	GLOSS
7. /ɕl/	myśl	/miɕl/	'a thought'
8. /tr/	łotr	/wɔtr/	'a rascal'
9. /tw/	plótł	/plutw/	'to weave, 3rd p. sgl. past'
10. /fr/	gofr	/gɔfr/	'a waffle'

SONORANT + OBSTRUENT			
1. /rf/	torf	/tɔrf/	'peat'
2. /mʂ/	zamsz	/zamʂ/	'suede'
3. /wʂ/	fałsz	/fawʂ/	'falsehood'
4. /rt/	tort	/tɔrt/	'a cream cake'
5. /jt͡ɕ/	pójdź	/pujt͡ɕ/	'to go, imp.'
6. /rt͡ʂ/	skurcz	/skurt͡ʂ/	'a cramp'
7. /nt͡s/	glanc	/glant͡s/	'lustre'
8. /lt͡s/	walc	/valt͡s/	'waltz'

SONORANT + SONORANT			
1. /mn/	hymn	/xɨmn/	'an anthem'
2. /rɲ/	czerń	/t͡ʂɛrɲ/	'blackness'
3. /wm/	hełm	/xɛwm/	'a helmet'
4. /rm/	karm	/karm/	'to feed, imp.'

Appendix 2 CC clusters – participants

NO.	SEX	AGE	LANGUAGES LEARNT
P1	F	23	German
P2	M	30	French
P3	M	18	German, French
P4	F	19	German, French
P5	F	22	French
P6	F	24	French (fluent)
P7	F	24	Italian, French
P8	F	23	German (fluent)
P9	M	23	French
P10	M	30	Spanish
P11	M	29	German, French
P12	M	20	French
P13	M	20	French, Spanish
P14	F	20	Spanish, Italian
P15	F	23	Italian, German
P16	M	18	French
P17	F	18	German, French
P18	F	20	German
P19	F	28	French, Japanese
P20	M	29	French, German, Italian
P21	M	30	French, Japanese
P22	M	26	French (fluent)
P23	F	30	French
P24	F	21	German, French
P25	F	24	German, French
P26	F	30	German (fluent), Spanish, Italian
P27	M	21	German
P28	M	25	German (fluent), French (fluent)
P29	F	24	French
P30	M	27	Spanish

Appendix 3 CC clusters – repair strategies

	CLUSTER	T	E VC₁C₂	E C₁VC₂	D	SC
			INITIAL CLUSTERS			
			OBSTRUENT + OBSTRUENT			
1.	/pt/	60 %	0 %	40 %	0 %	0 %
2.	/gb/	13.3 %	0 %	86.7 %	0 %	0 %
3.	/db/	40 %	0 %	60 %	0 %	0 %
4.	/gd͡ʑ/	13.3 %	0 %	86.7 %	0 %	0 %
5.	/t͡ʂk/	60 %	0 %	40 %	0 %	0 %
6.	/t͡sf/	86.7 %	0 %	0 %	0 %	13.3 % [sf]
7.	/d͡zb/	13.3 %	20 % [əzb]	0 %	0 %	66.7 % [zb]
8.	/d͡ʐd͡ʑ/	0 %	0 %	93.3 %	6.7 % [(d͡ʒ)d͡ʒ]	0 %
9.	/t͡ʂ/	73.3 %	0 %	20 %	6.7 % [(t)ʃ]	0 %
10.	/tf/	86.7 %	0 %	13.3 %	0 %	0 %
11.	/pʂ/	86.7 %	0 %	13.3 %	0 %	0 %
12.	/dv/	33.3 %	0 %	66.7 %	0 %	0 %
13.	/gʑ/	60 %	0 %	40 %	0 %	0 %
14.	/d͡ʑv/	6.7 %	20 % [əzv]	0 %	0 %	73.3 % [zv]
15.	/ʂp/	100 %	0 %	0 %	0 %	0 %
16.	/ɕp/	100 %	0 %	0 %	0 %	0 %
17.	/zb/	60 %	40 %	0 %	0 %	0 %
18.	/zd/	46.7 %	53.3 %	0 %	0 %	0 %
19.	/ft͡ɕ/	40 %	0 %	46.7 %	0 %	13.3 % [ft]
20.	/ft͡s/	20 %	0 %	40 % [fət]	0 %	40 % [ft]
21.	/ʂt͡ʂ/	0 %	0 %	0 %	0 %	100 % [ʃt]
22.	/ɕt͡ɕ/	60 %	0 %	0 %	0 %	40 % [ʂt͡ʃ]
23.	/vd͡ʑ/	13.3 %	0 %	86.7 %	0 %	0 %
24.	/zd͡ʑ/	40 %	46.7 %	0 %	0 %	13.3 % [ʂt͡ʃ]
25.	/zv/	73.3 %	13.3 %	0 %	0 %	13.3 % [sf]
26.	/xf/	20 %	0 %	0 %	73.3 % [(x)f]	6.7 % [kf]
27.	/xʂ/	13.3 %	0 %	0 %	86.7 % [(x)ʂ]	0 %
	AVERAGE	45.2 %	34.3 %		6.4 %	14.1 %

OBSTRUENT + SONORANT						
	CLUSTER	T	E		D	SC
			VC_1C_2	C_1VC_2		
1.	/vm/	6.7 %	86.7 %	0 %	0 %	6.7 % [fm]
2.	/dl/	20 %	0 %	73.3 %	0 %	6.7 % [tl]
3.	/dm/	40 %	0 %	60 %	0 %	0 %
4.	/zr/	40 %	0 %	40 %	0 %	20 % [sr]
5.	/zm/	33.3 %	33.3 %	0 %	0 %	33.3 % [sm]
6.	/vl/	46.7 %	0 %	33.3 %	0 %	20 % [fl]
7.	/zw/	46.7 %	20 %	0 %	0 %	33.3 % [sw]
8.	/t͡ɕm/	80 %	0 %	20 %	0 %	0 %
9.	/t͡sn/	33.3 %	0 %	6.7 %	0 %	60 %
10.	/t͡ʂw/	0 %	0 %	0 %	0 %	100 % [tw]
11.	/t͡sw/	26.7 %	0 %	0 %	0 %	73.3 % [tw]
12.	/ɕɲ/	46.7 %	0 %	0 %	0 %	53.3 % [ʃn]
13.	/tl/	86.7 %	0 %	0 %	6.7 % [t(l)]	6.7 % [kl]
14.	/ɕl/	100 %	0 %	0 %	0 %	0 %
AVERAGE		**43.3 %**	**26.7 %**		**0.5 %**	**29.5 %**

SONORANT + OBSTRUENT						
	CLUSTER	T	E		D	SC
			VC_1C_2	C_1VC_2		
1.	/rt/	0 %	100 %	0 %	0 %	0 %
2.	/lv/	0 %	0 %	100 %	0 %	0 %
3.	/wg/	0 %	100 % [ʊwg]	0 %	0 %	0 %
4.	/wb/	0 %	100 % [ʊwb]	0 %	0 %	0 %
5.	/wz/	0 %	100 % [ʊwz]	0 %	0 %	0 %
6.	/mʂ/	6.7 %	0 %	93.3 %	0 %	0 %
7.	/rd/	6.7 %	93.3 %	0 %	0 %	0 %
8.	/rv/	6.7 %	93.3 %	0 %	0 %	0 %
9.	/wk/	6.7 %	93.3 % [ʊwk]	0 %	0 %	0 %
10.	/mʐ/	26.7 %	0 %	73.3 %	0 %	0 %
AVERAGE		**5.4 %**	**94.6 %**		**0 %**	**0 %**

SONORANT + SONORANT						
	CLUSTER	T	E		D	SC
			VC_1C_2	C_1VC_2		
1.	/ml/	66.7 %	0 %	33.3 %	0 %	0 %
2.	/mr/	53.3 %	0 %	40 %	6.7 % [m(r)]	0 %
3.	/mn/	33.3 %	0 %	66.7 %	0 %	0 %
4.	/ln/	0 %	100 %	0 %	0 %	0 %
5.	/mɲ/	0 %	0 %	100 % [mən]	0 %	0 %
AVERAGE		30.7 %	68 %		1.3 %	0 %

FINAL CLUSTERS						
OBSTRUENT + OBSTRUENT						
	CLUSTER	T	E		D	SC
			C_1C_2V	C_1VC_2		
1.	/pt͡ʂ/	0 %	0 %	0 %	0 %	100 % [pt]
2.	/pt͡ɕ/	100 %	0 %	0 %	0 %	0 %
3.	/t͡ʂk/	100 %	0 %	0 %	0 %	0 %
4.	/t͡ʂp/	86.7 %	0 %	0 %	0 %	13.3 % [ʃp]
5.	/tʂ/	100 %	0 %	0 %	0 %	0 %
6.	/pʂ/	100 %	0 %	0 %	0 %	0 %
7.	/tf/	73.3 %	0 %	0 %	20 % [(t)f]	6.7 % [ts]
8.	/ft͡ʂ/	13.3 %	0 %	0 %	0 %	86.7 % [ft]
9.	/ʂt͡ʂ/	6.7 %	0 %	0 %	0 %	93.3 % [ʃt]
10.	/ɕt͡ɕ/	40 %	0 %	0 %	0 %	60 % [ʃt]
11.	/ʂp/	60 %	20 %	0 %	0 %	20 % [sp]
12.	/ft͡ɕ/	100 %	0 %	0 %	0 %	0 %
13.	/ɕp/	100 %	0 %	0 %	0 %	0 %
14.	/sf/	86.7 %	6.7 %	0 %	6.7 % [s(f)]	0 %
15.	/xf/	33.3 %	0 %	0 %	46.7 % [(x)f]	20 % [fk]
AVERAGE		66.7 %	1.8 %		4.9 %	26.7 %

OBSTRUENT + SONORANT					
CLUSTER	**T**	**E**		**D**	**SC**
		C_1C_2V	C_1VC_2		
1.	/kw/	0 %	100 %	0 %	0 %	0 %
2.	/dm/	6.7 %	93.3 %	0 %	0 %	0 %
3.	/sw/	6.7 %	93.3 %	0 %	0 %	0 %
4.	/çɲ/	6.7 %	93.3 % [ʃnə]	0 %	0 %	0 %
5.	/pɲ/	6.7 %	73.3 % [pnə]	0 %	6.7 % [p(ɲ)]	13.3 % [pn]
6.	/çm/	33.3 %	66.7 %	0 %	0 %	0 %
7.	/çl/	33.3 %	66.7 %	0 %	0 %	0 %
8.	/tr/	46.7 %	40 %	0 %	13.3 % [t(r)]	0 %
9.	/tw/	13.3 %	40 %	0 %	26.7 % [t(w)]	20 % [tf]
10.	/fr/	66.7 %	20 %	0 %	6.7 % [f(r)]	6.7 % [lf]
AVERAGE		**22 %**	**68.7 %**		**5.3 %**	**4 %**

SONORANT + OBSTRUENT					
CLUSTER	**T**	**E**		**D**	**SC**
		C_1C_2V	C_1VC_2		
1.	/rf/	93.3 %	0 %	0 %	6.7 % [(r)f]	0 %
2.	/mʂ/	100 %	0 %	0 %	0 %	0 %
3.	/wʂ/	93.3 %	0 %	0 %	0 %	6.7 % [ws]
4.	/rt/	100 %	0 %	0 %	0 %	0 %
5.	/ĵʨ/	100 %	0 %	0 %	0 %	0 %
6.	/rʨ/	80 %	0 %	0 %	0 %	20 % [rt]
7.	/nʦ/	80 %	0 %	0 %	0 %	20 % [nt]
8.	/lʦ/	40 %	0 %	0 %	0 %	60 % [lt]
AVERAGE		**85.8 %**	**0 %**		**0.8 %**	**13.3 %**

SONORANT + SONORANT					
CLUSTER	**T**	**E**		**D**	**SC**
		C_1C_2V	C_1VC_2		
1.	/mn/	6.7 %	0 %	93.3 %	0 %	0 %
2.	/rɲ/	13.3 %	86.7 % [rnə]	0 %	0 %	0 %
3.	/wm/	100 %	0 %	0 %	0 %	0 %
4.	/rm/	40 %	53.3 %	0 %	6.7 % [r(m)]	0 %
AVERAGE		**40 %**	**58.3 %**		**1.7 %**	**0 %**

Appendix 4 CCC clusters – experimental stimuli

INITIAL CLUSTERS			
CLUSTER	TARGET WORD	TRANSCRIPTION	GLOSS
OBSTRUENT + OBSTRUENT + OBSTRUENT			
1.	/bzd/	*bzdura*	/bzdura/	'nonsense'
2.	/pʂʈʂ/	*pszczoła*	/pʂʈʂɔwa/	'a bee'
3.	/stf/	*stwór*	/stfur/	'a creature'
4.	/tkf/	*tkwi*	/tkfi/	'to be stuck, 3rd p. sgl.'
5.	/vzg/	*wzgórze*	/vzguʐɛ/	'a hill'

OBSTRUENT + OBSTRUENT + SONORANT			
1.	/gʐm/	*grzmot*	/gʐmɔt/	'thunder'
2.	/pxl/	*pchli*	/pxli/	'flea'
3.	/skn/	*sknera*	/sknɛra/	'a miser'
4.	/sxl/	*schlać*	/sxlaʨ/	'to get drunk'
5.	/tkn/	*tknąć*	/tknɔ̃ʨ/	'to touch'
6.	/vbr/	*wbrew*	/vbrɛf/	'against'
7.	/vzl/	*wzlot*	/vzlɔt/	'ascent'
8.	/zgɲ/	*zgnić*	/zgɲiʨ/	'to rot'

OBSTRUENT + SONORANT + OBSTRUENT			
1.	/drg/	*drgać*	/drgaʨ/	'to twitch'
2.	/krf/	*krwi*	/krfi/	'blood, Gen. sgl.'

OBSTRUENT + SONORANT + SONORANT			
1.	/brn/	*brnąć*	/brnɔ̃ʨ/	'to wade'
2.	/smr/	*smród*	/smrut/	'stench'
3.	/zmɲ/	*zmniejsz*	/zmɲɛjʂ/	'to decrease, imp.'

SONORANT + OBSTRUENT + OBSTRUENT				
1.	/mɕt͡ɕ/	*mściwy*	/mɕt͡ɕivɨ/	'vindictive'

SONORANT + OBSTRUENT + SONORANT				
1.	/mdw/	*mdły*	/mdwɨ/	'insipid'
2.	/mgl/	*mglisty*	/mglistɨ/	'foggy'
3.	/mgɲ/	*mgnienie*	/mgɲɛɲɛ/	'a blink'

FINAL CLUSTERS				
	CLUSTER	**TARGET WORD**	**TRANSCRIPTION**	**GLOSS**
OBSTRUENT + OBSTRUENT + OBSTRUENT				
1.	/psk/	*Lipsk*	/lipsk/	'Leipzig'
2.	/stf/	*bóstw*	/bustf/	'a deity, Gen. pl.'

OBSTRUENT + OBSTRUENT + SONORANT				
1.	/xtr/	*blichtr*	/blixtr/	'tinsel'

SONORANT + OBSTRUENT + OBSTRUENT				
1.	/nʂt/	*kunszt*	/kunʂt/	'craft'
2.	/jst͡s/	*miejsc*	/mjɛjst͡s/	'a place, Gen. pl.'

Appendix 5 CCC clusters – participants

NO.	SEX	AGE	LANGUAGES LEARNT
P1	F	20	French
P2	F	21	French, German
P3	M	30	Spanish, French
P4	F	25	French
P5	F	22	German
P6	F	21	French
P7	M	30	French
P8	F	30	German
P9	F	29	French
P10	M	28	Japanese
P11	F	30	German, French, Dutch
P12	F	21	French, Spanish
P13	M	29	German
P14	F	30	French
P15	F	20	French, German

Appendix 6　CCC clusters – repair strategies

INITIAL CLUSTERS					
CLUSTER	**T**	**E**	**E & D**	**D**	**SC**
1.	/bzd/	20 %	73.3 % [bəzd]	0 %	0 %	6.7 % [pst]
2.	/pʂʈʂ/	13.3 %	53.3 % [pəsʈʃ]	0 %	0 %	33.3 % [pʃt] 13.3 % [psʈʃ] 20 %
3.	/stf/	60 %	40 % [stəf]	0 %	0 %	0 %
4.	/tkf/	26.7 %	46.7 % [təkf]	0 %	26.7 % [kf]	0 %
5.	/vzg/	13.3 %	73.3 % [vəzg]	13.3 % [əzg]	0 %	0 %
6.	/gʐm/	13.3 %	86.7 % [gəʒm]	0 %	0 %	0 %
7.	/pxl/	0 %	0 %	6.7 % [pəl]	93.3 % [pr] 26.6 % [pl] 66.7 %	0 %
8.	/skn/	33.3 %	66.7 % [skən]	0 %	0 %	0 %
9.	/sxl/	6.7 %	0 %	0 %	20 % [sl] 13.3 % [ʃl] 6.7 %	73.3 % [sfl]
10.	/tkn/	40 %	53.3 % [təkn]	6.7 % [kən]	0 %	0 %
11.	/vbr/	20 %	26.7 % [vəbr]	0 %	26.7 % [br]	26.6 % [fbr] 13.3 % [fpr] 13.3 %
12.	/vzl/	26.7 %	66.7 % [vəzl]	0 %	0 %	6.7 % [fsl]
13.	/zgɲ/	6.7 %	66.7 % [zgən]	0 %	0 %	26.6 % [skn] 13.3 % [zgn] 13.3 %
14.	/drg/	0 %	93.3 % [dərg] 53.3 % [drəg] 40 %	6.7 % [dəg]	0 %	0 %
15.	/krf/	6.7 %	26.7 % [krəf]	40 % [kəf]	26.7 % [kf] 20 % [kr] 6.7 %	0 %
16.	/mdw/	0 %	80 % [mədw]	20 % [məd]	0 %	0 %
17.	/mgl/	0 %	100 % [məgl]	0 %	0 %	0 %

INITIAL CLUSTERS					
CLUSTER	T	E	E & D	D	SC
18. /mɡɲ/	6.7 %	93.3 % [məɡn]	0 %	0 %	0 %
19. /mc͡tɕ/	0 %	93.3 % [məst͡ʃ]	0 %	0 %	6.7 % [mst͡ʃ]
20. /brn/	0 %	93.3 % [bərn] 60 % [brən] 33.3 %	0 %	6.7 % [bl]	0 %
21. /smr/	33.3 %	60 % [smər]	0 %	6.7 % [sr]	0 %
22. /zmɲ/	0 %	66.7 % [zmən]	6.7 % [əzn]	0 %	26.6 % [smn] 13.3 % [zmj] 13.3 %
AVERAGE	14.9 %	61.8 %	4.5 %	9.4 %	9.4 %

FINAL CLUSTERS					
CLUSTER	T	E	E & D	D	SC
1. /psk/	100 %	0 %	0 %	0 %	0 %
2. /stf/	46.7 %	0 %	0 %	53.3 % [st]	0 %
3. /xtr/	0 %	0 %	13.3 % [θtə]	86.7 % [θt] 33.3 % [ft] 26.7 % [xt] 26.7 %	0 %
4. /nʂt/	100 %	0 %	0 %	0 %	0 %
5. /jʂt͡s/	6.7 %	0 %	0 %	13.3 % [js]	80 % [jst]
AVERAGE	50.6 %	0 %	2.7 %	30.7 %	16 %

List of figures

List of tables

List of tableaux

221

References

Adler, A. N. (2006) Faithfulness and perception in loanword adaptation: a case study from Hawaiian. *Lingua* 116. 1024–1045.

Anderson, J. (1986) Suprasegmental dependencies. In Durand, J. (ed.) *Dependency and non-linear phonology*. London: Croom Helm. 55–133.

Anttila, A. (1998) Deriving variation from grammar. In Hinskens, F. L., van Hout, R. and W. L. Wetzels (eds.) *Variation, Change, and Phonological Theory*. Amsterdam: John Benjamins. 35–68.

Avery, P. & K. Rice (1989) Segment structure and coronal underspecification. *Phonology* 6(2). 179–200.

Baertsch, K. (2002) An optimality theoretic approach to syllable structure: the split margin hierarchy. PhD dissertation. Indiana University.

Baertsch, K. (2012) Sonority and sonority-based relationships within American English monosyllabic words. In Parker, S. (ed.) *The sonority controversy*. Berlin: De Gruyter Mouton. 3–37.

Bartmińska, I. & J. Bartmiński (1997) *Słownik wymowy i odmiany nazwisk obcych*. Bielsko Biała: PPU Park.

Bat-El, O. (1996) Selecting the best of the worst: the grammar of Hebrew blends. *Phonology* 13. 283–328.

Baugh, A.C. (1957) *A history of the English language*. New York: Appleton-Century-Crofts.

Bermúdez-Otero, R. (forthcoming) Stratal Phonology. In Hannahs, S. J. & A. R. K. Bosch (eds.) *The Routledge handbook of phonological theory*. Abingdon: Routledge.

Best, C. T. & W. Strange (1992) Effects of phonological and phonetic factors on cross-language perception of approximants. *Journal of Phonetics* 20. 305–330.

Bethin, C. (1992) *Polish syllables: the role of prosody in phonology and morphology*. Columbus: Slavica.

Bloomfield, L. (1933) *Language*. New York: Holt, Rineheart and Winston.

Boersma, P. (1998) *Functional Phonology: formalizing the interactions between articulatory and perceptual drives*. The Hague: Holland Academic Graphics.

Boersma, P. & S. Hamann (2009) Loanword adaptation as first-language phonological perception. In Calabrese, A. & L. W. Wetzels (eds.) *Loan Phonology*. Amsterdam & Philadelphia: John Benjamins. 11–58.

Brasington, R. (1997) Cost and benefit in loanword adaptation. *Working Papers in Linguistics* 3. 1–19.

Broselow, E. (1992) Transfer and universals in second language epenthesis. In Gass, S. M. & L. Selinker (eds.) *Language Transfer in Language Learning.* Amsterdam & Philadelphia: John Benjamins. 71–86.

Broselow, E. & H.-B. Park (1995) Mora conservation in second language prosody. In Archibald, J. (ed.) *Phonological acquisition and phonological theory.* Hillsdale: Erlbaum. 151–168.

Cho, Y. Y. & T. H. King (2003) Semisyllables and universal syllabification. In Fery, C & R. van de Vijver (eds.) *The Syllable in Optimality Theory.* Cambridge: Cambridge University Press. 183–212.

Chomsky, N. & M. Halle (1968) *The sound pattern of English.* New York: Harper & Row.

Clements, G. N. (1990) The role of the sonority cycle in core syllabification. In Kingston, J. & M. Beckman (eds.) *Papers in Laboratory Phonology I.* Cambridge: Cambridge University Press. 283–333.

Clements, G. N. & E. Hume (1995) The internal organisation of speech sounds. In Goldsmith, J. (ed.) *The handbook of phonological theory.* Cambridge: Blackwell. 245–306.

Crawford, C. (2009) Adaptation and transmission in Japanese loanword phonology. PhD dissertation. Cornell University.

Cruttenden, A. (2014) *Gimson's Pronunciation of English.* London & New York: Routledge.

Crystal, D. (2003) *The Cambridge encyclopedia of the English language.* Cambridge: Cambridge University Press.

Cyran, E. (2010) *Complexity scales and licensing in phonology.* Berlin: Mouton de Gruyter.

Cyran, E. & E. Gussmann (1999) Consonantal clusters and governing relations: Polish initial consonant sequences. In Hulst, H. van der & N. Ritter (eds.) *The syllable. Views and facts.* Berlin: Mouton de Gruyter. 219–247.

Davidson, L. (2001) Hidden rankings in the final state of the English grammar. In Horwood, G. & S. Kim (eds.) *Rutgers Linguistics Working Papers 2.* New Brunswick: Rutgers University. 21–48.

Davidson, L., Jusczyk, P. & P. Smolensky (2004) The initial and final states: theoretical implications and experimental explorations of Richness of the Base. In Kager, R., Pater, J. & W. Zonneveld (eds.) *Constraints in phonological acquisition.* Cambridge: Cambridge University Press. 321–368.

Davidson, L. & R. Noyer (1997) Loan phonology in Huave: Nativisation and the ranking of faithfulness constraints. *Proceedings of the West Coast Conference on Formal Linguistics* 15. 65–79.

Davidson, L. & M. Stone (2003) Epenthesis versus gestural mistiming in consonant cluster production: an ultrasound study. *Proceedings of the West Coast Conference on Formal Linguistics* 22. 165–178.

Davis, S. (1998) Syllable Contact in Optimality Theory. *Journal of Korean Linguistics* 23. 181–211.

Davis, S. & S.-H. Shin (1999) The syllable contact constraint in Korean: an optimality-theoretic analysis. *Journal of East Asian Linguistics* 8. 285–312.

de Lacy, P. (2006) *Markedness: reduction and preservation in phonology.* Cambridge: Cambridge University Press.

Dogil, G. & H. Luschützky (1990) Notes on sonority and segmental strength. *Rivista di Linguistica* 2(2). 3–54.

Dohlus, K. (2005) Phonetics or phonology: asymmetries in loanword adaptations - French and German mid front rounded vowels in Japanese. *ZAS Papers in Linguistics* 42. 117–135.

Donegan, P. (1978) On the natural phonology of vowels. PhD dissertation. Ohio State University.

Donegan, P. & D. Stampe (1979) The study of Natural Phonology. In Dinnsen, D. A. (ed.) *Current approaches to phonological theory.* Bloomington: IUP. 126–173.

Dressler, W. U. & K. Dziubalska-Kołaczyk (2006) Proposing morphonotactics. *Rivista di Linguistica* 18(2). 249–266.

Dukiewicz, L. (1995) Fonetyka. In Wróbel, H. (ed.) *Gramatyka współczesnego języka polskiego. Fonetyka i Fonologia.* Kraków: Wydawnictwo Instytutu Języka Polskiego PAN. 7–103.

Dupoux, E., Kakehi, K., Hirose, Y., Pallier, C. & J. Mehler (1999) Epenthetic vowels in Japanese: a perceptual illusion? *Journal of Experimental Psychology: Human Perception and Performance* 25. 1568–1578.

Dupoux, E., Pallier, C., Sebastian-Galles, N. & J. Mehler (1997) A destressing "deafness" in French? *Journal of Memory Language* 36. 406–421.

Durkin, P. (2014) *Borrowed words. A history of loanwords in English.* Oxford: Oxford University Press.

Dziubalska-Kołaczyk, K. (2002) *Beats-and-Binding Phonology.* Frankfurt am Main: Peter Lang.

Dziubalska-Kołaczyk, K. (2009) NP extension: B&B phonotactics. *Poznań Studies in Contemporary Linguistics* 45(1). 55–71.

Dziubalska-Kołaczyk, K. (2014) Explaining phonotactics using NAD. *Language Sciences* 46A. 6–17.

Elman, J. L., Diehl, R. L. & S. E. Buchwald (1977) Perceptual switching in bilinguals. *Journal of the Acoustical Society of America* 62. 971–974.

Fikkert, P. (1994) *On the acquisition of prosodic structure.* The Hague: Holland Academic Graphics.

Fisiak, J. (1970) The semantics of English loanwords in Polish. *Studia Anglica Posnaniensia* 2. 41–49.

Fisiak, J. (1975) Some remarks concerning the noun gender assignment of loanwords. *Biuletyn Polskiego Towarzystwa Językoznawczego* 35. 59–63.

Fleischhacker, H. (2005) Similarity in phonology: Evidence from reduplication and loan adaptation. PhD dissertation. University of California, Los Angeles.

Fujimura, O. & D. Erickson (1997) Acoustic phonetics. In Hardcastle, W. J. & J. Laver (eds.) *The handbook of phonetic sciences.* Oxford: Blackwell. 65–115.

Fujimura, O. & J. Lovins (1978) Syllables as concatenative phonetic rules. In Bell A. & J. B. Hooper (eds.) *Syllable and Segments.* Amsterdam: North-Holland. 107–120.

Gelderen, E. van (2006) *A history of the English language.* Amsterdam & Philadelphia: John Benjamins.

Giegerich, H. J. (1992) *English phonology: an introduction.* Cambridge: Cambridge University Press.

Goad, H. (2011) The representation of sC clusters. In Oostendorp, M. van, Ewen, C. J., Hume, E. & K. Rice (eds.) *Companion to phonology.* Oxford: Blackwell. 898–923.

Goad, H. (2012) sC Clusters are (almost always) coda-initial. *Linguistic Review* 29(3). 335–373.

Goad, H. & Y. Rose (2004) Input elaboration, head faithfulness and evidence for representation in the acquisition of left-edge clusters in West Germanic. In Kager, R., Pater, J. & W. Zonneveld (eds.) *Constraints in phonological acquisition.* Cambridge: Cambridge University Press. 109–157.

Goldsmith, J. A. (1990) *Autosegmental and metrical phonology.* Oxford: Blackwell.

Golston, C. & P. Yang (2001) White Hmong loanword phonology. In Fery, C., Dubach Green, A. & R. van de Vijver (eds.) *Proceedings of HILP 5.* Potsdam: University of Potsdam. 40–57.

Gouskova, M. (2001) Falling sonority onsets, loanwords, and syllable contact. *CLS* 37: 175-185.

Grosjean, F. (1982) *Life with two languages: an introduction to bilingualism*. Cambridge, MA: Harvard University Press.

Gussmann, E. (1997) Govern or perish: sequences of empty nuclei in Polish. In Raymond, H. and S. Puppel (eds.) *A Festschrift for Jacek Fisiak on his 60th birthday*. Berlin: Mouton de Gruyter. 1291–1300.

Gussmann, E. (2007) *The Phonology of Polish*. Oxford: Oxford University Press.

Gussmann, E. & J. Kaye (1993) Notes from a Dubrovnik café: I. The yers. *SOAS Working Papers in Linguistics and Phonetics* 3. 427–462.

Hall, N. (2011) Vowel epenthesis. In Oostendorp, M. van, Ewen, C. J., Hume, E. & K. Rice (eds.) *Companion to phonology*. Oxford: Blackwell. 1576–1596.

Hall, T. A. (1997) *The phonology of coronals*. Amsterdam & Philadelphia: John Benjamins.

Halle, M. & K. P. Mohanan (1985) Segmental phonology of Modern English. *Linguistic Inquiry* 16. 57–116.

Halle, M. & J.-R. Vergnaud (1980) Three-dimensional phonology. *Journal of Linguistic Research* 1. 83–105.

Harriott, P. & W. Cichocki (1993) Accentedness ratings of English loanwords by Acadian French listeners. *Revue quebecoise de linguistique* 22. 93–106.

Harris, J. (1990) Segmental complexity and phonological government. *Phonology* 7(2). 255–300.

Harris, J. (1994) *English sound structure*. Oxford: Blackwell.

Harris, J. (2006) The phonology of being understood: further arguments against sonority. *Lingua* 116(10). 1483–1494.

Haspelmath, M. (2009) Lexical borrowing: Concepts and issues. In Haspelmath, M. & U. Tadmor (eds.) *Loanwords in the World's Languages: A Comparative Handbook*. Berlin: De Gruyter Mouton. 35–54.

Haugen, E. (1950) The analysis of linguistic borrowing. *Language* 26. 210–231.

Haunz, C. (2007) Factors in on-line loanword adaptation. PhD dissertation. University of Edinburgh.

Heselwood, B. (1998) An unusual kind of sonority and its implications for phonetic theory. In Foulkes, P. (ed.) *Working Papers in Linguistics and Phonetics 6*. Leeds: University of Leeds. 68–80.

Hirano, H. (1994) A constraint-based approach to Korean loanwords. *Language Research* 30. 707–739.

Hoffer, B. L. (2002) Language borrowing and language diffusion: an overview. *Intercultural Communication Studies* 11. 1–37.

Hooper, J. (1976) *An Introduction to Natural Generative Phonology*. New York: Academic Press.

Howe, D. & D. Pulleyblank (2001) *Harmony as faithfulness*. Unpublished manuscript. University of British Columbia, Vancouver.

Hulst, H. van der (1984) *Syllable structure and stress in Dutch*. Dordrecht: Foris.

Ingram, J. & P. See-Gyoon (1998) Language, context, and speaker effects in the identification and discrimination of English /r/ and /l/ by Japanese and Korean listeners. *Journal of the Acoustical Society of America* 103. 1161–1174.

Itô, J. & A. Mester (1995) Japanese phonology. In Goldsmith, J. A. (ed.) *The handbook of phonological theory*. Oxford: Blackwell. 817–838.

Itô, J. & A. Mester (1999) The phonological lexicon. In Tsujimura, N. (ed.) *The handbook of Japanese linguistics*. Oxford: Blackwell. 62–100.

Itô, J. & A. Mester (2001) Covert generalisations in Optimality Theory: The role of stratal faithfulness constraints. *Studies in Phonetics, Phonology, and Morphology* 7. 273–299.

Jacobs, H. & C. Gussenhoven (2000) Loan phonology: perception, salience, the lexicon and OT. In Dekkers, J., van der Leeuw, F. & J. van de Weijer (eds.) *Optimality Theory: Phonology, Syntax, and Acquisition*. Oxford: Oxford University Press. 193–210.

Jakobson, R., Fant, G. & M. Halle (1952) *Preliminaries to speech analysis. The distinctive features and their correlates*. Cambridge, MA: MIT Press.

Jespersen, O. (1904) *Lehrbuch der phonetik*. Leipzig and Berlin: B. G. Teubner.

Jespersen, O. (1912) *Growth and structure of the English language*. Leipzig and Berlin: B. G. Teubner.

Kager, R. (1999) *Optimality Theory*. Cambridge: Cambridge University Press.

Kang, Y. (2003) Perceptual similarity in loanword adaptation: adaptation of English post-vocalic word-final stops in Korean. *Phonology* 20. 219–273.

Kang, Y. (2011) Loanword phonology. In Oostendorp, M. van, Ewen, C. J., Hume, E. & K. Rice (eds.) *Companion to phonology*. Oxford: Blackwell. 2258–2282.

Kaye, J. (1992) Do you believe in magic? The story of s+C sequences. *SOAS Working Papers in Linguistics and Phonetics* 2. 293–313.

Kaye, J., Lowenstamm, J. & J.-R. Vergnaud (1985) The internal structure of phonological elements: a theory of charm and government. *Phonology Yearbook* 2. 305–328.

Kaye, J., Lowenstamm, J. & J.-R. Vergnaud (1990) Constituent structure and government in phonology. *Phonology* 7. 193–231.

Kenstowicz, M. & H.-S. Sohn (2001) Accentual adaptation in North Kyungsang Korean. In Kenstowicz, M. (ed.) *Ken Hale: a life in language*. Cambridge, MA: MIT Press. 239–270.

Kenstowicz, M. & A. Suchato (2006) Issues in loanword adaptation: a case study from Thai. *Lingua* 116. 921–949.

Kiparsky, P. (1982) From Cyclic to Lexical Phonology. In Hulst, H. van der & N. Smith (eds.) *The Structure of Phonological Representations (Part I)*. Dordrecht: Foris. 131–175.

Kiparsky, P. (1985) Some consequences of Lexical Phonology. *Phonology Yearbook* 2. 85–138.

Kiparsky, P. (2000) Opacity and cyclicity. *The Linguistic Review* 17. 351–367.

Kuhl, P. (2000) A new view of language acquisition. *Proceedings of the National Academy of Sciences* 97. 11850–11857.

Kuryłowicz, J. (1952) Uwagi o polskich grupach spółgłoskowych. *Biuletyn Polskiego Towarzystwa Językoznawczego* 12. 221–232.

LaCharité, D. & C. Paradis (2005) Category preservation and proximity versus phonetic approximation in loanword adaptation. *Linguistic Inquiry* 36. 223–258.

Ladefoged, P. (1997) Linguistic phonetic descriptions. In Hardcastle, W. J. & J. Laver (eds.) *The handbook of phonetic sciences*. Oxford: Blackwell. 589–618.

Lahiri, A. & V. Evers (1991) Palatalization and coronality. In Paradis, C. & J.-F. Prunet (eds.) *The special status of coronals. Internal and external evidence*. New York: Academic Press. 79–100.

Levin, J. (1985) A metrical theory of syllabicity. PhD dissertation. Massachusetts Institute of Technology.

Lisker, L. (2001) Hearing the Polish sibilants [s š ś]: phonetic and auditory judgements. In Grønnum, N. & J. Rischel (eds.) *Travaux du Cercle Linguistique de Copenhague XXXI. To honour Eli Fischer-Jørgensen*. Copenhagen: C.A. Reitzel. 226–238.

Lombardi, L. (1991) Laryngeal features and laryngeal neutralization. PhD dissertation. University of Massachusetts Amherst.

Mańczak-Wohlfeld, E. (1995) *Tendencje rozwojowe współczesnych zapożyczeń angielskich w języku polskim*. Kraków: Universitas.

Mańczak-Wohlfeld, E. (2007) Rodzaj gramatyczny zapożyczeń angielskich w polszczyźnie. *Biuletyn Polskiego Towarzystwa Językoznawczego* 63. 39–48.

Mańczak-Wohlfeld, E. (2008) Morfologia zapożyczeń angielskich w językach europejskich. *Studia Linguistica Universitatis Iagellonicae Cracoviensis* 125. 113–120.

Massaro, D. W. & M. M. Cohen (1983) Phonological context in speech perception. *Perception and Psychophysics* 34. 338–348.

McCarthy, J. (1988) Feature geometry and dependency: a review. *Phonetica* 45. 85–108.

McCarthy, J. (2010) An introduction to Harmonic Serialism. *Language and Linguistics Compass* 4. 1001–1018.

McCarthy, J. & J. Pater (eds.) (2016) *Harmonic Grammar and Harmonic Serialism*. London: Equinox.

McCarthy, J. & A. Prince (1995) Faithfulness and reduplicative identity. *University of Massachusetts Occasional Papers* 18. 249–384.

McGuire, G. (2007) English listeners' perception of Polish alveopalatal and retroflex voiceless sibilants: a pilot study. *UC Berkeley Phonology Lab Annual Report*. 391–417.

Merriam-Webster.com (2017) https://www.merriam-webster.com (25 November 2017)

Miao, R. (2006) Loanword adaptation in Mandarin Chinese: Perceptual, phonological and sociolinguistic factors. PhD dissertation. Stony Brook University.

Millward, C. M. & M. Hayes (2011) *A biography of the English language*. Wadsworth: Cengage learning.

Mohanan, K. P. (1987) *The theory of Lexical Phonology*. Dordrecht: Reidel.

Murray, R. W. & T. Vennemann (1983) Sound change and syllable structure in Germanic phonology. *Language* 59. 514–528.

Oh, M. (2004) English stop adaptations as Output-to-output Correspondence. *Onin Kenkyuu* 7. 165–172.

Ohala, J. J. (1990) There is no interface between phonology and phonetics: a personal view. *Journal of Phonetics* 18. 53–71.

Oostendorp, M. van (1995) *Vowel quality and phonological projection*. PhD dissertation. Katolieke Universiteit Brabant.

Paradis, C. (1988a) On constraints and repair strategies. *The Linguistic Review* 6. 71–97.

Paradis, C. (1988b) Towards a theory of constraint violations. *McGill Working Papers in Linguistics* 5. 1–43.

Paradis, C. (1996) The inadequacy of faithfulness and filters in loanword adaptation. In Durand, J. & B. Laks (eds.) *Current trends in phonology: models and methods*. Salford: University of Salford Publications. 509–534.

Paradis, C. & D. LaCharité (1997) Preservation and minimality in loanword adaptation. *Journal of Linguistics* 33. 379–430.

Paradis, C. & D. Lacharité (2008) Apparent phonetic approximation: English loanwords in old Quebec French. *Journal of Linguistics* 44. 87–128.

Paradis, C. & J.-F. Prunet (eds.) (1991) *The special status of coronals. Internal and external evidence.* New York: Academic Press.

Parker, F. (1977) Perceptual cues and phonological change. *Journal of Phonetics* 5. 97–105.

Parker, F. & T. Walsh (1981) Voicing cues as a function of the tense/lax distinction in vowels. *Journal of Phonetics* 9. 353–358.

Parker, S. (2002) Quantifying the sonority hierarchy. PhD dissertation. University of Massachusetts Amherst.

Paul, H. (1891) *Principles of the history of language.* London: Longmans, Green and Co.

Peperkamp, S. (2005) A psycholinguistic theory of loanword adaptations. In Ettlinger, M., Fleischer N. & M. Park-Doob (eds.) *Proceedings of the 30th Annual Meeting of the Berkeley Linguistics Society.* Berkeley, CA: The Society. 341–352.

Peperkamp, S. & E. Dupoux (2002) Loanword adaptations: three problems for phonology (and a psycholinguistic solution). Paper presented at the North American Phonology Conference (Naphc), Concordia University, Montreal, 27 April 2002.

Peperkamp, S. & E. Dupoux (2003) Reinterpreting loanword adaptations: the role of perception. In Solé, M. J., Recasens, D. & J. Romero (eds.) *Proceedings of the 15th International Congress of Phonetic Sciences.* Barcelona: Causal Productions. 367–370.

Peperkamp, S., Vendelin, I. & K. Nakamura (2008) On the perceptual origin of loanword adaptations: experimental evidence from Japanese. *Phonology,* 25. 129–164.

Poplack, S. & D. Sankoff (1984) Borrowing: The synchrony of integration. *Linguistics* 22. 99–135.

Poplack, S., Sankoff, D. & C. Miller (1988) The social correlates and linguistic processes of lexical borrowing and assimilation. *Linguistics* 26. 47–104.

Price, P. J. (1980) Sonority and syllabicity: acoustic correlates of perception. *Phonetica* 37. 327–343.

Prince, A. & P. Smolensky (1993/2004) *Optimality theory: Constraint interaction in generative grammar.* Unpublished ms., Rutgers University & University of Colorado, Boulder. Published 2004, Oxford: Blackwell.

Pulleyblank, E. (1989) The role of coronal in articulator based features. *Papers from the Chicago Linguistics Society* 25. 379–393.

Puppel, S. (1992) The sonority hierarchy in a source-filter dependency framework. In Fisiak, J. & S. Puppel (eds.) *Phonological investigations.* Amsterdam & Philadelphia: John Benjamins. 467–483.

Radomski M. & K. Sydorenko (2016) Consonant deletion in online adaptation of Polish and Ukrainian consonant clusters by native speakers of English. In Szpyra-Kozłowska, J. & E. Cyran (eds.) *Phonology, its Faces and Interfaces.* Frankfurt am Main: Peter Lang. 261–275.

Rice, K. (1992) On deriving sonority: a structural account of sonority relationships. *Phonology* 9. 61–100.

Rose, S. (2000) Epenthesis positioning and syllable contact in Chaha. *Phonology* 17. 397–425.

Rose, Y. & K. Demuth (2006) Vowel epenthesis in loanword adaptation: representational and phonetic considerations. *Lingua* 116. 1112–1139.

Rowicka, G. (1999) *On ghost vowels. A Strict CV approach.* The Hague: Holland Academic Graphics.

Rubach, J. (1994) Affricates as strident stops in Polish. *Linguistic Inquiry* 25. 119–143.

Rubach, J. (2000) Glide and glottal stop insertion in Slavic languages: a DOT analysis. *Linguistic Inquiry* 31. 271–317.

Rubach, J. & G. Booij (1990) Syllabic structure assignment in Polish. *Phonology* 7. 121–158.

Sagey, E. (1986) The representation of features and relations in non-linear phonology. PhD dissertation. Massachusetts Institute of Technology.

Samek-Lodovici, V. & A. Prince (1999) *Optima.* (Technical Reports of the Rutgers Center for Cognitive Science). Rutgers University.

Sapir, E. (1921) *Language: an introduction to the study of speech.* New York: Harcourt, Brace and World.

Sawicka, I. (1974) *Struktura grup spółgłoskowych w językach słowiańskich.* Wrocław: Ossolineum.

Sawicka, I. (1985) Syllabic structure in Slavic languages. *Rocznik Slawistyczny* XLV. 3–9.

Sawicka, I. (1995) Fonologia. In Wróbel, H. (ed.) *Gramatyka współczesnego języka polskiego. Fonetyka i Fonologia.* Kraków: Wydawnictwo Instytutu Języka Polskiego PAN. 107–198.

Scheer, T. (1999) On constraints vs. non-circular approaches to word-initial clusters. In Rennison, J. & K. Kühnhammer (eds.) *Phonologica 1996.* The Hague: Holland Academic Graphics. 289–304.

Scheer, T. (2004) *A lateral theory of phonology. What is CVCV, and why should it be?* Berlin: Mouton de Gruyter.

Schwartz, G. (2010) Phonology in the signal – unifying cue and prosodic licensing. *Poznan Studies in Contemporary Linguistics* 46(4). 499–518.

Schwartz, G. (2012) Glides and initial vowels within the Onset Prominence representational environment. *Poznan Studies in Contemporary Linguistics* 48(4). 661–685.

Schwartz, G. (2013) A representational parameter for onsetless syllables. *Journal of Linguistics* 49(3). 613–646.

Schwartz, G. (2015) Who needs a nucleus? Tashlhiyt Berber syllabification in the Onset Prominence representational environment. *Poznan Studies in Contemporary Linguistics* 51(2). 247–290.

Selkirk, E. (1982) The syllable. In Hulst, H. van der & N. Smith (eds.) *The Structure of Phonological Representations (Part II).* Dordrecht: Foris. 337–383.

Selkirk, E. (1984) On the major class features and syllable theory. In Aronoff, M. & R. Oehrle (eds.) *Language Sound Structure.* Cambridge, MA: MIT Press. 107–136.

Seo, M. (2011) Syllable contact. In Oostendorp, M. van, Ewen, C. J., Hume, E. & K. Rice (eds.) *Companion to phonology.* Oxford: Blackwell. 1245–1262.

Shaw, P. (1991) Consonant harmony systems: the special status of coronal harmony. In Paradis, C. & J.-F. Prunet (eds.) *The special status of coronals. Internal and external evidence.* New York: Academic Press. 125–157.

Shinohara, S. (1997) Analyse phonologique de l'adaptation japonaise de mots etrangers. These de doctorat. Universite Paris III.

Silverman, D. (1992) Multiple scansions in loanword phonology: evidence from Cantonese. *Phonology* 9. 289–328.

Soares, C. & F. Grosjean (1984) Bilinguals in a monolingual and a bilingual speech mode: the effect on lexical access. *Memory and Cognition* 12. 380–386.

Sohn, H.-S. (2001) Optimization of word-final coronals in Korean loanword adaptation. In Fery, C., Dubach Green, A. & R. van de Vijver (eds.) *Proceedings of HILP 5.* Potsdam: University of Potsdam. 159–177.

Stangel, K. (2013) The comparison of bisegmental representations of sC clusters in English. *Anglica. An International Journal of English Studies* 22(2). 27–40.

Steriade, D. (1982) Greek prosodies and the nature of syllabification. PhD dissertation. Massachusetts Institute of Technology.

Steriade, D. (2001/2008) The phonology of perceptibility effects: the P-map and its consequences for constraint organisation. In Hanson, K. & S. Inkelas (eds.)

The nature of the word: studies in honor of Paul Kiparsky. Cambridge, MA: MIT Press. 151–180.

Szpyra J. (1995) *Three tiers in Polish and English phonology*. Lublin: Wydawnictwo UMCS.

Szpyra-Kozłowska, J. (1998) The sonority scale and phonetic syllabification in Polish. *Biuletyn Polskiego Towarzystwa Językoznawczego* LIV. 65–82.

Szpyra-Kozłowska, J. (2015) Input to loanword adaptation of anglicisms in Polish. In Bloch-Rozmej, A. & A. Bondaruk (eds.) *Spotlight on Melody and Structure in Syntax and Phonology*. Lublin: KUL. 305–329.

Szpyra-Kozłowska, J. (2016a) Pozajęzykowe czynniki kształtujące fonetyczną i fonologiczną adaptację anglicyzmów we współczesnej polszczyźnie. *Poradnik Językowy* 2. 21–37.

Szpyra-Kozłowska, J. (2016b) Wewnątrzjęzykowe mechanizmy fonologicznej polonizacji zapożyczeń angielskich. *Poradnik Językowy* 6. 61–76.

Szpyra-Kozłowska, J. (2016c) Perception? Orthography? Phonology? Conflicting forces behind the adaptation of English /ɪ/ in loanwords into Polish. *Poznań Studies in Contemporary Linguistics* 52(1). 511–549.

Szpyra-Kozłowska J. & M. Radomski (2014) Between non-native speaking and native listening skills. Perceived phonetic properties of foreign-accented Polish. In Chodkiewicz, H. & M. Trepczyńska (eds.) *Language Skills: Traditions, Transitions and Ways Forward*. Newcastle upon Tyne: Cambridge Scholars Publishing. 179–195.

Szpyra-Kozłowska J. & M. Radomski (2016) English ash in loanwords into Polish. Factors behind two patterns of adaptation. In Szpyra-Kozłowska, J. & E. Cyran (eds.) *Phonology, its Faces and Interfaces*. Frankfurt am Main: Peter Lang. 277–295.

Ulrich, C. (1997) Loanword adaptation in Lama: testing the TCRS model. *Canadian Journal of Linguistics* 42. 415–463.

Vendelin, I. & S. Peperkamp (2006) The influence of orthography on loanword adaptations. *Lingua* 116. 996–1007.

Vennemann, T. (1988) *Preference laws for syllable structure and the explanation of sound change: With special reference to German, Germanic, Italian, and Latin*. Berlin: De Gruyter Mouton.

Weinreich, U. (1970) *Languages in contact: findings and problems*. The Hague: Mouton.

Wells, J. C. (2008) *Longman Pronunciation Dictionary*. 3rd edition. Pearson Longman.

Werker, J. F. & R. C. Tees (1984) Phonemic and phonetic factors in adult cross-language speech perception. *Journal of the Acoustical Society of America* 75. 1866–1878.

Winford, D. (2003) *An introduction to contact linguistics*. Oxford: Blackwell.

Winter-Froemel, E. (2008) Studying loanwords and loanword integration: two criteria of conformity. *Newcastle Working Papers in Linguistics* 14. 156–176.

Witalisz, A. (2013) English linguistic influence on standard and American varieties of Polish: a comparative study. *Studia Linguistica Universitatis Iagellonicae Cracoviensis* 130. 327–346.

Yildiz, Y. (2005) The structure of initial /s/-clusters: evidence from L1 and L2 acquisition. In Tzakosta, M., Levelt, C. & J. van der Weijer (eds.) *Developmental paths in phonological acquisition. Leiden papers in Linguistics 2.1.* Leiden: University of Leiden Center for Linguistics. 163-187.

Yildiz, Y. (2010) *Age effects in the acquisition of English onset clusters by Turkish learners: an optimality-theoretic approach.* Newcastle upon Tyne: Cambridge Scholars Publishing.

Yip, M. (1993) Cantonese loanword phonology and Optimality Theory. *Journal of East Asian Linguistics* 2. 261–291.

Yip, M. (2002) Necessary but not sufficient: perceptual influences in loanword phonology. *Journal of the Phonetic Society of Japan* 6. 4–21.

Zydorowicz, P. (2010) Consonant clusters across morpheme boundaries: Polish morphonotactic inventory and its acquisition. *Poznań Studies in Contemporary Linguistics* 46(4). 565–588.

Zydorowicz, P. & P. Orzechowska (2017) The study of Polish phonotactics: measures of phonotactic preferability. *Studies in Polish Linguistics* 12(2). 97–121.

Zydorowicz, P., Orzechowska, P., Jankowski, M., Dziubalska-Kołaczyk, K., Wierzchoń, P. & D. Pietrala (2016) *Phonotactics and morphonotactics of Polish and English. Theory, description, tools and applications.* Poznań: Wydawnictwo Naukowe UAM.

Sounds – Meaning – Communication

Landmarks in Phonetics, Phonology and Cognitive Linguistics

Edited by Jolanta Szpyra-Kozłowska

www.peterlang.com